PROMISE
— of —
ARMINIAN
Theology

ESSAYS IN HONOR OF
F. LEROY FORLINES

EDITED BY
MATTHEW STEVEN BRACEY
& W. JACKSON WATTS

RANDALL HOUSE
— ACADEMIC —

114 Bush Rd | Nashville, TN 37217
randallhouse.com

ISBN-13: 9780892659944

TABLE OF CONTENTS

Part III: Ethics, Culture, and the Church

Part IV: Personal Tributes

CELEBRATING A HERO
OF THE
FREE WILL BAPTIST FAITH

Matthew Steven Bracey

Cheap-easy believism, the four basic relationships and values, the inescapable questions of life, short list and long list legalism, the total personality, and "the boys downstairs": These are just a few of the many "Forlinesisms" that many of us hold dear. Unlike other volume contributors, I did not formally study under F. Leroy Forlines (b. 1926) during my matriculation at Welch College. Instead I have come to know him by virtue of his yet-to-be-published secularism project (see chapter nine). Since he invited me to edit this work in 2012, I have spent countless hours poring over his manuscript, sitting in his office, and learning from this hero of the Free Will Baptist faith (see Heb. 11).

I have learned that he, at nearly ninety years of age, is indeed a man of Christian character, integrity, and wisdom. He is a man at whose feet we should sit, listen, and learn. And he is a man in whom we see a love for Christ, His church, and His world. For all of his professional life, Mr. Forlines has served the Free Will Baptist denomination. He attended Free Will Baptist Bible College (now Welch College) as a student in the late 1940s and early 50s, and began teaching there a few years later. Since then—through teaching, writing, and serving—he has given the denomination direction, and Classical Arminianism shape (also called Reformation Arminianism or Reformed Arminianism). In many respects, Mr. Forlines is a Renaissance man, for he has bequeathed to us writings on a wide variety of topics, as this book illustrates. For these reasons and more, its contributors have collaborated to celebrate and honor him with this festschrift, entitled *The Promise of Arminian Theology: Essays in Honor of F. Leroy Forlines*. The term "festschrift" literally means a celebratory writing (*fest* 'celebration' + *schrift* 'writing'). We who stand indebted to Mr. Forlines aim to celebrate his life, work, and legacy.

The Promise of Arminian Theology comprises four sections, which include eleven chapters and three tributes. In each chapter, the authors honor Mr. Forlines by exploring some aspect of his work through summary, synthesis, analysis, and critical engagement. In each tribute, the authors honor him through the stories they have shared and the lessons they have learned from him. Through this approach, we hope to demonstrate Mr. Forlines's emphasis on the total personalities of people as thinking, feeling, acting beings. These chapters and tributes, along with their respective subjects, will show Mr. Forlines's total personality; and inspire (we hope) readers' total personalities as the gospel is for the whole person—thoughts, affections, and choices.

In this volume, we aim not simply to honor Mr. Forlines for what he has handed down to us, but also to honor him for the foundations he has laid for present and future generations toward Christian faithfulness. We hope to inspire Free Will Baptists, as well as the church generally, to remember from whence they have come, and to build upon what they have received. With the biblical authors, may we be faithful to receive, hold, and pass down the faith that was once for all entrusted to the saints (Jude 3; see also 1 Cor. 11:2; 2 Thess. 2:15). Indeed, we are thankful for what Mr. Forlines has given us, and we hope to pass it on to those who come after us.

In section one of this book, the authors consider important foundations in Forlines's theology. In chapter one, Andrew Ball affirms Forlines's theological methodology and presuppositions, and introduces the "Forlinesean trifecta." Next, Phillip Morgan reviews what roles worldview, culture, epistemology, and apologetics assume in Forlines's work.

Section two gives attention to particular theological themes that surround the gospel. Kevin Hester analyzes Forlines's discussion of conditional election in chapter three, highlighting the importance that an influence-response model of personality plays in a Reformed Arminian understanding of this doctrine. Jesse Owens follows with a chapter on atonement and justification, in which original sin, imputed guilt, penal satisfaction, and general atonement are affirmed in a Forlinesean scheme. In chapter five, Barry Raper outlines sanctification and spirituality in Forlines's work, showing how sanctification ultimately is related to restoration, and supporting a down-to-earth spirituality that emphasizes ordinary means of grace in spiritual growth. Next, David Outlaw addresses the topics of conditional perseverance and the possibility of apostasy in chapter six. Finally, Matthew McAffee reviews the progressive covenantal approach to eschatology that Forlines espouses. These chapters show that Forlines is faithful to biblical orthodoxy, as well as the General/Free Will Baptist tradition. They also distinguish Forlines's theology from Wesleyanism on the one hand and Calvinism on the other.

Section three, which includes chapters eight through eleven, considers Forlines's contributions to ethics, secularism, ministry, and counseling—the outworking of the gospel in the church and world. W. Jackson Watts examines Forlinesean ethics in chapter eight, demonstrating how the principles Forlines has given, such as the four basic relationships and four basic values, provide helpful paradigms for facing today's world. I share an overview of Forlines's exploration into secularism in chapter nine, illustrating how Forlines hopes to help the church understand the culture in which it ministers, and inspire fundamental change in society. In chapter ten, Christopher Talbot outlines what Forlines has said about the church's mission, ministry, and communication of the gospel. Then, in chapter eleven, Edward E. Moody, Jr. reviews Forlines's contributions to counseling and psychology with an aim toward understanding and helping people both inside and outside of the church.

Section four concludes the volume with three personal tributes. Jon and James Forlines pay tribute to both Leroy and Fay Forlines for the principles their parents instilled in them as children. Robert E. Picirilli honors Forlines as a colleague and friend. J. Matthew Pinson celebrates him for his indispensable mentorship.

We believe the foundation that Mr. Forlines has laid offers great promise for the future. Thus we have called this project *The Promise of Arminian Theology*. Contrary to the misconceptions present in some scholarship and traditions regarding Arminius and Arminians, Forlines's work demonstrates that Reformed Arminian theology is biblically faithful, theologically coherent, and spiritually robust. It reveals a theology that offers hope and promise for God's people in numerous areas of life and ministry. This project has been a long time in the making. The work has been hard and challenging, yet rewarding. As the volume editors, W. Jackson Watts and I are grateful for the sacrifices that the other contributors have made to help make this festschrift possible. Collectively, we are thankful for what F. Leroy Forlines has given to us and to the church, and we celebrate him as a hero of the Free Will Baptist faith.

PART I
PROLEGOMENA

CHAPTER ONE

THE THEOLOGICAL METHOD OF F. LEROY FORLINES

Andrew Ball

Why Method Matters

There are many reasons to be thankful for F. Leroy Forlines's theological legacy. One is his rich and unique method, that is, the way he *does* theology. Devoting attention to Forlines's method is important because it makes explicit what every theology is laden with: underlying presumptions (i.e., predispositions, presuppositions, biases, assumptions, prerogatives, etc.) that motivate the questions and, hence, the technique used to get answers. If we consider theological method essentially as a "philosophy of how to do theology,"[1] then it should seem obvious that it cannot be done in a vacuum as if isolated from those starting presumptions. Rather, they will determine the method. For instance, if a theologian comes to the theological task believing the canon of Scripture is not historically reliable, then the Bible will not be *the* central part of the method in the way that it would be to someone who affirms its inerrancy.

Before charting Forlines's method, we must be mindful to resist the "Enlightenment urge" to assume that a theology's value is somehow determined by how objective or neutral its methodology is. Forlines is not concerned with objectivity per se, not only because he assumes that it is impossible, but more importantly because it is undesirable. That urge rests on the faulty assumption that neutrality and impartiality are epistemic virtues to be exemplified in every sort of study, including theology. They are not.

One reason is that even though our thoroughly modern culture privileges the epistemic values and methods of empirical science as being the absolute standards for any research project, there are some areas for which the scientific method cannot offer right answers, such as theology. A second reason is that one cannot do theology from a completely neutral standpoint anyway because its very nature—the project of answering the inescapable questions of life—engages the total personality, which is one's entire being: "Thinking and feeling must be found together" because "we are deeply concerned and involved" in our search for truth.[2]

For Forlines, theology communicates a panoramic picture of reality—a "worldview"—that articulates an intelligible account of all truth.[3] Theology, then, is very *subjective* in the sense that its very purpose is staked in meeting the deepest needs of the human person, that being which bears God's very image.[4] As such, a theology, and especially the method that brings it to life, has real-world ramifications.

Forlines's *magnum opus*, The Quest for Truth (hereafter *Quest*),[5] best displays his method. *Quest* is a holistic theology that begins by recognizing the foundational (and inescapable) questions that arise out of our *imago Dei* humanness, and then shows how biblical Christianity ultimately provides the best answers to these questions. Even though *Quest* may be known more for its distinctive Classical Arminian and Free Will Baptist perspective, our appreciation for it extends beyond that; its conclusions are outgrowths of a much deeper theological project explicitly grounded in metaphysical and epistemological convictions regarding what truth is and how we can access it. Frankly no other single-volume text in the Arminian tradition has ever presented theology quite in this way.

Understanding the Context

Forlines's life has spanned nearly ninety years. Born in 1926, he finished college in 1952, graduate school in 1959, seminary in 1962, and graduate school again in 1972.[6] In 1953, he began teaching at his *alma mater*, Welch College. He retired officially (but never practically) from that post in 1992.[7]

Considering the theological context of this time, Forlines was heavily shaped by the fundamentalist-modernist controversy over the Bible's status. The fundamentalist[8] conviction that Scripture is completely reliable and ultimately authoritative rubbed against modernists' embrace of "higher criticism," which essentially treated it as any other humanly-authored text. Many of the old institutions went with the modernists, and this created a huge gap in orthodox biblical education. New Bible colleges and seminaries were then spawned for the purpose of upholding scriptural authority, and for the most part[9] American evangelicalism continued to defend the veracity of Scripture throughout the rest of the twentieth century.

It is no understatement that this particular issue has been at the heart of Forlines's work. Early on, he and longtime colleague Robert Picirilli published a pamphlet that warned of modern theology's influence.[10] For Forlines and Picirilli, the problem was that modernism's forcing of the scientific method upon Scripture[11] resulted in its "willing[ness] to deny any of the fundamental doctrines of Christianity."[12] Because of this it was a "tool that Satan is using to destroy the doctrinal foundation[s] [of] the virgin birth of Christ, His deity, the blood atonement, and Christ's bodily resurrection."[13] Hence, he who approaches Scripture in any other way except "simply to believe what [God] has revealed" is "a fool and vainly self-confident."[14] Concerned that we not become fools, Forlines would again publish on this subject in each of the following two decades,[15] his views finally culminating in *Quest*.

A related issue that Forlines addressed during this time was Karl Barth's neo-orthodoxy. On the surface, Barth's work seemed to offer some promise as a response to the modernist theological method noted above since he rejected it outright. He did so, however, not because he believed in the inerrancy of the biblical text itself, but because he thought that God's Word is not actually the text. Rather, it is Christ revealed through the medium of the text. Forlines argued in 1978 that this nuanced position identifies Scripture not as "content revelation," but as a "reflection of the Bible writers about their *encounter* with God."[16] Hence, in neo-orthodoxy there is no "message" since "the Bible is a record of revelation, but not revelation [itself]."[17]

This view has many problems. One is that it assumes the text itself (and one's faith based on that text) to be "irrational" unless coupled with an existential encounter between God and the reader.[18] What exactly is an "existential encounter" with God through Scripture? What does that even mean? As J. I. Packer has noted, Barth considers Scripture as mere "instrumentality in God's hands as his means of channeling to us in his specific word *of the moment*."[19] However, the obvious problem here is that if it just depends on the word *of the moment*, a person "can be a slippery eel when it comes to pinning him down about his theology."[20] Furthermore, there is a methodological inconsistency here since the neo-orthodox thinker "may have considerable liberty in what doctrine he subscribes to" so long as this neo-orthodox dogma about "revelation and the Bible" is itself inflexible.[21]

Forlines utterly rejected *neo*-orthodoxy for the same reasons that he rejected the modernists' *non*-orthodoxy: both positions reject the veracity and authority of God's revealed Word as it stands, as God's divine revelation to humanity, the text of which communicates His truth and will to persons in the way that rational agents normally and usually comprehend truth, in language and prose. Both the *non* and *neo*-orthodox positions are dangerous, "not for what [they] believ[e], but because of what [they] deny."[22]

Along with these theological struggles were problems in American society. Though Forlines has lived through one of America's greatest eras of optimism that began with the end of the Great Depression and carried on to the post-war boom years, he also experienced the beginning of the moral crisis that explicitly began in the 1960s and still continues today. It is significant that Forlines's own theological reflections take this into account. At one point, he bemoans the new American attitude toward "truth." Whereas the culture he grew up in "was strongly influenced by Christian thought," it is now the case that pluralism and relativism are the norms.[23] The "prevailing mood of doubt and uncertainty in today's culture" somewhat rigs the game in its attempt to preclude any "sure and satisfactory answers to the inescapable questions of life" that are part and parcel of finding "meaning in life."[24] The theological task, then, should strive to diffuse this mood by exposing it for what it is. Once this is accomplished, the possibility will be opened for getting the right answers.

The Problem that Motivates the Method

As noted Forlines's theology is motivated by the fact that "there has been a major shift in worldview thinking on the grassroots level in [his] lifetime."[25] Defining "worldview" as one's "explanation of the whole of reality,"[26] Forlines notes society's transition from being largely "informed by Christian thought . . . morals and ideals" to now being under the "powerful force" of "secular thought."[27] What is so problematic about this is that since "the only truth a person can discover is that which is allowed by his epistemology,"[28] the particular epistemology with which a person works inevitably achieves (or precludes) certain kinds of truth. For instance, if one wholeheartedly accepts the modernist paradigm that "Truth exist[s] and that it [can] be found by reason [alone],"[29] then he will be prevented from knowing anything beyond the reach of what his own cognitive abilities (by themselves) can get for him through mere observation.

Forlines borrows Francis Schaeffer's distinction between lower and upper story (e.g., think of a building) knowledge.[30] The former has those things that "can adequately be studied by the mind as it reflects upon the data of observation and experience" as its objects; and the latter is concerned with that which empirical observation can never get us—higher-order knowledge about answers to "the inescapable questions of life"[31] such as, "Is there a God? If so, what is He like? How can I know Him? Who am I? How can I tell right from wrong?"[32] and so on. The big problem here, however, is not only that privileging the lower-story's standards as normative ultimately rules out any possible answers to upper story questions, but even more devastating is that this paves the way for the current postmodern attitude that "neither believes in nor desires to find ultimate [i.e., upper-story] Truth."[33] It has hence declared the upper story not to even be within the bounds of human rationality, but that it is unintelligible and groundless. As Forlines notes, the epistemological transition from an optimistic modernism to a pessimistic postmodernism is because of modernism's "fail[ure] to produce Truth."[34]

The great problem, then, is not just that the possibility of truth is denied (although this is bad enough), but that such a denial forecloses our ability to have the rational worldview that "human beings are in desperate need of"[35] since "the human heart cries out for more than the hopelessness and despair of postmodernism."[36] Forlines's theological task is a response to this by showing how a full-orbed, scripturally based, orthodox, evangelical worldview is the most rational and intelligible one since only it truly meets the needs of persons.

The Forlinesean Trifecta

Three important methodological assumptions, intimately connected, undergird how Forlines does theology: (1) God, (2) truth, and (3) the human person.

God

In one sense an understanding of God is the foundational assumption of Forlines's method because it gets at the heart of the above noted epistemological problem by firmly laying the cornerstone for a Christian (and hence, truthful) worldview. The postmodern problem is that God is not knowable, and thus, the very concept of God is irrational. Forlines's response to this, however, is that "if there is a God, the only hope of knowing Him would be for Him to reveal Himself to us."[37] Fortunately for us He has indeed done so in two important ways.

First, Forlines utilizes the biblical understanding of God's general revelation to all of those who have been made in His image (Gen. 1:26) and thus share a "rational (Col. 3:10) and a moral likeness (Eph. 4:24)" with Him.[38] General revelation is simply "the revelation of God in the created order and the basic nature of man."[39] Although it does not communicate the gospel itself—that is, truths about God's redemption[40] and restoration for humanity through Christ—it nevertheless communicates some things about God that "does help prepare a person for the reception of the message of redemption."[41] Forlines refers to Romans 1–2 as the primary scriptural source for our understanding about how general revelation informs our moral knowledge. Romans 1:32 is a clear statement that "people do know the judgment of God" and 2:14-15 confirms that "no one can plead ignorance of God's law because it is written on the heart of every human being."[42] Romans 1:18 reveals that even though the carnal man suppresses the knowledge of God, "suppressed knowledge is nevertheless knowledge."[43] That we bear God's image implies that our design includes some knowledge about the kind of being God must necessarily be. Through general revelation, "people grasp . . . that God is eternal, powerful, holy, just, caring, and fair," even if they "deny [His] existence."[44] As such we are not a blank slate regarding knowledge of God: "we have not been hurled into space to drift aimlessly" but have "been preprogrammed by God with a knowledge of [Him] and what He is like."[45]

Second, Forlines is wholly committed to the more important claim that God has also revealed Himself through special revelation, which Forlines defines as "God communicat[ing], in a direct way, knowledge of Himself and His plan to a particular person or group."[46] Special revelation is "necessary" because "God is personal."[47] After all, "God's revelation is presented . . . as a record of God speaking, acting, and dealing with His people," and so "we see truth demonstrated in terms of relationships."[48] God wishes to communicate specific truths to us, and the most important truth that His special revelation communicates to us is the "basic theme of the message of redemption."[49]

Holy Scripture

What exactly is "special" revelation? For Forlines it is God's inspired, infallible, and inerrant communication that takes its form in the canon of Scripture. This is an extremely important methodological assumption for Forlines because his affirmation of the Bible's veracity is why he can use Scripture in doing theology.

Forlines affirms that the Holy Scripture is *inspired*. Its authorship has a "divine origin" such that the text itself is a result of God's "breathing" (2 Tim. 3:16) through the human writers, reflecting their own various skills and personalities.[50] As such Forlines's use of Scripture is based on his conviction that its inspiration should be understood as *verbal plenary*[51]—the words of the entire canon are completely inspired by God. It is not the case that inspiration extends only to the thoughts of the human authors and so the words themselves are just tools or instruments (this is a claim that borders on the edge of the neo-orthodoxy discussed earlier where, in that scheme, "there is no content revelation"[52]). Rather, Forlines affirms that "words" are the very means through which God communicates true propositions about Himself.[53] This is very good news for us because through written and spoken language we convey and process ideas. God has chosen this basic means of communication in order to communicate His will to us. So long as we grasp the "normal laws of language,"[54] we have a place to begin to understand what God has said.

However, the Bible is not just inspired; it is *inerrant*. For Forlines this means "what it affirms to be true is true."[55] There are several reasons for this. One is that it "gives not the slightest hint that error is affirmed anywhere in its pages,"[56] and actually, it does the opposite. Jesus, for instance, did not consider the Old Testament to contain any error whatsoever (Matt. 5:18; John 10:35).[57] Second, God's very character forces us to recognize that He is nothing short of truth, and so whatever He says must necessarily be true. This is affirmed in the fact that "God cannot lie (Num. 23:19, Tit. 1:2)" given His complete "holiness and righteousness."[58] Because of this, whatever He says must be true, which gives Forlines a sure basis for his conviction about inerrancy: "We do not believe that the Bible is the Word of God because it is inerrant. Rather, we believe the Bible is inerrant because we believe that it is the Word of God."[59]

Total Personality

The third assumption underlying Forlines's theology is an anthropological one regarding our nature. As rational beings, not only are we capable of possessing true propositions, but also truth as such has the potential to affect us psychologically, emotionally, and praxeologically. This is just a fact of our *imago Dei* ontology. Being made in God's image means we are rational beings, but it also means we are more than rational. For Forlines God's revelation communicates to our total personality. So, when we intake or discover truth, our entire being is involved in the process, not just our mind. Our total personality is "concerned with thinking (the activity of the mind), feeling (the activity of the heart, which refers to the seat of our emotions), and acting (the activity of the will)."[60] And even though we can conceptually abstract each of these activities from each other for the purpose of discussing them, "we cannot [effectively] separate the[ir] activity" from one another because "the activity of each is deeply involved in the other"; they are "a functional unity."[61]

In an unpublished paper that was widely circulated among many of his undergraduate theology students, Forlines explains this interconnectedness:

> While every part of the person is important, the mind is the gateway to the personality. Ideas are presented to the mind. As the mind thinks about these ideas, attitudes are developed in the heart. In the heart we feel the reality of things. The heart registers the value we place on things. We feel that things are important or unimportant. In its functions, the heart is dependent upon the mind. The will acts from the thinking of the mind and the feeling of the heart. Appropriate action comes from a prepared heart and mind. The priority of the mind over the heart and will is in keeping with what the Bible says about truth and knowledge [Jn. 8:32, Jn. 17:17].[62]

Two interesting points follow about the total personality. First, Forlines seems to prioritize the mind because it is one's initial epistemic input. In other words, the mind is something akin to the fresh-air intake vent in your home's heating system that takes the new (i.e., unprocessed) air to your furnace's burner. Similarly, the mind takes in ideas—all sorts of ideas. This is why the life (and health!) of the mind is extremely important.

Second, Forlines suggests that the individual aspects of the personality—mind, heart, will—should not be considered as individual processes per se, but as sections or aspects of one complete concurrent process. The way this works is that once ideas (i.e., inputs) enter into the initial part (i.e., the mind) of the process (i.e., total personality), they are not independently processed there before being sent on to the next part of the procedure. Instead, each part is simultaneously processed in its respective way, having an instantaneous effect on the total personality. Each part of the process, then, *always* functions together simultaneously as one complete, coherent process. This process is not analogous to an assembly line, but is more like an electrical circuit. This is what I take Forlines to mean when he says that neither part of the total personality can be separated from one another. It is an instantaneous and inextricably packaged deal. When Forlines claims that "truth is for the total personality,"[63] he means that truth is not merely for the mind, but for the entire person. Truth is not only a mere epistemic good, but also an emotional and praxeological good. This is why it is not a "mere mental exercise," but also "experience oriented."[64]

The Interconnectedness of the Trifecta

These three methodological assumptions are not distinct from one another in a hard and fast way, but manifest much overlap. It would be fruitful for our study to trace this out some more in order to get a better glimpse of this aspect of Forlines's methodology.

Remember that when Forlines asks the student to "allow [his] total personality to enter the study,"[65] in effect, he is asking him to allow his total being to be impacted freely by truth. However, there is a specific reason that he asks the question in this way. Forlines's stated purpose in *Quest* for presenting his theology the way he does is to provide reasons for how the Christian worldview an-swers (and how it is superior to) postmodern despair. Given the challenges that postmodernism presents, specifically its challenge against "the very existence of truth," it "must be met with an appeal to the total personality"[66] because any "system that proposes to explain the whole of reality (or a worldview) must prove to be satisfactory to our total personality."[67] Here, his assumptions about God, Scripture, and humanity coalesce.

One way to approach this coalescence is through our thoughts about God. We have already noted Forlines's claim that God has revealed Himself, and that if He has revealed Himself, what has been revealed is necessarily accessible to those with whom He wishes to communicate. Special revelation is a specific way He has revealed His message of redemption. And it is striking that given the way human beings are constituted (i.e., total personality), special revelation speaks to persons' total personalities. In other words, this is not a fluke, but a specific design on both counts, persons and Scripture. The God Who speaks is Himself a *person* and "is personal."[68]

To be made in the image of God not only means that our personalities mirror (to a lesser degree, of course) God's personality, but it also assumes the more basic premise that "we are designed beings."[69] Moreover, because we are designed as such we "are not blank tablets" and "we have not been hurled into space to drift aimlessly," but rather, "we have been preprogrammed by God with a knowledge of God and what He is like."[70] God does not just design us to be like Him in certain ways, but He has designed us with preloaded data that can never be erased because it is *written into our very being*. God's self-revelation to man speaks into that being—it speaks to the total personality—because that Word itself is data designed in such a way to communicate to the kind of being (i.e., a person) that can understand and process that data. This "personal God Who has created man in His own image"[71] has created us with the capacities that are able to understand God's communication, just as if He is communi-cating with Himself.

Consider the existence of *a priori* beliefs, which (roughly) are the kinds of beliefs we have *prior* to (or, apart from) any particular perceptual experience or observation. For Forlines some of the preloaded data that is written onto our very being are *a priori* beliefs about God and what He necessarily must be like. For instance, we have a built-in belief that if there is a God, He must be perfect, holy, fair, just, and sovereign.[72] These are necessary qualities of God, given our *a priori* definition of the concept of God. Is it possible to think of God in a way that is less than these things? Sure, but as Forlines notes, one has to "divorce the mind from the rest of his personality"[73] in order to do this, which leads us to the exact same kind of despair that postmodernism points to. We can attempt to divorce the life of our minds from the rest of the aspects of our personalities and run each as separate processes, but the rest of our personality cries "foul!" when we attempt such detachments. They are merely attempts to do what could only work in an "irrational universe" where "man is hopeless."[74]

If we recognize our *a priori* beliefs about what God must be like, as well as the pre-programmed questions (i.e., the inescapable ones) that flow from the needs of our total personalities, then "if there is a book that can rightly be called God's Word, it is without error . . . whatever this book affirms is true."[75] How can we know this? Not because we have (or need) some way of scientifically verifying Scripture's truth-claims, but because "our whole being is repulsed by the idea of a book that is the Word of God being less than inerrant."[76] Given our *a priori* understanding of the concept of God, specifically that His communication to us must be (1) personal (since He is a person and we are persons) as well as (2) without error (since a necessary property of God is complete and utter truth), His revelation must then necessarily speak to our whole beings truly.

This takes us to the Bible. Forlines writes:

> [It] is addressed to the total personality, not just to the mind. The Bible must be studied in the arena of life. You bring the Bible to life and you bring life to the Bible. You bring the Bible to your pains and you bring your pains to the Bible. When

the Bible is properly understood, it makes us free (Jn. 8:32). It gives meaning and purpose to life. We have something to live for, and we have something to die for.[77]

Along these lines, Forlines affirms the canon of Scripture as God's genuine special revelation because it "self-authenticates" itself.[78] Given the makeup and needs of a total personality, the Bible speaks into that because it was written to do that. It speaks to our very being in a way that no other book does. A personal God wrote it for the "total personality" needs of His personal creation.

> Our interest is kindled because of the inescapable questions which represent unquenchable longings. The message of the Bible sounds like what our innermost being needs. In the Bible we see answers to our inescapable questions. In the Bible we see provisions for our needed experiences. It speaks to our total personality. We see it as an alleviation of our lostness. . . . The reasonableness of our faith in Scripture is also shown by the way in which the Bible fits into a functioning system of Truth (or worldview). When we believe God, the Bible, Jesus Christ, and man with his needs, it all fits together. There is togetherness, cohesiveness, and interrelatedness.[79]

Forlines's Practice of Doing Theology

With the above trifecta in his methodological toolkit, Forlines utilizes a particular praxis for the specific nuts and bolts work of theology—that is, for coming to his theological claims. This process is twofold. First, he ultimately is concerned with what Scripture has to say about an issue. And given the discussion in the previous section, we know why he places such emphasis on what Scripture says. Biblical exegesis, then, is central to his project.

Second, his humility is manifested in his recognition that his own work stands on the shoulders of others' work, whether he agrees with them or not. This is why so many of his arguments are crafted as a conversation with what others have thought about an issue. His work reflects his desire to show deference to what other serious scholars have already said, but challenging them when he finds their arguments and/or exegesis lacking. In this way, his work is critical.

Exegetical

Consider, for instance, how Forlines explicitly develops his position on the topic of perseverance (an issue dealt with in chapter six). Forlines offers his own argument on the matter, but not before (or without) considering the best exegesis for both sides of the issue. In *Quest*, he begins his discussion by explaining the scriptural grounding of two opposing views, the traditional Calvinist view of perseverance and the more popular doctrine of "once saved, always saved." He painstakingly investigates and exegetes passages often used to substantiate those views: John 10:28-29; Romans 8:35-39, 11:29; and Philippians 1:6, just to name a few.[80] He then carefully exegetes the ones that support apostasy as being a very real possibility: Hebrews 6:4-6, 10:26-29; 2 Peter 2:20-22; Colossians 1:21-23; and John 15:2, 6.[81] Forlines does not base the crux of his argument on how it fits into his theological system, but on what Scripture has to say about the issue at hand because he (rightly) assumes that "truth is an integrated and harmonious whole."[82] There is no need to defend any "system." Hence, there is no need to color any scriptural exegesis for the purpose of the system, or for the prerogative of the system's adherent.

Critical

Even though Forlines's theology ultimately is exegetically based, it is not solely exegetical. He is very explicit about being part of a larger conversation with other theologians, past and present. Of course, not everyone does this. Some (but thankfully very few) exhibit a jaded sort of biblical interpretation where their own hubris guides their abilities, and so long as a particular rendering is merely possible (and works to achieve their prerogative), it does not matter how far it is outside of the spectrum of 2000+ years of serious theological discourse. Forlines recognizes the naïveté of doing theology in a bubble. He knows the history of theology, and all of the arguments and trends and shifts, and his reasoning reflects this.

Also, he does not merely gloss over those with whom he sympathizes, or wholesale reject those with whom he disagrees. Rather, he takes a critical perspective, correcting the erring arguments while respecting and appreciating the arguer. A short list includes people such as John Calvin, James Arminius, Charles Stanley, Zane Hodges, John Gerstner, Louis Berkhof, R. C. Sproul, I. Howard Marshall, Robert Shank, and Wayne Grudem, among others.[83] Forlines presents his work as a dialogue with key thinkers on all sides of an issue. He does not make it easy for himself. He intentionally deals with the best argument from the best thinkers, but that is why his work is so valuable.

Where Do We Go from Here?

Given all that has been noted above, what may be the most unique and original aspect of Forlines's method is his explicit use of basic anthropological facts about human nature as premises for his argument about our need for (and the purpose of) theology. Seen this way, theology is not just the warp and woof of scholars, but the milk and meat of *every* Christ follower. It meets the needs of our total personality. We need theology because we need God.

In reflecting on how this fits into the history of theological methodology, an interesting question surfaces: to what extent is a methodological use of "total personality" implicitly utilized given the kind of theology one is doing? I still get the sense (even though this may perpetuate an unfortunate stereotype) that most streams of Reformed Calvinist theologies tend to assume more on the "rational" part of the anthropological spectrum, whereas many streams in Arminian theology implicitly focus on the psychological-emotional side of the spectrum. And what I mean here is that they privilege each, respectively, as the paradigm within which theological truth claims are processed.

Forlines, however, considers the *whole* person with *all* of his attributes, and crafts a theology that takes it all into account, speaking to the whole person because God speaks to the whole person. One question that deserves further study is whether this assumption is an upshot of the kind of Reformed Arminian worldview that has influenced Forlines. Specifically, is Forlines's holism uniquely Reformed Arminian in that it navigates between the extremes of ultra-rationalistic Reformed and ultra-experiential non-Reformed streams? Further work on this would be fascinating, especially if done so with an eye toward understanding its impact on the church, both universal and local, regarding its mission to make disciples of Jesus Christ. We will do a great disservice if we fail to take up the mantel Forlines has given us and carry it onward—doing it not for ourselves, but for the Church.

---

[1] David K. Clark, *To Know and Love God* (Wheaton: Crossway, 2003), 24.

[2] F. Leroy Forlines, *The Quest for Truth: Answering Life's Inescapable Questions* (Nashville: Randall House, 2001), 3; hereafter *Quest*.

[3] Ibid., 100.

[4] One's "total personality" is drawn into the theological enterprise because the questions it seeks to answer are the most important ones relative to one's own existence and well-being. Hence, approaching theology in the same way that one might approach a research project about fuel-cell technology is not appropriate, for instance.

[5] While this essay relies on several works by Forlines, it extrapolates his method in *Quest*, since that is his most comprehensive work.

[6] Jack Williams, "No Excuses, No Regrets," *One Magazine* (Oct/Nov, 1996).

[7] Ibid.

[8] By "fundamentalist" I am invoking its original designation regarding the five *fundamental* propositions central to the historic, Christian faith. Originally drafted by the Presbyterian Church USA in 1910 (and eventually accepted by all theological conservatives), they are: (1) the canon of Scripture is inspired of God and hence inerrant; (2) Christ was born of a virgin; (3) Christ's death atoned for man's sin; (4) Christ arose bodily; and (5) Christ's miracles are a historical fact. (See the Minutes of the 1910 General Assembly of the Presbyterian Church USA, 272-73).

[9] Not all would, of course; Forlines notes Harold Lindsell's controversial 1976 exposé of evangelical institutions that eventually rejected their original commitment to biblical inerrancy. See *Quest*, 22-23; Harold Lindsell, *The Battle for the Bible* (Grand Rapids: Zondervan, 1978).

[10] Leroy Forlines and Robert Picirilli, *Orthodoxy, Modern Trends, and Free Will Baptists* (Nashville: Free Will Baptist Bible College, 1957).

[11] By "scientific method," Forlines and Picirilli mean the empirical study of theology, whereas the epistemological methods that govern empirical science also are carried over to study

Scripture and theology. Forlines will later argue that empiricism as a means for trying to answer life's inescapable questions is utterly inadequate. As such, he does not dismiss the proper role of empirical research in the domains for which it is best suited; but to use it beyond its proper (limited) role has utterly disastrous consequences.

[12] Forlines and Picirilli, 6.

[13] Ibid., 38.

[14] Ibid., 41.

[15] See Forlines, *Issues Among Evangelicals* (1968) and *Inerrancy and the Scriptures* (1978), both published by the Commission on Theological Liberalism of the National Association of Free Will Baptists, Nashville, TN.

[16] Forlines, *Inerrancy and the Scriptures*, 24; italics added; hereafter *Inerrancy*.

[17] Ibid.

[18] Ibid.

[19] J. I. Packer, *Truth and Power* (Wheaton: Harold Shaw, 1996), 116; italics added.

[20] Forlines, *Inerrancy*, 25.

[21] Ibid., 25.

[22] Ibid., 12.

[23] Forlines, *Quest*, 1.

[24] Ibid., 1.

[25] Ibid., 7.

[26] Ibid.

[27] Ibid., 9.

[28] Ibid.

[29] Ibid., 14.

[30] This distinction is akin to Immanuel Kant's distinction between objects of the *noumenal* realm (unknowable) and the *phenomenal* realm (knowable). See Kant's chapter "Analytic of Principles" in *Critique of Pure Reason*.

[31] Forlines, *Quest*, 7.

[32] Ibid., 1.

[33] Ibid., 14.

[34] Ibid.

[35] Ibid., 40.

[36] Ibid., 30.

[37] Ibid., 31.

[38] F. Leroy Forlines, *Romans*, The Randall House Bible Commentary, gen. ed. Robert E. Picirilli (Nashville: Randall House, 1987), 57.

[39] Forlines, *Quest*, 32.

[40] Ibid., 95.

[41] Ibid., 36.

[42] Ibid., 34.

[43] Ibid., 35.

[44] Ibid., 36.

[45] Ibid., 33.

[46] Ibid., 32.

[47] Ibid., 37.

[48] Ibid., 39.

[49] Ibid., 37.

[50] Ibid., 47.

[51] Ibid., 48.

[52] Ibid., 62.

[53] Ibid., 49.

[54] Ibid., 52.

[55] Forlines, Inerrancy, 15.

[56] Forlines, Quest, 54.

[57] Ibid., 55.

[58] Ibid.

[59] Ibid., 63.

[60] Forlines, Inerrancy, 10.

[61] Ibid., 10; see also Forlines, Quest, 55.

[62] F. Leroy Forlines, A Theological Approach to Personality (Nashville: Free Will Baptist Bible College, n.d.).

[63] Forlines, Quest, 3.

[64] Ibid.

[65] Ibid., 30.

[66] Ibid., 64.

[67] Ibid., 18.

[68] Ibid., 31.

[69] Ibid., 33.

[70] Ibid.

[71] Ibid., 52.

[72] Ibid., 56; see also Forlines, Inerrancy, 10-13.

[73] Forlines, Quest, 56.

[74] Ibid., 57.

[75] Ibid., 56.

[76] Ibid.

[77] Ibid., 53-54.

[78] Ibid., 108.

[79] Ibid., 108-09.

[80] Ibid., 269-76.

[81] Ibid., 276-88.

[82] Ibid., 5.

[83] Ibid., 269-99.

CHAPTER TWO

WORLDVIEW AND CULTURE IN THE THOUGHT OF F. LEROY FORLINES

Phillip T. Morgan

Seaside swimmers are well acquainted with the infamous riptide. This occurs when a section of sand bar, loosened by the continuous advance and retreat of ocean waves, finally gives way and rushes out to sea. The first signal to swimmers of this event is the almost instantaneous disappearance of the ground beneath them. They are then swiftly swept out to sea, sometimes finding that they are more than a mile offshore. The immediate loss of firm ground beneath their feet and the outrushing current overwhelm the mind, and the tide pulls them under. In fact, many have even died from being caught in such an event. They keep their heads above water, but are swept so far out to sea that they are unable to swim back to shore before their strength expires. The only hope is to find firm footing as soon as possible.

Undeniably, the twentieth century experienced a cultural riptide of extreme magnitude. Many were caught in modernity's outrushing vortex, which has become known as postmodernity. This anti-worldview rejects any coherent, systematic understanding of reality. Christians who did not realize what was happening looked around at the end of the twentieth century only to find the vast expanse of postmodern relativism and pluralism separating them from the sure footing they thought existed. However, some refused to go with the current and held firmly to biblical foundations. F. Leroy Forlines is an exemplar of those who have resisted the tide.

Raised during the Great Depression, Forlines was schooled in high ideals by his family and community, and later by Welch College. Though "times were hard," he describes a culture that intuitively lived out a Christian worldview that permeated American society.[1] Influenced by both Carl F. H. Henry and Francis Schaeffer, Forlines expanded upon what he had received by diligently developing a robust, intentional worldview that could withstand the twentieth century's cultural changes.

Forlines understands cultures as embodied thought systems. Because modernism and Christianity had similar assumptions about the nature of absolute truth and its implications for everyday life, even secular elements of American society were not usually radically incompatible with Christianity. Therefore, when Forlines began developing his worldview as an adult, he firmly understood what a Christian worldview should resemble. He found that the ideals, morals, and truth commitments, which he was raised to extol, could be maintained despite modernism's failures and postmodernism's relativism. But they could be maintained only by holding to the convictions that God is personal and has communicated with man through the Bible. From this revelation we can learn Who God is, who we are, and what our lives should look like. The result is a robust, holistic worldview that embraces all of life and seeks to transform the culture around us.

Epistemology

In *The Quest for Truth* (hereafter *Quest*),[2] Forlines begins with epistemology, which entails "the most basic questions that must be dealt with."[3] Epistemology is the study of how we acquire and test knowledge. It addresses how we know what we know and is central to worldview development. Because Forlines's work flows from his epistemology, we will address it first by sketching the historical and cultural context of his work and his engagement therein.

Empiricism's Failure

Though Forlines begins his analysis of the epistemological debate with Copernicus, we will begin earlier. Schaeffer stated that Thomas Aquinas's (1225-1274) work "opened the way" for the division of knowledge.[4] Prior to Thomas, epistemology was guided by the thought of Augustine of Hippo (354-430), who held that we must first believe in order to understand: *Crede ut intelligas*.[5] This means that every person has a subjective starting position from which they observe the universe. However, Thomas embraced neo-Aristotelian thought, synthesizing it with Augustine and positing that observation of the natural world could lead to knowledge of God and universal truth. Thomas thus opened the way to dividing knowledge into two categories: grace (God, heaven, unseen things, man's soul, universals) and nature (created things, earth, visible things, man's body, specifics).[6] In *Quest*, Forlines adopts Schaeffer's interpretation of the Thomistic divide as an upper and lower story division of knowledge.[7] As Forlines describes it, the upper story contains "the inescapable questions of life: knowledge of God, universals, moral knowledge, religious knowledge, meaning and purpose for life, etc.," whereas the lower story contains "particulars, mathematics, mechanics, the physical sciences, etc."[8]

Forlines analyzes the effects of this epistemic break with Copernicus (1473-1543). Working within the new divided paradigm, Copernicus's observations led him to posit that the earth revolved around the sun rather than the sun around the earth. The ensuing debate led people to perceive science as autonomous from Christianity and special revelation.[9] As Forlines writes, "In the minds of many reason aided by experience and observation (empiricism) had triumphed over theology. God was no longer necessary."[10] Seventeenth and eighteenth century Christians unwittingly began to imbibe this new divided epistemology. According to George Marsden, "By the end of the eighteenth century, American Protestants of almost all sorts had adopted this two-tiered worldview, founded on an empiricist epistemology, with the laws of nature below, supporting supernatural belief above. They thus had worked out a modern version of the Thomist synthesis of reason and faith."[11] This was not immediately seen as problematic, primarily because the vast majority of scientists initially accepted biblical conclusions.

The autonomy of science and reason became much plainer after Charles Darwin's *On the Origin of Species* (1859). Soon Herbert Spencer (1820-1903) applied evolutionary theory to life and thought. Forlines writes, "The evolutionary principle was viewed as the key to understanding religion, morals, sociology, economics, and all other areas of life."[12] Since man is reduced to a "product of natural causes through the process of evolution," he can define his own morality and religion or non-religion.[13]

Friedrich Nietzsche (1844-1900) drove these ideas to their logical conclusion when he proclaimed that God was dead. Forlines points out however, "The atheism to which Nietzsche referred was not ontological atheism (the denial of God's actual existence). It was epistemological atheism."[14] This is because those who have already "limited data for rational thought to observation and experience" can only believe in a God Who is "merely an appendage to their worldview."[15] Nietzsche simply realized that a God Who is disconnected from life is no different than an absent God. For Forlines, that is the logical conclusion of empiricism. As he puts it, "I believe the epistemology of empiricism is the parent and atheism as a worldview is the child."[16]

Empiricism's failure to discover knowledge of God or absolute truth eventually became apparent. Though men and women continued to adhere to an empiricist epistemology, they rejected the possibility of reason and absolute truth. They lost any hope that they could find answers to their deepest needs. This worldview or anti-worldview became known as postmodernism.

Responding to Empiricism's Failure

If empiricist epistemology leads to atheism and a postmodern view of truth, it cannot be a tenable Christian epistemology. According to Forlines empiricism's fatal flaw was not its use of logic, but rather its starting assumptions.

Empiricism begins with the assumption that observation and experience are the only ways to acquire knowledge. Therefore, empiricists reject "divine revelation and innate ideas as valid sources for data" with the intent of acquiring a neutral or objective starting point.[17] However, the concept of a "neutral platform from which to start" is fallacious.[18] Forlines states, "We cannot start from 'nowhere.' We must start from somewhere."[19] Empiricism's refusal to admit special revelation could never allow an investigator to discover a personal God Who has revealed Himself through personal communication. "An inadequate epistemology [has] shut him off from a knowledge of God," Forlines explains.[20] The "*only* truth a person can discover is that which is allowed by his *epistemology*."[21] Further compounding the situation by disregarding innate ideas, empiricism was unable to posit a system capable of fulfilling man's deepest needs.

Forlines thus rejected empiricist epistemology for a nuanced presuppositionalism.[22] Like Augustine he contends that belief precedes understanding. This is evident in his statement that the "*only* truth a person can discover is that which is allowed by his *epistemology*."[23] A person's preexisting assumptions inevitably inform his or her acquisition of knowledge. Here Forlines asserts that empiricism, like presuppositionalism, is "faith-knowledge."[24] Yet Forlines does not thereby reject reason. "Human beings are deeply rational," he states.[25] "When reason is used with sincerity, diligence, and integrity, it is necessary and valuable in determining the truth or falsity of a worldview."[26] Therefore, Forlines sees reason as necessary in determining the validity of his type of presuppositional worldview.

Influences on Forlines's Thought

Forlines's epistemological thought built upon and worked along similar lines as the "evangelical renaissance." This movement was partially birthed from the work of the Dutch Reformed theologian, Abraham Kuyper (1837-1920).[27] Thinkers like Schaeffer and Henry drew from Kuyper their understanding that "any discipline is built on starting assumptions and that Christians' basic assumptions should have substantial effects on many of their theoretical conclusions in a discipline."[28] Especially influential for Schaeffer was Kuyper's understanding of the importance of presuppositions:

> The distinction between the true science and the false science lies not in the arena where people perform their investigations, but in the manner with which they investigate, and in the principle from which people begin to investigate. Sin has not only corrupted our moral life, but has also darkened our understanding. The result can only be that anyone attempting to reach scientific knowledge with that darkened understanding is bound to acquire a distorted view of things, and thereby reach false conclusions.[29]

Kuyper believed two sciences would result from the differing starting platforms of Christian (true) science and non-Christian (false) science. Both use reason to reach their conclusions. However, because their starting positions differ, both groups proceed logically, and yet come to differing conclusions. Thus two conflicting worldviews may be scientific and rational, if each is consistent with its starting premises.

Marsden considers the debate over how "Christian scholars pursue science" as the "overshadowing" theme of twentieth century evangelicalism.[30] This debate centered on Benjamin B. Warfield's (1851-1921) rejection of Kuyper's model.[31] Those who took the Warfield line continued to believe that "one science or rationality" could be shared by all humanity.[32] Warfield also held that Christianity's truths could be demonstrated rationally from an objective empiricist epistemology. Forlines disagrees. Concerning the perceived proofs of God's existence, he suggests, "The arguments for the existence of God do not prove in the absolute sense of the word."[33] Overall Forlines best fits in the Kuyperian camp.

Sources of Data

Having formulated an epistemology, Forlines makes a definitive decision concerning the sources of data to be used: "The question to be decided by epistemology is: 'What are the sources of data?' Everybody recognizes the validity of observation and experience as a valid source of data. The question is: What about Divine revelation and innate knowledge?"[34] Forlines believes that empiricism's rejection of innate knowledge and divine revelation is destructive.[35] If there is a God, He must either be impersonal or personal. If He is impersonal, then we cannot know Him, since an impersonal God cannot communicate, and we cannot find Him through the use of our five senses.[36] However, "if God is personal, He can speak."[37] Therefore, the only way we can know Him is through His communication with us. Forlines thus accepts divine revelation as a source of knowledge.

Having settled the question of divine revelation, Forlines turns to innate knowledge. He contends that we have God's moral law in our hearts (Rom. 2:14-15). Though depravity vitiates innate knowledge of God's moral law, we "will never inform a blank space in a person's mind when you tell him or her that adultery, lying, and stealing are wrong."[38] People may have different ideas about what these are, but they are never completely ignorant of them. Forlines believes these innate ideas should also be allowed as sources of data.

Forlines's epistemology has developed through serious consideration. By tracing the history of empiricism's divided knowledge and analyzing its basic assumptions, he concludes that empiricism can only produce atheism or agnosticism (see chapter nine). However, if divine revelation is accepted, it was possible to include God from the beginning. This approach assumes God is personal and has communicated with man through divine revelation and innate knowledge, which is the basis of Forlines's worldview. Before addressing his worldview, though, we first need to consider his primary tool for constructing it.

Apologetics

Because his epistemological model asserts that all worldviews begin with different preconceived ideas, Forlines's approach to apologetics is to test each worldview as a whole for validity. Accordingly, a worldview is valid only if it is "satisfactory to our total personality as thinking, feeling, acting beings."[39] Though the total personality has always been important in Forlines's work, he perceives personality as growing in importance in recent years.

Protecting Total Personality

Forlines demands the total personality be addressed because most philosophers and theologians detrimentally separate logic from life. He recalls he "was not familiar with anyone who had come up with a test that would forthrightly demand that a true worldview must be effectively life related."[40] Due to his own "deep struggles in bringing Truth and life together," Forlines demands that any system claiming to explain all of reality should also engage the whole person as a thinking, feeling, acting being. The test Forlines eventually developed to verify worldview validity asks four questions:

> (1) Does it answer the *inescapable questions of life?* (2) Is there internal consistency, i.e., is the structure logically related to the foundation? Do all the parts fit consistently together? (3) Is there causal adequacy? i.e., are the causes adequate to produce the effects attributed to them? (4) Does it conform to that which is undeniably true? If a worldview cannot answer the *inescapable questions of life*, it is not worthy of our consideration.[41]

The *inescapable questions of life* deal with humanity's deepest needs: "Is there a God? If so, what is He like? How can I know Him? Who am I? Where am I? How can I tell right from wrong? Is there life after death? What should I and what can I do about guilt?"[42] Because these questions address our deepest needs, they involve our emotions, actions, and thoughts. We cannot "have peace and satisfaction" without finding "answers to these questions that our total being will accept."[43]

Purely logical systems offer conclusions against which our emotions cry out. Forlines writes, "The heart is the seat of the emotions. It is through our hearts that what we know with our minds becomes real. In our hearts we feel value and disvalue."[44] Therefore emotions validate thought systems claiming to offer a holistic philosophy of the world. However, emotion is not the only test. Any worldview that offers answers to life's inescapable questions must also be reasonable. Forlines contends, "We are so constructed that we cannot set reason aside."[45] "Even those who propose to set reason aside give reasons for it," he points out.[46] Those who try to deny reason and unified truth do damage to themselves: "It is painful and creates problems. Our inner being cries out for meaning and purpose in life."[47] Reason has at least three demands: First, a worldview must be internally consistent. The worldview's embodied results must be consistent with its presuppositions and development, and no tenet may contradict any other. Second, the proposed causes must be capable of producing the "effects attributed to them."[48] If the causes proposed are incapable of producing the expected effects, the worldview is insufficient. Finally, worldviews cannot make assertions that contradict what is undeniably true of reality. If a worldview asserts propositions contrary to reality, it must be rejected.

Because Forlines's worldview test addresses reason, emotions, and actions, it protects the whole person. Any worldview disregarding man's emotions and intuitions as illusory ignores something vital. On the other hand, if man's emotions and intuitions are satisfied and reason is sacrificed, then again the whole person is destroyed. Lastly, any worldview that satisfies humanity's need for reason and emotion, but demands actions impossible to fulfill, is useless. Any worldview that divides the whole person fails to correspond with that which is undeniably true of humans.

Cultural Adjustments

Interestingly Forlines's worldview test manifests itself in two ways. Each is designed for a different culture. Earlier in life Forlines worked within a culture that still held modernism's promises. Therefore, the test appearing in *Biblical Systematics* (hereafter *Systematics*) (1975) was in the format reproduced above. However, by *Quest's* publication in 2001, Forlines had made two slight changes to his test. First, the internal sufficiency demand is reworded in the second test, though the question's substance is the same.[49] Second, Forlines reorders the test's four prongs; this change is more important. He explains why he did this: "In 1975, modernism was being challenged, but it had not been dethroned. With the emphasis that was given to reason in modernism," the original order "was fitting."[50] The first test "was a rational test of coherence."[51] We can see then that Forlines was engaging the whole person in the early test, and realizing that modernism demanded reason above all else, structured his test to engage the person of that day. In his words, it "addressed . . . the modernist secular paradigm."[52]

In the intervening years though, postmodernism had "dethroned" modernism.[53] By 1990 postmodernism ruled American culture. Forlines describes the cultural revolution of the 1960s-1990s as responses resulting from the realization that "reason and science had not been able to minister to the deep inner needs of human nature."[54] He sympathetically describes the despair of those involved in this paradigm shift in *Quest*: "Those who switched to postmodernism did so because they had supped at the table of modernism and went away starved."[55] Forlines responded to the change in the culture's needs around him. In the second iteration of his worldview test, he demands fulfillment of humanity's deepest needs first. He states, "It became apparent that the test: Does it answer the *inescapable questions of life?* should be the first test."[56] Even in 1975 he believed a worldview should answer these questions. However, cultural changes encouraged him to emphasize the section of his test that most closely dealt with the people's needs he was trying to reach. Despite differing emphasis and structural order, Forlines consistently tests his own worldview against these demands. No step in his worldview is allowed to forgo the demands of the whole person.

A Robust Holistic Worldview

Forlines constructs his worldview from his epistemology and apologetics. He rejects the optimistic hope that we can retain empiricism as a means of proving the Christian worldview's claims. Instead, he embraces an approach similar to Kuyper's presuppositionalism as a way to investigate and build a worldview from within. Forlines begins by offering four basic presuppositions upon which he relies throughout his worldview construction. Though these presuppositions are honored from the beginning, each must also prove its validity in turn. Forlines refers to these propositions as his "platform"; we might also think of them as growing organically from his epistemology. If we think of his epistemology as the root system of his worldview, then his first postulate is the stalk's base. From this grows the next three presuppositions, finally blossoming into a holistic worldview that vibrantly addresses all of life.

God Exists and Has Revealed Himself to Us

Forlines's base postulate is a more precisely defined expression of his epistemological decision to accept divine revelation and innate knowledge. Forlines accepts the existence of a personal God as a presupposition because any other starting point cannot satisfactorily answer life's inescapable questions. Forlines contends that God's divine revelation is present in the Bible and person of Jesus Christ. He also clarifies that innate knowledge, observation, and personal experience are part of God's general revelation. These elements work together to communicate to man in a manner he can comprehend.

After applying his worldview test to modernism and postmodernism, Forlines finds them woefully insufficient. However, the existence of a personal God passes. According to Forlines, if a personal God exists, the only way to know Him is through personal communication. Therefore, Forlines posits: (1) "If there is a God, He is a perfect being"[57]; and (2) "if there is a book that could rightly be called God's Word, it is without error, or stated positively whatever it affirms is true."[58] These *a priori* beliefs arise from our whole person—mind, heart, and actions. Although a person could conceive of a God Who "is less than perfect, holy, just, and fair," he or she could only do so if they "divorce the mind from the rest of [their] personality."[59]

Forlines's second proposition flows from his first: Anything claiming to be God's perfect Word must be inerrant. He states, "I believe it to be a self-evident truth that any book that would be the Word of God would be inerrant."[60] He does not deny that there are people who "do not believe in Biblical inerrancy."[61] But he contends, "Such people have at least been faced with the question of inerrancy from their own inner being."[62] Here again the needs of the total personality are the test. Yes, a person can come to a belief that God's Word is errant, but he or she can do so only by rejecting their deepest emotional and intuitive demands: "Our whole being is repulsed by the idea of a book that is the Word of God being less than inerrant."[63] Forlines's reason for ascertaining whether the Bible is inerrant is similar to J. I. Packer's: "Biblical *inerrancy* and biblical *authority* are bound up together. Only truth can have final authority to determine belief and behavior, and Scripture cannot have such authority further than it is true."[64] Biblical inerrancy is so important because biblical authority demands it.

Having established his second proposition, Forlines discusses general revelation as exhibited in nature and man's existential experience. In his analysis of Romans 1:19, Forlines concludes that Paul "is telling us that God *is known* [innately] through general revelation."[65] The content of innate knowledge develops in Forlines's thinking over time. In 1975, he wrote that God's glory, eternal power, and divine attributes can be gathered from general revelation, leaving man with "no defense for his sinning."[66] Beyond this brief summation Forlines offers two definitive comments, "(1) Man, as a sinner, has not properly read what may be known of God through general revelation"; and, "(2) The story of redemption is not written in general revelation. Redemption revelation must be special revelation."[67]

By 2001 Forlines had developed his treatment of general revelation considerably. In *Quest* he addresses the debate over the interpretation of *gnostos* in Romans 1:19, concluding that "people *do* have knowledge [*gnostos*] of God and morals," which is innate.[68] The innate knowledge of God and morals can be suppressed as Romans 1:32 states, but *"suppressed knowledge is nevertheless knowledge."*[69] This innate knowledge of God manifests itself in life's inescapable questions and morality. C. S. Lewis similarly wrote concerning moral knowledge: "It seems, then, we are forced to believe in a real Right and Wrong. People may be sometimes mistaken about them . . . but they are not a matter of mere taste and opinion."[70]

Concerning innate knowledge of God, Forlines's thinking has also developed. In *Systematics* Forlines unequivocally states, "I do not believe that the knowledge of God is innate."[71] However, he came to decide that he had a "misunderstanding of the meaning of 'innate.'"[72] His original understanding was that this term meant that newborns have knowledge of God, which seemed unreasonable. But he came to decide that innate knowledge of God more aptly describes a "natural" quality of belief in God.[73] We may choose not to believe in God because of environmental influences, but our natural inclination is toward belief in God.[74] Beyond our innate ideas of God and morality, Forlines contends that knowledge can be gained by "observation and experience."[75] These produce the knowledge that Forlines suggested in *Systematics*. Therefore, the main development in Forlines's treatment of general revelation concerns innate knowledge. His approach to innate knowledge also provides an excellent foundation for building a robust Reformed Arminian approach to natural law, which still needs to be done.

God's Revelation Is for Man, and Can Be Known By Man

The second postulate in Forlines's worldview may seem redundant. However, he correctly believes it essential. The knowledge of the origins and nature of man are important. The Bible gives both. It is written to man so that he might understand himself in relation to God, himself, other people, and creation (Forlines's four basic relationships). "Revelation takes the guess work out of identification," Forlines writes.[76] Instead identification "comes to us as a 'given' from the Creator Himself. The real nature of man's personality and what it takes to meet those needs will never be discovered by observation and experimentation. It must come to us as a 'given.'"[77] Forlines states that the Divine revelation of man's origins and nature are "integrally related to the Christian system."[78] This is because the Bible offers us directions for "running the human machine," as C. S. Lewis puts it.[79] Forlines adds, "We need proper prescriptions for our lives."[80] Thus Forlines draws on the Bible for his approach to all of life.

Of special import to Forlines's worldview are these two scriptural truths: (1) man has fallen from his original estate, and (2) God sent His Son in the person of Jesus Christ to offer redemption. According to Forlines, man being created in God's image has two aspects: constitutional (personhood) and functional (personality). After the Fall, man's functional likeness was vitiated so we no longer think, feel, and act in ways that are pleasing to God. Therefore, "a new birth is required for man's salvation."[81] The incarnation of Jesus not only offers a means of restoration to our prior relationship with God, but also a way to rehabilitate our functional likeness to God so that we might live new lives. Jesus offers a whole new life of thoughts, feelings, and actions—an embodied, holistic worldview for man that is integrated and harmonious.

Truth Is an Integrated and Harmonious Whole

The necessity for integration and harmony arises from the nature of a worldview. Worldviews are systems of thought that claim to explain all of reality. A worldview that fails to be harmonious and fully integrated can only offer a splintered explanation. Forlines elaborates on this third postulate, "One of the most important things to observe about a system is that nothing in a system can be fully identified without reference to other parts of the system. Every part of a system is tied into the system by relationships to other parts."[82] As we have seen Forlines determines that the Christian worldview offers an integrated and harmonious whole that is cohesive and interrelated. Therefore, the Christian worldview has implications for all of life.

All of Life's Experiences

If Forlines's epistemology is the root system of his worldview, his first three presuppositions would be the stem and the last a blossom. The existence of a personal God Who has communicated with man in a comprehensible and holistic manner finds its embodiment in all of life's experiences. According to Forlines, "All of life's experiences operate within the framework of four basic relationships and involve four basic values."[83] This model completely embraces every aspect of a man's or woman's life. Everything we think, feel, or do occurs with at least one or more of these relationships. Man's creation, Fall, and redemption all affect these four relationships.

Forlines's four basic values—holiness, love, wisdom, and ideals—guide us within these relationships.[84] These four values relate to one another in a complex manner. Holiness is the most demanding. Forlines describes it as "inflexible" because it demands separation from sin.[85] Love, wisdom, and ideals must bow to holiness's demands.[86] However, holiness also promotes chastened love, godly wisdom, and high ideals. These values are always present in the four basic relationships and guide our actions (see chapter eight). As Charles Colson states, "Our choices are shaped by what we believe is real and true, right and wrong, good and beautiful."[87] Like Colson, Forlines's worldview is comprehensive or holistic—truth for life—and it must be lived out through understanding and engaging culture.

Describing culture, Forlines writes, "Culture as such may be neutral since culture is capable of reflecting the values of any world view, but a particular culture is never neutral. It reflects the values of the world view (or views) of the people who make it up."[88] Since culture is never truly neutral, it is subject to scrutiny. Discussing the importance for teachers and preachers to study the prevailing culture, Forlines writes, "No matter what we study, it will always be studied in a context and will be addressed to a context. The Bible does not change, but the context in which it is studied and preached does change."[89] Forlines states further, "It is the responsibility of those of us who teach Bible and Theology to make ourselves aware of the world-view thinking that is shaping the thinking and behavior of people in our society and in our churches."[90] Forlines thus shows a kinship with Schaeffer who also believed that we share the gospel more persuasively by understanding the prevailing culture.[91] In both men's analysis, the surrounding culture had changed drastically during the twentieth century.[92]

Both Forlines and Schaeffer located the cause of the dramatic twentieth century paradigm shift in the secular world's rejection of modernism. This rejection was not complete, but only served to reject the possibility of absolute truth. Forlines contends this development was inevitable:

> If man is the product of natural causes through the process of evolution, when it comes to matters relating to the moral and the religious, he is a blank tablet. He can choose his own morals and religion, or decide not to be religious at all. He might encounter some difficulty from others, but he would not be in conflict with any internal design. Assuming this to be true, the highest happiness for the human race would be accomplished by recognizing these matters to be strictly personal, and making no attempt to suggest that one person's opinion might be any better than another's.[93]

Empiricism could only lead to postmodernity; if either an internal design or a moral God does not exist, then morality is only a matter of personal preference. Forlines also notes the vehemence with which assertions of individual morality were interpreted, "The worst thing that any person could do is to say that another person is wrong. Those who do such things are bigots. Bigotry is wrong!"[94] Forlines wrote those words in 1989, but his analysis has been proven accurate over the intervening years.

In a 2012 interview, sociologist Christian Smith described the findings of his research into teenagers' spiritual lives. His results match almost precisely what Forlines predicted in 1989: "If there is something that is objectively morally right or wrong, you certainly could not impose it upon anyone. That is what the assumption is, that it would be an imposition. It could not be something that one person could use to influence another person because that would be coercive."[95] Smith continues, "So the underlying moral commitment here is that nobody should make anyone else feel bad."[96] The result of such rejection is the anti-worldview in which we live and breathe.

This anti-worldview has had dramatic effects on our culture. Forlines often explains the dramatic shift in values that he has experienced in his lifetime.[97] Concerning morals and ideals he states, "When it comes to morality and ideals, the *culture* that I was brought up in did a better job of training people than the *church* does now."[98] Since that time the "weakening of the influence of orthodox thought" has effected a "weakening of the influence of morality on the conscience, and many forms of immorality are defended as being right."[99] If morals have suffered under postmodernity's reign, ideals have become nonexistent. "Ideals are considered to be in a neutral area where only personal opinion and preference prevail. All of this could have been predicted. It is not simply a happenstance of culture," Forlines writes.[100] "It was inherent in epistemological atheism. When there is a denial of truth that makes some actions either right or wrong, certainly there is no reason left to insist on politeness."[101] Therefore, ideas define and guide the imaginations and actions of the people living within a culture, just as they also express people's values.

Forlines also sees this effect in the arts. "When you erase purpose and meaning from life," Forlines explains, "what you have is chaos, confusion, absurdity, pessimism, and despair. All of this shows through in modern art."[102] A culture does not simply embody its ideals in its morals and actions, but also in its art and music. Forlines writes, "Since music is art, I think we could say that much of modern music is anti-music, or non-music."[103] What does Forlines mean by music? "I am referring here to the music as distinguished from the lyrics or words. The message of the words is easier to analyze than the message of the music, but the music also conveys a message or a worldview."[104] Here Forlines makes clear that both the content and form of art reflects an artist's worldview. As James K. A. Smith has perceptively noted, all of these factors work together to produce a "secular liturgy," which "operates with a more holistic, affective, embodied anthropology . . . than the Christian church tends to assume!"[105] Forlines also contends that evangelism has become more difficult since the 1930s and 1940s. Now people must first be convinced of the reality of sin before they can be told they need a Savior.[106]

Another aspect of this problem has resulted from many Christians choosing to imbibe the culture rather than faithfully witnessing against it. Ken Myers portrayed this capitulation as "an amphibious position where [Christians] want to be in both worlds—the bitter sweet delight of basking in ambivalence."[107] As Forlines points out, postmodernism has "been around a long time."[108] However, postmodernism's influence has moved outside the academy and into the world, and unfortunately its "influence is not limited to unbelievers. The thinking and behavior of many Christians has also been polluted."[109]

Within our churches, Forlines describes a "significant moral decline"[110] present in our dulled consciences and complete disregard for "ideals of beauty and excellence."[111] Concerning these ideals, why have so many Christians made a "deliberate attempt to go with the flow of the culture?"[112] Forlines suggests this development reflects the "thought that we can reach more people with the gospel if we tailor our [worship] services and our lifestyles to allow about anything that is not a direct violation of the moral laws of the Ten Commandments."[113] He suggests further, "In fact you are considered a hindrance to the growth of the church if you feel disposed to have any concern for beauty, excellence, and propriety."[114]

Forlines manifests his concerns for these very ideals by denying the appropriateness of certain musical forms for worship because "Christianity has implications for every area of life."[115] The method of most churches is simply to do "what gets the job done. The end justifies the means."[116] Forlines points out that this approach has the distinct danger of producing a "shallow, superficial concept of Christianity."[117] Forlines is consistent with Lewis, who says, "The standard of permanent Christianity must be kept clear in our minds. . . . In fact, we must at all costs *not* move with the times."[118] When Christians do "move with the times," Henry has noted it "obscures the comprehensive and cohesive nature of the Biblical view."[119]

However, this does not mean that Forlines advocates a withdrawal from the public square. Forlines's approach to cultural engagement is what many evangelicals call "transformational." Forlines states directly, "I think we are supposed to be transforming the secular culture rather than to be transformed by it. I think in recent years the church has been transformed by secular culture more than the church has transformed secular culture."[120] He believes we must start by finding "what changes our culture has experienced that have resulted from a departure from Christian world view-thinking."[121] Once assessed, "We must work to bring those departures back under the influence of Christian thought. We dare not let secular thought change us. If we surrender at this point, we will fail to accept our responsibility to be the salt of the earth."[122] James K. A. Smith agrees, "There is something inherently irresponsible about [cultural] withdrawal."[123] Smith suggests that we should "center" ourselves in a robust Christian worldview, for "from that space we then lean out and are sent into these other more fraught contexts to bear witness and collaborate. I think meaningful cultural labor will require collaboration and that means we need to be out there."[124]

Yet Forlines is cautious about the amount of collaboration in which Christians can faithfully engage. When considering Carl F. H. Henry's proposals for collaboration, Forlines cautions that "he has strained to keep dialogue."[125] Instead we need to heed Lewis's call for an attack on the "enemy's line of communication. What we want is not more little books about Christianity, but more little books by Christians on other subjects—with their Christianity *latent*."[126] The goal is to engage all areas of life Christianly. As an example Forlines writes about our engagement with politics:

> The separation of church and state does not mean that Christianity has no political implications. The political implications have to be studied in the context of the period of time in mind. Certainly the political set up of Christ's future king-

dom will take a different form than what we now have. However, the present time is a chief concern in this discussion. . . . If we separate the church and state, we cannot expect the state to take on the responsibility of preaching the Gospel. We can expect the state to create an atmosphere in which a person can freely serve God and develop himself spiritually. It is a Christian's responsibility to exercise his influence to be sure that this atmosphere prevails.[127]

Forlines agrees with Myers that Christians should "encourage cultural habits that go against the grain" of the prevailing culture.[128] We must use our influence to seek to change, reshape, and transform the culture around us into a more Christlike kingdom. Forlines concludes that this is essential for Christians, "If we do not put the changes in our culture that have occurred in the last few decades under the scrutiny of Scripture, and cull out what is in conflict with Scripture, secularism will transform us. That is the reverse of what should be. The next generation of believers will pay for our failure."[129]

Conclusion

The twentieth century was a difficult century for those who lived through it. A paradigm shift of rare magnitude occurred and many only realized what was happening after it was too late. F. Leroy Forlines, however, determined in his heart to hold to the firm ground of biblical Christianity when it began to shift. Working concurrently with thinkers like Carl F. H. Henry and Francis Schaeffer, Forlines developed a Christian worldview that is equally robust and coherent. Like those before him, Forlines believes that God's Word informs all of life and gives rise to a holistic worldview. He therefore constructed a worldview that organically grew from his brand of presuppositionalism. The flowering of this worldview results in a full-bodied embrace of transformational Christianity. We are transformed by God through the person of Jesus Christ and the Bible. We then turn and transform the culture around us spreading redemption as far as the curse is found.

[1] F. Leroy Forlines, *The Quest for Truth: Theology for A Postmodern World* (Nashville: Randall House, 2001), 417; hereafter *Quest*.

[2] *Quest* is largely a development of Forlines's 1975 monograph, *Biblical Systematics* (hereafter *Systematics*). I have attempted to work out of *Systematics*, referring to *Quest* only in cases of difference. Ideally this suggests some lines of development in his thinking. In certain instances I deal with these developments directly, but generally I have left this task to the reader.

[3] Forlines, *Quest*, 7.

[4] Francis A. Schaeffer, *Escape from Reason: A Penetrating Analysis of Trends in Modern Thought* (1968; repr., Downers Grove: InterVarsity, 2006), 13; see also Bradley G. Green, *The Gospel and the Mind: Recovering and Shaping the Intellectual Life* (Wheaton: Crossway, 2010), 98-99.

[5] Augustine of Hippo, "Tractate on John 29," in *The Fathers of the Church: St. Augustine Tractates on the Gospel of John 28-54*, trans. John W. Rettig (Washington D.C.: Catholic University of America Press, 1993) 18; https://books.google.com/books?id=QKWH9Qr_hnAC&printsec=frontcover&source=gbs_ge_summary_r&cad=0#v=onepage&q&f=false; accessed June 19, 2015; Internet.

[6] Schaeffer, *Escape from Reason*, 13-14.

[7] Francis A. Schaeffer, *The God Who Is There*, 2nd ed. (1982; repr., Downers Grove: InterVarsity, 1998), 83.

[8] Forlines, *Quest*, 8.

[9] Ibid., 10.

[10] Ibid., 11.

[11] George M. Marsden, *Understanding Fundamentalism and Evangelicalism* (Grand Rapids: Eerdmans, 1991), 131.

[12] Leroy Forlines, "The Responsibility of the Bible Department as It Relates to World View Thinking" (unpublished manuscript, 1989), 2.

[13] Ibid., 9.

[14] F. Leroy Forlines, "Dealing with the Influence of Epistemological Atheism" (paper presented at the National Association of Free Will Baptists Commission for Theological Integrity Theological Symposium, Nashville, TN, October 25, 1996), 7.

[15] Ibid., 7.

[16] Ibid., 2.

[17] Forlines, *Quest*, 8.

[18] Ibid., 5.

[19] Ibid.

[20] Ibid., 9.

[21] Ibid.

[22] Forlines's approach to presuppositionalism is of an Augustinian caliber similar to that of Edward John Carnell, Carl F. H. Henry, Ronald H. Nash, and Francis Schaeffer. However, an association of his work with Cornelius Van Til's hard transcendental argument would be incorrect.

[23] Forlines, *Quest*, 9.

[24] F. Leroy Forlines, *Biblical Systematics: A Study of the Christian System of Life and Thought* (Nashville: Randall House, 1975), 80.

[25] Forlines, *Quest*, 95.

[26] Ibid.

[27] Marsden, 150-51; Mark Noll, *The Scandal of the Evangelical Mind* (Grand Rapids: Eerdmans, 1994), 216-17; James K. A. Smith, *Letters to A Young Calvinist: An Invitation to the Reformed Tradition* (Grand Rapids: Brazos, 2010), 96-105.

[28] Marsden, 151.

[29] Abraham Kuyper, *Wisdom & Wonder: Common Grace in Science & Art*, trans. Nelson D. Kloosterman, eds. Jordan J. Ballor and Stephen J. Grabill (Grand Rapids: Christian's Library Press, 2011 [1905]), 52.

[30] Marsden, 150-51.

[31] Ibid., 123.

[32] Ibid., 151.

[33] Forlines, *Systematics*, 73.

[34] Forlines, "Dealing with the Influence of Epistemological Atheism," 2.

[35] Ibid., 10.

[36] Forlines, *Systematics*, 12.

[37] Ibid.

[38] Forlines, "Dealing with the Influence of Epistemological Atheism," 10.

[39] Forlines, *Systematics*, 9.

[40] Forlines, *Quest*, xv.

[41] Ibid. 18.

[42] Forlines, *Systematics*, 1.

[43] Ibid.

[44] Leroy Forlines, *Morals and Orthodoxy* (Nashville: Commission on Theological Liberalism National Association of Free Will Baptists, 1974), 11.

[45] Forlines, *Systematics*, 70.

[46] Ibid.

[47] Ibid.

[48] Ibid., 75.

[49] Ibid., 9; Forlines, *Quest*, xv.

[50] Forlines, *Quest*, xv.

[51] Ibid.

[52] Ibid., xiii.

[53] Ibid., 16.

[54] Ibid., xv.

[55] Ibid., 14.

[56] Ibid., xv.

[57] F. Leroy Forlines, *Inerrancy and the Scriptures* (Nashville: Commission on Theological Liberalism National Association of Free Will Baptists, 1978), 10; hereafter *Inerrancy*.

[58] Ibid. 11.

[59] Ibid.

[60] Ibid.

[61] Ibid.

[62] Ibid.

[63] Ibid.

[64] J. I. Packer, *Beyond the Battle for the Bible* (Westchester: Cornerstone, 1980), 17.

[65] Forlines, *Quest*, 35.

[66] Forlines, *Systematics*, 13.

[67] Ibid.

[68] Forlines, *Quest*, 34.

[69] Ibid., 35.

[70] C. S. Lewis, *Mere Christianity* (New York: Macmillan, 1943), 20.

[71] Forlines, *Systematics*, 73.

[72] Forlines, *Quest*, xvi.

[73] Ibid., 103.

[74] Ibid.

[75] Ibid., 36.

[76] Forlines, *Systematics*, 109.

[77] Ibid.

[78] Ibid., 87, 108-09.

[79] Lewis, *Mere Christianity*, 69.

[80] Forlines, *Systematics*, 108.

[81] Ibid., 113.

[82] Ibid., 109.

[83] Ibid., 6.

[84] F. Leroy Forlines, *Biblical Ethics: Ethics for Happier Living* (Nashville: Randall House, 1973), 38.

85 Ibid., 46.

86 Ibid., 48.

87 Charles Colson and Nancy Pearcey, *How Now Shall We Live?* (Carol Stream: Tyndale House, 1999), 13.

88 Forlines, "The Responsibility of the Bible Department," 3.

89 Ibid., 1.

90 Ibid.

91 Schaeffer, *The God Who Is There*, 175.

92 For support of Forlines's and Schaeffer's cultural decline narrative from a broader witness pool, see Roy Rosenzweig and David Thelen, *The Presence of the Past: Popular Uses of History in American Life* (New York: Columbia University Press, 1998), 38, 135-137.

93 Forlines, "The Responsibility of the Bible Department," 9.

94 Ibid.

95 Christian Smith, interview by Ken Myers, *Mars Hill Audio Journal* 112 (June 2012).

96 Ibid.

97 See Forlines, *Quest*, 19-22, 27-29, 411-12, 415-24, 444-45.

98 Ibid., 19.

99 Forlines, *Morals and Orthodoxy*, 3-4; see also Rosenzweig and Thelen, *The Presence of the Past*, 135-37.

100 Forlines, "Dealing with the Influence of Epistemological Atheism," 14.

101 Ibid.

102 Ibid., 12.

103 Ibid., 13.

104 Ibid.

105 James K. A. Smith, *Desiring the Kingdom: Worship, Worldview, and Cultural Formation* (Grand Rapids: Baker Academic, 2009), 24.

106 Forlines, *Quest*, 19-20.

107 James K. A. Smith, interview by Ken Myers, *Mars Hill Audio Journal* 123 (November, 2014).

108 Forlines, "The Responsibility of the Bible Department," 2.

109 Ibid.

110 Forlines, *Morals and Orthodoxy*, 8.

111 F. Leroy Forlines, "A Plea for Unabridged Christianity," *Integrity: A Journal of Christian Thought* 2 (Summer 2003): 85-102, 90.

112 Ibid., 90.

113 Ibid.

114 Ibid., 85-102, 98.

[115] Leroy Forlines, *Issues Among Evangelicals* (Nashville: Commission on Theological Liberalism National Association of Free Will Baptists, 1968), 73; see also Leroy Forlines, *Cheap-Easy Believism* (Nashville: Commission on Theological Liberalism National Association of Free Will Baptists, 1975), 16.

[116] Forlines, "Dealing with the Influence of Epistemological Atheism," 15; see also Forlines, "A Plea for Unabridged Christianity," 98.

[117] Forlines, *Cheap-Easy Believism*, 15.

[118] C. S. Lewis, "Christian Apologetics," in *God in the Dock: Essays on Theology and Ethics*, ed. Walter Hooper (Grand Rapids: Eerdmans, 1970), 92.

[119] Carl F. H. Henry, "The Christian Scholar's Task in a Stricken World," *Christian Scholar's Review*, 17 no. 4 June 1988, 487.

[120] Leroy Forlines, "Critique of the Hybel Seeker Service" (unpublished manuscript, 1994), 2.

[121] Forlines, "The Responsibility of the Bible Department," 3.

[122] Ibid.

[123] James K. A. Smith, interview by Ken Myers.

[124] Ibid.

[125] Forlines, *Issues Among Evangelicals*, 76.

[126] Lewis, "Christian Apologetics," 93.

[127] Forlines, *Issues Among Evangelicals*, 74.

[128] Kenneth A. Myers, *All God's Children and Blue Suede Shoes: Christians and Popular Culture* (1989; repr., Wheaton: Crossway, 2012), 182.

[129] Forlines, "The Responsibility of the Bible Department," 3; underline removed.

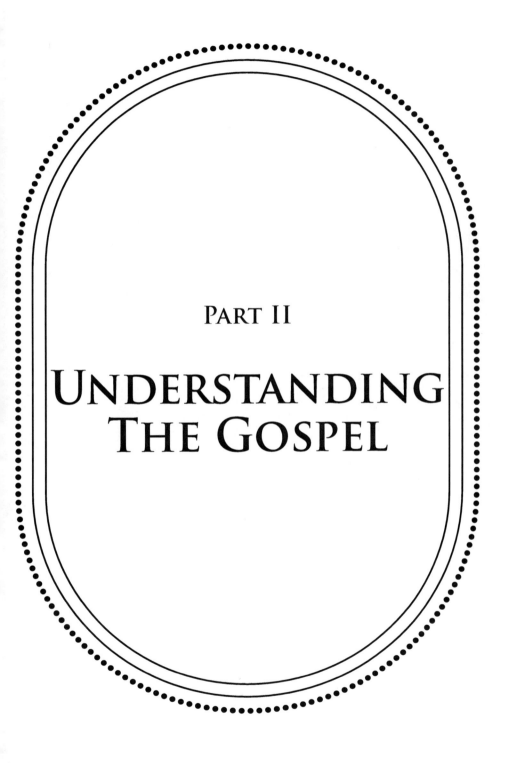

PART II

UNDERSTANDING THE GOSPEL

CHAPTER THREE

ELECTION AND THE INFLUENCE AND RESPONSE MODEL OF PERSONALITY

Kevin L. Hester

The task of theology is to explicate and systematize human thought about the inscrutable God. Theologians ask questions that are not easily answered by a simple review of revelation. God's ways are not our ways, and His thoughts are not our thoughts (Isa. 55:8). For example, theologians have identified three theological mysteries that have been the source of intense theological debate since the early church. These mysteries are the unity and distinction of the godhead in the Trinity, the union of the two natures in Christ, and the relationship between human freedom and divine sovereignty.

The councils of Nicea (325) and Constantinople (381) declared the essential unity of the Trinity, and the full personhood and divinity of each member.[1] The councils of Ephesus (431) and Chalcedon (451) defined Christology over against Nestorianism and Apollinarianism, arguing that the Son has two complete natures united in one person without confusion or change.[2] Numerous local councils against Pelagius and his followers established the sovereignty of

God in salvation, the depravity of humanity, and the necessity of grace. The Second Synod of Orange (529) defined the nature of the relationship by positing universal guilt and depravity and the necessity of grace in all aspects of salvation. At the same time, the canons denied predestination to damnation and affirmed that grace could indeed be resisted, emphasizing human cooperation after conversion.[3]

The uneasy conclusions of the Second Synod of Orange have never been fully satisfying. Throughout Christian history the debate has persisted in ways that the issues of the Trinity and Christology have not. It is seen in disputes with Gottschalk and his condemnation, the early rivalry between the Dominicans and the Jesuits, and in the competing Protestant traditions of Calvinism and Arminianism.

Calvinism has emphasized God's sovereignty, arguing for a soteriology that affirms total depravity, unconditional election, limited atonement, irresistible grace, and perseverance.[4] Arminianism, driven by an emphasis upon the full personality of humanity, has traditionally asserted a total universal depravity that is redeemable by prevenient grace (sometimes referred to as deprivation), conditional election, unlimited atonement, resistible grace, and conditional perseverance with the possibility of apostasy. Both schools of theology assert Scripture's primacy and work to build their theology upon it. Space will not allow even a cursory review of the numerous works (theological and exegetical) that have been and will continue to be published as part of this debate.[5] However, the topic of election provides us, not simply with the opportunity to review F. Leroy Forlines's contribution to this debate, but to delineate his theological method and soteriology as a *via media* between Calvinism and Wesleyan Arminianism. He distinguishes his position from Calvinism by arguing for conditional election, and from Wesleyan Arminianism by teaching individual rather than corporate election. Forlines's work on election finds its synthesis between poles of tension in Scripture, theology, and Christian experience.

Forlines's *Via Media*

Forlines's 1975 *Biblical Systematics* says little about election.[6] Chapter 12, "The Condition of Salvation," probably affords the best opportunity to raise this theological distinctive, but there is no reference to it. The only listing of the term "election" is in chapter 13, "Continuance in Salvation," and even there it is mentioned only as an element of distinction between Calvinism and Forlines's Reformed Arminianism.[7] The placement, though non-substantive in nature, demonstrates his approach to the concept of election, as it will be later unfolded in his *Quest for Truth*. Election, when it is considered, is reviewed in light of its place in Reformed soteriology. For Forlines, election is important as it manifests itself practically in ministry and in the experience of salvation in the life of the believer.

In *The Quest for Truth* (hereafter *Quest*),[8] Forlines treats the topic in a discussion of God's sovereignty, human ability (in relation to the doctrine of depravity and repentance/faith), and its ultimate relationship to apostasy. In chapters 15-17 of *Quest*, Forlines addresses election. His broad, systematic approach is seen in the placement of his discussion after perseverance. He recognizes this is far from ordinary and explains that "a discussion of decrees and election should draw from a thorough study of the doctrines of Scripture, God, man, and salvation both in its provision and application."[9]

Forlines proceeds to introduce Calvinist and Arminian understandings of election in chapter 15, where he enters a philosophical discussion of the nature of determinism and free will.[10] This approach is drawn from his emphasis upon the full personality of the human person as created in God's image. Whereas most Calvinists begin their discussion of election by reviewing God's sovereignty and most Wesleyan Arminians focus on free will, Forlines centers on the relationship between God and those whom He wishes to redeem. The *via media* he takes argues that election narrates a burgeoning relationship between God and the elect,[11] both of whom must be recognized in their full personhood. He argues that God has created humanity in His own image as a personal being with the ability to think, feel, and act and relates to humanity in this way.

Influence and Response

Forlines argues that Calvinism teaches a cause and effect relationship between God and humanity as an outgrowth of its teaching on God's sovereignty.[12] This is an oversimplification of the relationship.[13] He states that the question of whether humanity has free will is misplaced.[14] Instead, the question should be, "Does God deal with fallen man as a person?"[15] If so, then God must recognize His creative purposes in humanity. God is unable (because He is unwilling) to "cause" a person to act in a particular way, though God readily makes appeals and seeks strongly to influence these free responses.[16] The Calvinistic understanding of election as determinative is rightly viewed as a systemic necessity.[17] Denying the full personhood of humanity, it also raises concerns from human experience. If God's sovereignty is defined to say that God is the cause of faith, then there is no possibility for a negative response. This belies the human perception of consideration and undercuts the authenticity of the act of faith. "Whether we want to think of the act of willing as the function of a faculty of the person or simply the person making a choice," Forlines writes, "the fact remains that the ability of choice is part of being a person."[18]

When Calvinism's view of God's sovereignty in election is extended to include the reprobate, it necessitates God being the ultimate cause of things that are clearly expressed in Scripture as contrary to His will. Our perception of evil is a clear indication of human freedom expressed contrary to God's will.

> To say that human beings always respond properly to divine influence would say something about God, as the one who does the influencing, that I do not think we want to say. We cannot attribute all that is happening in the world to the influence of God. Nor, can we make Him the cause or the determiner of all that is happening. This is the kind of thinking that inclines many to atheism. It is unthinkable that a sover-

eign, holy, just, fair, and loving God would be the determining cause of everything that is happening in our world. There is something within us that rebels against such a thought.[19]

Forlines rightly raises questions about human responsibility when, according to Calvinism, God causes all human acts. To demonstrate, he references Feinberg and says that the Calvinist position means that God is the "cause not only of faith on the part of those who believe, but also for the sins of dishonesty, murder, rape, etc. The reason the person is responsible for such action, though it is 'causally determined,' is that he did what God caused him to do freely, not by constraint."[20]

Experience of Salvation

Forlines also rejects the Calvinistic framework for election based upon the Christian experience of repentance and faith in conversion. The Calvinistic view of election in response to total depravity means that God grants faith to the believer as a result of regeneration. He then notes that for Calvinism regeneration (the first aspect of sanctification) precedes justification. However, this is a logical and a theological impossibility. One cannot separate regeneration from sanctification or sanctification from justification. Scripture is clear that the condition for justification is repentance and faith. For regeneration to precede the biblically mandated conditions for the application of Christ's atonement calls into question the basic premise of the satisfaction view of the atonement.[21]

Forlines's insistence upon the satisfaction view of the atonement also raises questions for Calvinism's view of unconditional election. In his discussion of Ephesians 1:4, Forlines contrasts the Calvinist reading of this text with the *ordo salutis* of supralapsarianism and infralapsarianism: "In Calvinism, the elect were chosen by God . . . before the decree to provide atonement. They were His at that very moment. In both Supralapsarianism and Infralapsarianism, the decision to elect some and reprobate others precedes the decree to provide redemption."[22] But how could a holy God establish a relationship with fallen persons without atonement? This would violate God's holiness, "the foundation on which the satisfaction view of atonement rests."[23]

Forlines concludes his discussion of the Calvinistic understanding of election with an analysis of its assertion that faith's possession as a gift necessitates unconditional election.[24] Calvinism's insistence is driven by the connection between total depravity, election, and a number of seemingly clear passages of Scripture that indicate human inability to come to God (John 6:44; 14:6) and that faith is a "gift" (Eph. 2:8). This is perhaps the most frequent charge laid against those who hold conditional election. If faith is a not a "gift" then justification must be based in a human work in contradiction to Ephesians 2:8. Many Calvinists argue that those who teach conditional election are semi-Pelagians in disguise.[25]

Scripture

Forlines demonstrates the central role Scripture plays in his theological method through his discussion of saving faith.[26] In discussing the Holy Spirit's role in salvation, Forlines does not shy away from the Johannine passages mentioned above. A common challenge to Arminians from Calvinists is that they hold a weak view of depravity. This is not altogether true. Wesleyan Arminians teach the necessity of a prevenient grace that is generally applied.[27] In distinction from Wesleyan Arminianism, Forlines argues that the effects of depravity necessitate a prevenient grace that is individually applied.[28] Though he does not fully develop this concept, Forlines ties prevenient grace to God's means of grace found in Scripture and the testimony of believers: "There must be a move toward man on God's part before there can be a move toward God on man's part. . . . The Holy Spirit must take the Word of God and work in the human heart and mind to prepare the heart and mind before there can be the response of faith from a sinner."[29]

In this way Reformed Arminianism is closer to Calvinism than Wesleyan Arminianism. The remaining distinction is that the result of faith is not guaranteed. This is the result of Forlines's emphasis upon Scripture and his influence and response model of God's relationship with humanity: "The preparation of the mind and heart by the Word of God and the Holy Spirit creates a framework of possibilities in which a person can respond in faith to Jesus Christ. The response of faith is not guaranteed, but it is made possible."[30]

This influence and response model of relationships also informs Forlines's interpretation of Ephesians 2:8. He does not shy away from viewing faith as a gift because it is impossible without God's work. This never, however, contradicts the sinner's personality as a thinking, feeling, and acting being.

> Faith is called a gift because it cannot be exercised without the work of the Holy Spirit. At the same time, it is a response of the person in such a way that it is a response of his or her personality. It is in a real sense his own action. If a human being is to be treated as a person, in some real sense the action must be the person's own regardless of how much divine aid may be given. Otherwise, a human being has been reduced to a subpersonal being.[31]

Forlines defends himself from the accusation of Pelagianism by insisting that salvation is only through Christ and His atonement. The means of the application of salvation in no way undercut the necessity of the atonement, or undermine the authenticity of the human response. "We must distinguish between the 'condition' and the 'ground' of salvation. Salvation is grounded solely in the death and righteousness of Christ provided by atonement . . . and imputed to the believer's account in justification. It is conditioned on the response of faith in Christ alone."[32]

Having thus defined the context of his view of election in an influence and response model and having raised objections to the Calvinist understanding of unconditional election, Forlines then turns to an interpretation of election in Scripture, embracing it as a biblical doctrine. He engages more biblical passages and discusses more biblical terms than would be possible for us to review here. Instead of summarizing each passage, I will synthesize his five primary conclusions.

1. Election takes place in eternity past.[33]

Forlines sees God's action in election as occurring in eternity past. He draws a parallel between Christ's election as the sacrificial lamb elected "before the foundation of the world" (1 Pet. 1:20) with 1 Peter 1:2 where Peter addresses those who were "elected by God the Father . . . to be obedient to Jesus Christ and to be sprinkled with His blood" to argue that both elections occurred in God's plan of atonement from the beginning of time.[34] "God was not caught off guard by the fall of the race into sin," he writes.[35] "The plan of redemption was already made and determined before the fall of Adam and Eve took place in the chronological order of events. What was planned and determined in eternity past took place when Jesus died on the cross."[36]

God's elective purposes are eternal by their nature. God's foreknowledge accompanies and informs God's actions. God's sovereign purposes in election are attendant with His purposes in creation and in redeeming His creation once fallen. Forlines cites the following verses as teaching the eternal nature of God's decrees: Romans 8:30; 9:23-24; Acts 4:28; 1 Corinthians 2:7; Ephesians 1:5, 11; and 1 Peter 1:2, 20. He bemoans the theological loss to Arminianism for failing to teach adequately a biblical view of predestination. Election, after all, touches upon the heart of the gospel:

> Predestination is just as essential for Classical Arminianism as it is for Calvinism. If there is no predestination, there is no gospel. Our gospel says that God has predestinated salvation for everyone who believes in Jesus Christ and He has predestinated that all who do not believe in Jesus Christ will be condemned to eternal death. . . . It is the fault of Arminians that we have almost forfeited the word predestination to the Calvinists.[37]

Forlines's perspective on the eternality of God's decrees leads to a traditional schema of the ordo salutis.[38] He quotes Thiessen approvingly to argue that the biblical decrees include: (1) creation; (2) permission of the fall; (3)

provision of salvation for all; and (4) application of salvation to all who believe.[39] What Forlines provides therefore is a form of sublapsarianism modified to fit his view of conditional election. Again, Forlines's conclusions show his synthesis between the Reformed tradition and Wesleyan Arminianism with a tendency toward the Reformed side of the spectrum. This orientation is also seen in his belief that election is best understood individually.

2. Election is individual.[40]

Forlines draws his basic model of influence and response to define his understanding of Paul's teachings in Romans and Jesus' teaching found in John's gospel. He underscores the fact that Jesus' and Paul's emphasis in light of their Jewish context was to demonstrate the need for an individual response of faith. Against Jewish views of corporate election,[41] Jesus taught the necessity of individual salvation. This is perhaps best seen in Jesus' words to Nicodemus regarding the means of salvation in John 3, but Forlines sees this consistently presented throughout the Gospel (4:14; 6:25-29, 35, 51; 7:37-39; 10:7-11, 27-30, and 14:6).

This concept then serves as the backdrop for the use of the terms *eklegomai* (choose), *helkuo* (draw), and *didomi* (give) throughout John's Gospel. The word *eklegomai* is always used in reference to Christ's choosing of the twelve disciples (6:70; 13:18; 15:16, 19). While many understand this term in reference to the apostolic office, Forlines adds that it still poses no problem for conditional election because Jesus' choosing does not rule out a response from the disciples. Each disciple chosen still had to decide to follow. The point is to indicate "any response on the part of any individual is a response to divine initiative."[42]

This emphasis upon divine initiative is seen in John's use of the term *helkuo* (draw). Jesus indicated that He would draw all men to Himself in John 12:32, and in John 6:44 we read, "No one can come to me unless the Father who sent me draws him." Led by his view of depravity and the necessity of prevenient grace, Forlines readily adopts Yarbrough's understanding of John 6:44 as a "forceful attraction."[43] Depravity necessitates such a work of the Holy

Spirit, but Forlines's influence and response model assures the possibility of rejecting this call.

The term *didomi* (give) is handled similarly. John teaches that the Father gives believers to Jesus (John 6:37), He gives disciples the ability to come to Jesus (6:65), and Jesus gives eternal life to those who come to Him (10:28). Again, we see John's focus on individual belief and on the divine initiative of the offer of salvation. Jesus and His atonement are the basis for eternal life, which is the terminus of the Father's offer of salvation. The Father's drawing leads to this result in believers; yet these passages do not require unconditional election.

> It was extremely clear that Jesus rejected any concept of the corporate election of all Jews. It was also clear that salvation was experienced on an individual basis. If salvation is experienced on an individual basis, it follows that since God is the same yesterday, today, and forever that election in eternity past would have been on an individual basis. . . . Salvation is conditioned on faith in Jesus Christ as Lord and Savior. Calvinists do not deny that justification is conditioned on faith in Christ. Is not justification required for election? If faith is the condition for justification now, why would it not be viewed that way in eternity past?[44]

3. Election is the work of God.

Forlines is committed to the biblical teaching that salvation has its beginning and end in God. God's sovereignty extends to all things. Salvation is based in God's work and not humanity's: "The whole plan of salvation from beginning to end is the work and plan of God."[45] The divine initiative in salvation as expressed in John's Gospel finds its fulfillment in God's sovereignty as expressed in such passages as Jeremiah 18:1-4, Romans 9:15, and Philippians 2:13. Forlines insists that election outlines God's plan and work in salvation so biblical passages like these emphasize that the Father is always salvation's cause and the Son's passive and active obedience are always salvation's basis.

This is confirmed in Forlines's reflection on Romans 8:29-30. The terminus of election is the believer's conformity to the image of the Son, or in other words, glorification.[46] In verse 30 we see a biblical *ordo salutis* as Paul moves from grace to grace in calling, justification, and glorification. The aorist tense employed indicates the certainty of this process as an act of God.[47] Forlines understands that though this passage is not an "exhaustive treatment of the doctrine of salvation," it does outline God's action in salvation as the reason believers should not fear God's absence in the face of any and all circumstances.[48]

This passage need not be read as teaching unconditional election. He asserts that the calling mentioned here (read in light of Acts 17:30 and Romans 10:11-13) should not be confined to the elect. Instead, such passages indicate "a call that extends to all men."[49] He adds, "No one is justified who was not first called." In dialogue with John Murray he asserts,

> The very nature of a call means that it is the activity of the one who extends the call. Justification is a divine act in which God declares us righteous based on the death and righteousness of Christ. The foundation of our justification is solely the merits of Christ rather than our own. But if Murray wants to insist that there is no involvement of the human personality in meeting the condition of faith as it relates to justification, I must differ with him. However, this verse says nothing about faith.[50]

"In Calvinism, regeneration precedes faith. The person is regenerated and then he believes and is justified. In Arminianism, the person believes, then he is justified and regenerated."[51]

4. Election is according to God's foreknowledge.

Forlines distinguishes his thought from Calvinism on the word *proginosko* (to foreknow). Most Calvinists see this term and *proorizo* (to predestine) as essentially synonymous.[52] In Calvinism God's foreknowledge is tied directly to God's decretive purposes. God knows the future because God has decreed the future and His sovereignty ensures that these things will necessarily occur.[53] Forlines asserts that God's foreknowledge is "not to be equated with divine causality"[54] although it does take under its purview God's active engagement in accomplishing His purposes.[55] In this way God's foreknowledge renders the subject of His foreknowledge as certain without making it necessary.[56]

Forlines reviews all seven places in the New Testament where this term or its roots are used. He defines the term to mean "prior knowledge" when used in reference to humanity as in 2 Peter 3:17 and Acts 26:5.[57] He distinguishes his understanding of foreknowledge as simple prescience from the Calvinistic perspective of God's foreknowledge as decretive and "efficacious."[58] He discusses this comparison as he works through Acts 2:23 and 1 Peter 1:20. In each place Calvinists view the term *proginosko* as synonymous with God's determining counsel. In both places God's foreknowledge regards Christ's crucifixion and atonement. Forlines takes this term as "instrumental," arguing that "God did not see the future as a passive observer."[59] Instead, God's foreknowledge included His decrees, His redemptive work, and the contingent choices of free beings. God's sovereignty and indeed God's wisdom are manifested in time as His plan is executed according to His foreknowledge.

While Forlines does not doubt that Christ's sacrifice was preplanned and ordained by God in eternity past, he rejects that the use of this term in these passages is teaching this truth. He says,

> The plan of God to provide atonement through the death of
> Christ was foreknown by God in eternity past. For this to have
> been *foreknown* meant, of course, Jesus was chosen for the pur-
> pose of providing atonement by His death and that it was *pre-*

planned, predetermined, and *prearranged.* All of these concepts, while true, are true by necessary inference from the nature of God and from the direct teaching of Acts 2:22 and 4:28, not by the meaning and use of *proginosko.* Calvinism's insistence that *proginosko* and *prognosis* are to be taken as synonymous with predestination is without foundation both from biblical usage and from use outside the Bible.[60]

Forlines continues to apply this instrumental understanding of *proginosko* in Romans 8:29 and 11:2. In both instances election is based in the instrumentality of God's foreknowledge of faith.[61] At the same time, he recognizes that foreknowledge in these passages moves beyond simple prescience to an intimate, personal knowledge: "God foreknew the elect with affection, or he foreknew them as being His."[62] These two concepts are not mutually exclusive, which Arminius demonstrates when commenting on Romans 8:29:

> He who is not in Christ, can not be loved in Christ. But no one is in Christ, except by faith; for Christ dwells in our hearts by faith, and we are ingrafted and incorporated in him by faith. It follows then that God acknowledges His own, and chooses to eternal life no sinner, unless He considers him as a believer in Christ and as made one with him by faith.[63]

Foreknowledge is connected to election as we learn here and in 1 Peter 1:2. What is not apparent is "what in foreknowledge formed the basis of election."[64] Certainly this foreknowledge would include faith and perseverance in that faith. This is the response of most Arminians on this topic.[65] Forlines is careful not to press his exegesis too far. In addition he takes great pains to argue that God's foreknowledge is not the passive viewing of a static God. Instead God's foreknowledge, and its connection to election, reveals His nature, His actions, and the contingent (though influenced) responses of free persons. God's foreknowledge includes:

(1) The result of His creative activity and His divine influence. (2) The result of the devastating effects of sin. (3) The result of the response that human beings would give as a result to the redemptive work of Jesus Christ, the ministry of the Holy Spirit, the ministry of the Word of God, and the ministry of the redeemed. (4) The result of all of the influences that would come from all sources outside Himself. (5) The result of all the influence that He would bring on people through His power and His infinite wisdom.[66]

The connection between foreknowledge and election brings us to Forlines's final assertion that election is conditional rather than unconditional.

5. Election is conditional.

The theological concept of election is a systemic one that touches on soteriology. In Arminianism salvation is based on faith, and election is the result; in Calvinism salvation is by election, and faith is the result. The exegetical arguments used by each are read through these lenses. Arminianism focuses upon the believer's experience and the passages teaching that salvation comes by grace through faith. Faith is viewed as the condition for salvation. Passages on election are read in this context. The Calvinist system focuses on passages related to election and foreknowledge and reads passages related to faith's instrumentality in salvation in this context.

In chapter sixteen of *Quest*, Forlines reviews passages instrumental to the Calvinist understanding of unconditional election and argues that they do not necessitate the position. Instead, they can be consistently interpreted with conditional election in view. Two major examples of his work in this area follow.

Romans 9

One of the quintessential passages thought to teach unconditional election is Romans 9. Forlines gives significant treatment to this passage in its historical and cultural context to develop his major interpretive key for this passage. He reasons that we can only apprehend Paul's meaning when we grasp his opponents' position. In Romans Paul has shown that both Gentiles and Jews are saved only by faith in Christ. Forlines argues that Paul's opponents believed in the "unconditional corporate election of all Jews," based on their understanding of the Abrahamic covenant as unconditional.[67] Paul's question in verse 14 finds its meaning in this context. Paul's burden is that "large numbers of Jews, who were the Covenant People of God would be lost and under God's wrath."[68] Rather than seeing this as an unjust failure of God, Paul bases this in God's conditional election according to foreknowledge. Though the Jews had received the unconditional promise of the Abrahamic covenant and the blessing of the Law, salvation had always been mediated through faith.[69] The role of faith in salvation had revealed that, "not all who are descended from Israel belong to Israel" (9:6).

As he moves into 9:10-13, Paul teaches that the past revealed that "not even all of Isaac's descendants made up the Covenant Seed of Abraham," revealing that God "could also determine that not all of the Covenant Seed of Abraham through Jacob would be saved."[70] Paul is not dealing with why some people are elected and some are not; instead he is speaking to the question of why not everyone who was physically descended from Abraham through Jacob was coming to faith in Christ. Forlines understands Paul as expressing that election is eternal, as we have seen above, and that election is not based on works.[71]

Forlines asserts that Paul begins teaching that election is individual with 9:15. He interprets the singular construction of *hon an* (whom) as a reference to individuals. This quotation of Exodus 33:19 is taken by many as a direct assertion of unconditional election.[72] Forlines asks, "On whom does God will to show mercy and compassion?"[73] Citing Acts 16:30-31 he answers, "God is choosing whom He wills when He chooses to show His mercy in salvation toward the one who believes in Jesus as his Lord and Savior."[74] He continues, noting that salvation is not by works as if any person could ever merit salvation; but that faith, unlike works, is the condition of salvation. As a condition it should never be confused with the ground of salvation, which is always Christ's atonement.[75] One's response to God's gracious call and His prevenient grace will lead to mercy or hardening as is indicated in 9:19. This hardening is both the free act of the one who rejects and the judicial confirmation of that rejection by God.[76]

Forlines argues that Paul returns to his emphasis on the eternal nature of God's election and its individual application in 9:19-24. His influence and response model of God's interaction shows the reciprocity of God's actions and human response. In 9:31-33 Paul revisits the problem of the Jewish rejection of God in Christ. He makes clear that this problem does not rest in election, but in the refusal of the unbelieving Jews to exercise faith in Christ. In so doing Paul also enlightens us to the answer of whether the election that he has been discussing is unconditional or conditional. This passage clearly ties election and faith together. Election is conditioned on faith.[77]

Ephesians 1

In Ephesians 1:3-14 Paul issues a doxology on the believer's blessings by virtue of union with Christ. These blessings include predestination, adoption, redemption, forgiveness, an inheritance, and the sealing of the Holy Spirit. Paul connects election with salvation "in Christ." Calvinists have seen here a basis for unconditional election. Especially important are 1:4, which says that God chose believers in Christ "before the foundation of the world," and 1:5, which indicates that believers are predestined for adoption as His children.

Forlines has no difficulty in asserting the individual aspects of election or its eternality as we have seen above. He is unwilling, however, to cede this passage to those who would advocate unconditional election. Two central problems follow this reading. First, election cannot precede God's provision and application of the atonement. He reasons that God's holiness demands humanity's guilt be reconciled before a believer is united to Christ. To think otherwise violates God's holiness and clear biblical teaching that faith instrumentally unites believers to Christ.[78]

Second, the believer's union with Christ is the object of this election. A believer's election is "in Him."[79] The text "does not say that we (believers) were chosen *to be in Christ*."[80] Election is in view of Christ's election (1 Pet. 1:20-21) and its benefits come to believers through the instrumentality of faith.

> In our study of atonement and justification, difference was made between the *ground* of justification and the *condition* of justification. The same distinction must be made in election. The *ground* of election is that God foreknew us as being in Christ (in union with Christ). Thus, He chose us *in Christ*. That is what Ephesians 1:4 tells us. Since the condition for being in Christ is *faith in Christ*, it is necessarily implied that God foreknew that the person would meet the *condition* of faith in Christ.[81]

Theological Response to Calvinism

Chapter seventeen in *Quest* provides "Scriptural Support for Conditional Election." Forlines continues his review of important theological terms and biblical passages pertaining to election.[82] Much of the material is responsive to Calvinism and lacks a substantive constructive argument.[83] Forlines falls short of demonstrating conditional election, but again defines important biblical and theological terms such as election and foreknowledge and interprets them consistently with conditional election. He closes the chapter however with important theological arguments for conditional election that provide a significant contribution to the discussion. Though building a strictly exegetical argument for conditional election is difficult, Scripture is plain in its presentation of the means of salvation. This serves as our guide in developing this theological concept.

> It is true that the Bible does not specifically say that foreknown faith was the condition of election in eternity past. The Cal-

vinist is correct when he says that the Bible does not tell us
why God chose the elect. However, silence on why God chose
the elect gives no support for unconditional election. . . .
Since God is the same yesterday, today, and forever means
that if we know why God chooses people now, we can reason
back to why God chose the elect in eternity past . . . It is
abundantly clear that salvation is by faith now . . . if salvation
is conditional now, it necessarily leads to the conclusion that
election in eternity past was conditional. The burden of proof
is upon those who think otherwise.[84]

Forlines summarizes his argument for conditional election by noting the
theological background of election in salvation, the universal call, and the extent of the atonement. He notes that election in Ephesians 1:4 is election to
a position "in Christ." Our position in Christ comes about by the facility of
faith. Foreknown faith is the basis for election.[85] The gospel's universal call and
God's desire for all persons to be saved indicate that the distinguishing factor
among the elect and reprobate is faith in a Messiah universally offered for all.[86]
The extent of the atonement (John 3:16; 1 Tim. 2:6; Heb. 2:9; and 1 John 2:2)
indicates the conditional nature of election as well. If God wills all persons'
salvation, the only possible explanation for the failure of all persons to believe
is human freedom and conditional election.

Horizons for a Forlinesean Understanding of Election

Throughout his discussion on election, Forlines makes important contributions to the Reformed Arminian perspective and the theological study of
the topic more generally. Most important is his reliance upon an influence
and response framework for understanding salvation. The role of experience
in his theological method is unique and speaks well to the postmodern world.
At the same time, his theological method is committed to the centrality of
Scripture, and his exegetical work is noteworthy for a theologian. He does not

limit himself to a review of the work of biblical specialists and refuses simply to proof text his theological assertions. In reference to Romans 9, his exegesis reinterprets and prefigures the modern debate on Paul's understanding of the law and the Jewish understanding of salvation.

His work on election is also foundational for the modern Reformed Arminian perspective. Forlines carves out his own niche between Calvinism and Wesleyan Arminianism. Unconstrained he develops a broadly Reformed understanding of election that embraces election as individual and eternal, and emphasizes the necessity of grace in salvation. Though nuanced Forlines maintains an essentially Arminian conclusion that views election as conditioned upon foreseen faith and perseverance. His reading of election before time according to the experience of the believer's salvation in time is connected by the eternal nature of the immutable God and serves to advance the argument in favor of conditional election.

Forlines's work is groundbreaking and serves as the first modern presentation of Reformed Arminianism on election. It opens the possibility of advance in the areas of prevenient grace and double predestination in an Arminian scheme, setting the stage for more advanced exegetical work on predestination and election. The question of perseverance is also impacted by his study, which poses some intriguing questions on the relationship between election and a practical theology, emphasizing its necessity. Forlines's work establishes a vista from which those who follow can see a bit further back into the eternality of God and a bit further ahead in the theological process of the application of salvation.

---

[1] The council of Nicea declared the Father, Son, and Holy Spirit *homoousios* (consubstantial). Tertullian, followed by Augustine, reflected on the Trinity as *una substantia tres personae* (one essence, three persons). See Tertullian, *Adversus Praxeas*, 26; and Augustine, *De Trinitate*, 7.

[2] The Chalcedonian formula described the Son as being "truly God and truly man"; *homoousios* (consubstantial) with the Father; having two natures without confusion,

change, division, or separation; and united in one person and subsistence. See Henry Bettenson, *Documents of the Christian Church* (London: Oxford University Press, 1947), 73.

[3] See "Grace," in F. L. Cross and E. A. Livingstone, *The Oxford Dictionary of the Christian Church*. 3rd rev. ed. (London: Oxford University Press, 2005), 700-02.

[4] These doctrines, often referred to by the acronym TULIP, were first defined at the Synod of Dort (1618-1619) in response to James Arminius's teachings. See Aza Goudriaan and Fred van Lieburg, eds., *Revisiting the Synod of Dordt*, Series in Church History and Religious Culture, vol. 49 (Leiden: Brill, 2011).

[5] Those new to this topic will find the following introductory work helpful: Chad Owen Brand, ed., *Perspectives on Election: Five Views* (Nashville: Broadman & Holman, 2006).

[6] F. Leroy Forlines, *Biblical Systematics: A Study of the Christian System of Life and Thought* (Nashville: Randall House, 1975).

[7] Ibid., 207, 224-25.

[8] F. Leroy Forlines, *The Quest for Truth: Answering Life's Inescapable Questions* (Nashville: Randall House, 2001); hereafter *Quest*.

[9] Ibid., 303.

[10] Ibid., 314-20; 325-28. Forlines discusses hard and soft determinism as identified in numerous Calvinist authors. He posits that Calvinist insistence on a liberty of spontaneity without a liberty of indifference is unhelpful since Calvinism builds upon a cause and effect model, which means that "all we see happening in today's world is in exact conformity to the desire of a holy and loving God" (337). Readers interested in Calvinist and Arminian understandings of these issues will find the following works helpful: Paul Helm, "The Philosophical Issue of Divine Foreknowledge," in *The Grace of God The Bondage of the Will: Historical and Theological Perspectives on Calvinism*, 2 vols., eds. Thomas R. Schreiner and Bruce A. Ware (Grand Rapids: Baker, 2005), 2.485-97; and William Lane Craig, *The Only Wise God: The Compatibility of Divine Foreknowledge and Human Freedom* (Eugene: Wipf & Stock, 2000). Craig adopts what is essentially a Molinist, middle knowledge view of compatibilism.

[11] One of the only other works to establish a similar *via media* between Calvinist and Arminian theories of election is Norman Geisler, *Chosen But Free: A Balanced View of Divine Election* (Minneapolis: Bethany House, 1999). This work was not particularly well received because of his use of hyperbole on both ends of the theological spectrum.

[12] The Calvinistic demand that God's sovereignty requires a cause and effect understanding of election actually reveals a smaller view of sovereignty. Forlines explains, "In the *influence* and *response* approach, God does not depend upon omnipotence alone to execute His sovereignty. He depends upon wisdom. It takes far more wisdom for God to be sovereign within the framework of influence and response than it does within the framework of cause and effect" (Forlines, *Quest*, 291).

[13] Ibid., 312.

[14] Ibid., 313.

[15] Ibid.

[16] Ibid.

[17] Ibid., 312.

[18] Ibid., 315. Forlines does not press this argument as forcefully as I think possible. If humans have the perception of freedom, and Scripture seems to confirm this perception in invitations to respond to God's call, it would seem to necessitate a non-constrained choice. Otherwise God appears to be deceiving humanity.

[19] Ibid., 320. We see in this argument and in his insistence upon an influence and response model as opposed to a cause and effect model good examples of the existential component of Forlines's basic theological method.

[20] Ibid., 309. Forlines is responding here to John S. Feinberg, "God Ordains All Things," in *Predestination and Free Will: Four Views of Divine Sovereignty and Human Freedom*, eds. David Basinger and Randall Basinger (Downers Grove: Intervarsity, 1986). See especially pp. 24-25, 32.

[21] Forlines, *Quest*, 339. "If a person is consistent in developing the implications of the satisfaction view of the atonement, it is clear that God cannot perform the act of regeneration (an act of sanctification) in a person before he or she is justified. God can move in with His sanctifying grace only after the guilt problem is satisfied by justification." See also, where following a quote from Berkhof, Forlines says, "Calvinists do not teach that the elect are justified before they experience faith. They teach that the person for whom Christ died will certainly be justified, but they do not consider a person justified until he experiences faith as the condition of justification. Thus, the atonement is provisionary until it is applied" (207).

[22] Ibid., 401.

[23] Ibid. Forlines is following an assertion developed by James Arminius in his "An Examination of the Treatise of William Perkins Concerning the Order and Mode of Predestination." See *The Writings of James Arminius*, ed. James Nichols and W. R. Bagnall, 3 vols. (Grand Rapids: Baker, 1956), 3.279-525; see especially 3.314.

[24] Forlines argues that the Calvinist understanding of unconditional election, in addition to being systemically required, is built upon three assumptions that he answers in turn: "1. That the sovereignty of God requires unconditional election and thus precludes conditional election. 2. That total depravity precludes the response of faith from a sinner unless he is first regenerated by the Holy Spirit. 3. That salvation is free precludes conditional election" (*Quest*, 341).

[25] Though rarely printed in serious academic texts, this view is often seen in popular writings of writers like R. C. Sproul, John Piper, and Michael Horton.

[26] The argument of this section from *Quest* is incomplete. Other than insisting upon his adherence to the satisfaction view of the atonement and belief that justification is a gift (341), Forlines does not speak directly to the issue. He does deal fairly comprehensively with some of these passages later in chapters 16 and 17. The material found above is developed from his discussion of the condition of salvation in chap-

ter 13. It is likely that in his mind, his attention to the topic at this place justified its virtual exclusion in his discussion of election.

27 For a modern introduction to a Wesleyan Arminian version of prevenient grace, see W. Brian Shelton, *Prevenient Grace: God's Provision for Fallen Humanity* (Anderson: Warner, 2014).

28 Forlines, *Quest*, 385-86.

29 Ibid., 257. The best presentation of prevenient grace from a Reformed Arminian perspective, though he does not like the term, preferring instead "pre-regenerating grace," is found in Robert E. Picirilli, *Grace, Faith, and Free Will: Contrasting Views of Salvation; Calvinism and Arminianism* (Nashville: Randall House, 2002), 153-60. Picirilli also associates pre-regenerating grace with the hearing of the gospel. More work needs to be done on this important doctrine from the Reformed Arminian perspective.

30 Forlines, *Quest*, 257.

31 Ibid.

32 Ibid., 368; see also Picirilli, 177-81.

33 Forlines notes that both Calvinism and Arminianism agree that whenever election occurs, the process of justification is tied to faith. God's election before time does not render a member of the class of the elect in union with Christ (and therefore "saved") until faith is demonstrated in time. "I have no quarrel with the idea that in some sense all of God's decisions are eternal. But His decisions are based on a prior knowledge of what He will do. He has not performed an act until He actually does it. . . . In both Calvinism and Arminianism, a person is not justified in the sight of God until he believes" (*Quest*, 261).

34 Ibid., 402; see also 397. More will be said below about the purpose of this election where Forlines disagrees with Calvinism, but his statements in view of the timing of the decree to elect place him within the broad stream of the Reformed tradition.

35 Ibid., 397.

36 Ibid.

37 Ibid., 394. Interestingly Forlines embraces double predestination. The difference is that in both cases election is conditional: "I am not averse to double predestination as such. What I reject is unconditional double predestination. I believe in conditional double predestination. On the condition of foreknown faith in Christ, God has predestinated believers to eternal life. He has on the condition of foreknown sin and unbelief predestinated unbelievers to eternal damnation. Apart from such predestination, we cannot assure the believer of eternal life or the unbeliever of eternal damnation" (374). Picirilli makes a similar claim in *Grace, Faith, Free Will*: "Reprobation is corollary to election. Unlike the Calvinistic system, the Arminian system makes election and reprobation essentially parallel (although as opposites). Election is gracious and eternal, founded in Christ, and conditional and personal in application. Reprobation is just and eternal, punitive (punishment for sin), and conditional and personal in application. The major non-parallelism is that election

requires the included foreordination of the administration of the means to faith: namely, the Word and the Spirit; reprobation requires nothing more" (59).

[38] Forlines's inclusion is uncommon among Arminians. Robert Picirilli notes, "Arminians have not been as concerned as Calvinistic theologians to provide a detailed *ordo salutis* or order of salvation. There is no good reason to avoid such a discussion, however." He goes on to list his own *ordo salutis*, which is different from Forlines's. Picirilli instead focuses upon the human appropriation of salvation rather than God's eternal decrees in giving the following outline: "calling = prevenient grace, conversion, including: a. repentance, b. faith, justification, regeneration, sanctification" (159-60).

[39] Forlines, *Quest*, 343; see also Henry C. Thiessen, *Introductory Lectures in Systematic Theology*, 1st ed. (1949), 344-349. Forlines notes that this work's position on election as conditional was modified by Doerksen the editor of subsequent editions. See Forlines, *Quest for Truth*, 513, n. 26.

[40] Forlines's embrace of individual election is based upon his reading of Scripture, which will be seen below. His view stands him in stark contrast with Wesleyan Arminians who teach corporate election. One of the best presentations of the Wesleyan understanding may be found in William W. Klein, *The New Chosen People: A Corporate View of Election* (Grand Rapids: Zondervan, 1990). See also Robert Shank, *Elect in the Son: A Study of the Doctrine of Election* (Springfield: Westcott, 1970), 45-55.

[41] More will be said on this topic in the material below, especially in relation to our discussion of Romans 9 and Forlines's contributions to a Jewish, cultural understanding of election in the first century.

[42] Forlines, *Quest*, 384.

[43] Ibid., 386; see Robert W. Yarbrough, "Divine Election in the Gospel of John," in *The Grace of God, the Bondage of the Will*, eds. Thomas R. Schreiner and Bruce A. Ware, 2 vols., (Grand Rapids: Baker, 1995), 1.47-62.

[44] Forlines, *Quest*, 383.

[45] Ibid., 368.

[46] Ibid., 392. Forlines misses an opportunity to point out that many passages related to predestination and election have their terminus in different aspects of the believer's salvation experience. In contrast to Calvinism, which seems to envision election only as related to the atonement proper, Scripture asserts that believers are predestined "to be conformed to the image of His Son" (Rom. 8:29), "for adoption as sons" (Eph. 1:5), and foreknown "for obedience to Jesus Christ and for sprinkling with his blood" (1 Peter 1:2), among others.

[47] Ibid., 378. This certainty by no means indicates that apostasy is not a real possibility. It does however indicate that election extends from foreseen faith to continuance in faith until death. The number of the elect and the number of those who have been regenerated and experience forgiveness of their sins at one time are not the same. I would argue that the elect will by definition persevere until the end because God's foreknowledge in election is dependent upon persevering faith. For-

lines does not himself draw out this distinction, and more work needs to be done to establish the connection between God's foreknowledge and divine election in regard to perseverance and apostasy.

[48] Ibid., 379.

[49] Ibid., 378.

[50] Ibid. Forlines is engaging with John Murray in his *The Epistle to the Romans*, 2 vols., in The New International Commentary on the New Testament, gen. ed. F. F. Bruce (Grand Rapids: Eerdmans, 1982), 1.320.

[51] Forlines, *Quest*, 270.

[52] As just one example see B. B. Warfield, "Predestination," in *Biblical Doctrines* (New York: Oxford University Press, 1929) who says, "'Foreordain' and 'predestinate' are exact synonyms, the choice between which can be determined only by taste" (4).

[53] L. Berkhof, *Systematic Theology* (Grand Rapids: Eerdmans, 1939). He says, "God has decreed all things, and has decreed them with their causes and conditions in the exact order in which they come to pass; and His foreknowledge of future things and also contingent events rests on His decree" (67-68).

[54] Forlines, *Quest*, 333.

[55] Ibid., 335.

[56] Ibid. This fine philosophical distinction is not fully explained. God's knowledge of future contingent events is certain because God's foreknowledge is infallible. However, foreknown events are not "necessary" because they are dependent upon the free choices of contingent beings that have not yet been actuated. See Picirilli, *Grace, Faith, Free Will* (especially chapters 3 and 4) and his "Foreknowledge, Freedom, and the Future," *Journal of the Evangelical Theological Society* 43:2 (June 2000), 259-71. For an excellent, though dated, discussion of these philosophical terms in an Arminian system see Richard Watson, *Theological Institutes* (New York: Nelson and Phillips, 1850), I: 378-81.

[57] Forlines, *Quest*, 395.

[58] Ibid.

[59] Ibid., 396.

[60] Ibid., 398.

[61] Ibid., 399; see also Forlines, *Romans*, The Randall House Bible Commentary, gen. ed. Robert E. Picirilli (Nashville: Randall House, 1987).

[62] Forlines, *Quest*, 399.

[63] Arminius, 3.314.

[64] Forlines, *Quest*, 400.

[65] For just two examples see Jack W. Cottrell, "Conditional Election" in Clark H. Pinnock, ed., *Grace Unlimited* (Minneapolis: Bethany Fellowship, 1975), 51-73; and, Shank, 108-52.

[66] Forlines, *Quest*, 335.

[67] Ibid., 349. This receives a thorough treatment in this text (347-90) and much of this material is drawn from Forlines's work, *Romans*. Much of what Forlines says prefigures modern debates about the nature of Judaism in the first century and Paul's understanding of the Law. See E. P. Sanders, *Paul and Palestinian Judaism* (Philadelphia: Fortress, 1977). Forlines briefly interacts with Sanders (354-55), but his work is based on observations developed in his own unpublished thesis, "A Study of Jesus' Encounter with the Pharisees," Th.M. Thesis, Chicago Graduate School of Theology, 1970.

[68] Forlines, *Quest*, 347.

[69] Ibid., 356. Forlines is reflecting upon Paul's teaching regarding the Law's inability to justify (3:20); its revelation of the wrath of God (4:15); and its propensity to stir up sins (5:20; 7:5).

[70] Ibid., 359.

[71] Ibid., 362.

[72] See Thomas R. Schreiner, "Does Romans 9 Teach Individual Election unto Salvation," in *Still Sovereign: Contemporary Perspectives on Election, Foreknowledge, and Grace*, eds. Thomas R. Schreiner and Bruce A. Ware (Grand Rapids: Baker, 2000), 89-106.

[73] Forlines, *Quest*, 367.

[74] Ibid.

[75] Ibid., 368-69.

[76] Ibid., 370-71. I recall Forlines offering the illustration that "the same sun that hardens the clay melts the butter." In other words God's call and the free offer of salvation can have different results in the lives of different people whose hearts are freely inclined to accept or reject His wooing.

[77] Ibid., 376.

[78] Ibid., 400-02. Forlines argues that Calvinism errs in not distinguishing the condition and the ground for union with Christ. He says, "The *condition* for being chosen for the application of the benefits of atonement is faith in Christ. The *ground* for being chosen is being in Christ" (374).

[79] Picirilli refers to this as the "Christocentricity" of election where he makes a number of helpful observations. See his *Grace, Faith, Free Will*, 66, 68-69; See also Shank, *Elect in the Son*, 27-45, where he likewise refers to the Christocentric nature of election pointing out that Christ is the elect one (28), the foundation of election (31) and is therefore instrumental in election (32-43) and comprehensive in election (43-45).

[80] Forlines, *Quest*, 401. A third argument could be leveraged against Calvinism here. Ephesians 1:4 indicates through a purpose clause (*hoti*) that election was not to salvation but to a relationship with Christ toward the end of the believer's sanctification. Thus believers may be "holy and without blame before him in love."

[81] Ibid., 403.

[82] Forlines's discussion of biblical terms is helpful, but often confined to particular passages. Picirilli's discussion though similarly constrained has greater clarity, "foreordination (predestination) therefore seems clearly to refer to *what* happens in salvation rather than *who* is saved. 'Election' sees the saved as people God has chosen; 'predestination' refers to what He has chosen them for" (68; see especially 65-122). Also helpful is I. Howard Marshall, "Predestination in the New Testament," in Clark H. Pinnock, ed., *Grace Unlimited* (Minneapolis: Bethany Fellowship, 1975), 127-43.

[83] A more summative and synthetic positive presentation of conditional election from a Reformed Arminian perspective may be found in Picirilli, *Grace, Faith, Free Will*, 53-58. Picirilli likewise deals with Romans 9 and Ephesians 1. Though his review of Romans 9 is much more limited than Forlines's, what he presents on Ephesians 1 is less reactionary to Calvinism and more constructively oriented (66-78). Reformed Arminians await a satisfactory full-length, systematic treatment of conditional election.

[84] Forlines, *Quest*, 403.

[85] Ibid.

[86] Ibid., 404-05.

CHAPTER FOUR

FORLINES'S THEOLOGY OF ATONEMENT AND JUSTIFICATION

Jesse F. Owens

"But now . . . " Those words signal a seismic transition in chapter three of Romans (3:21)—a transition that signals hope for humanity where there formerly was none. Paul is on the verge of elaborating what it means for mankind to be made right with God through faith in the person and work of Jesus Christ. The biblical and theological term for this is justification. Accompanying the doctrine of justification is Christ's payment for sin, or the atonement, which stands at the center of the doctrine. Since the atonement rests at the center of justification, it also rests at the very heart of the gospel. Therefore, atonement and justification are not doctrines reserved for ivory tower discussions among professional theologians and pastors. They are cosmic realities that, properly understood, have the power to "grip the heart" by showing us the seriousness of sin, the righteousness of Christ, and the holiness and love of God.[1] They are places where we tread carefully, reflect deeply, and quite often find ourselves brought prostrate in awe of the fact that "while we were still sinners, Christ died for us" (Rom. 5:8).

This chapter will explore Leroy Forlines's theology of atonement and justification. We will note his emphases on related doctrinal features, such as penal satisfaction, imputation, and the necessity of absolute righteousness. We will also briefly survey earlier Arminian theologies of atonement in figures such as John Goodwin, John Wesley, Thomas Helwys, Thomas Grantham, and Thomas Monck some of which are congruent with Forlines's view, and some of which are not. This chapter will also address the extent of the atonement from a historical and theological perspective. Ultimately the reader will find that Forlines's theology of atonement and justification is firmly rooted in both Scripture and the Reformed (or Classical) Arminian tradition.

Tracing Forlines's Theology of Atonement and Justification

Since the Reformation, three views of the atonement have been dominant: the governmental view, the moral influence view, and the penal satisfaction view.[2] The governmental view contends that Christ's death operates as a public display of God's righteous judgment of sin, and that faith itself is counted for righteousness. The moral influence view focuses primarily on the role of Christ's death as a means of drawing persons to God through a radical display of love and self-sacrifice. Finally the penal satisfaction view maintains that Christ's death was substitutionary (that is, Christ died in the place of sinners) and that God's holiness required such a payment for the forgiveness of sins. Furthermore, most adherents to the penal satisfaction view maintain that sinners are made righteous through Christ's righteousness, which is imputed to the sinner through faith in Him.[3]

Unfortunately many assume that all Arminians embrace the governmental view of the atonement.[4] Such is not the case for Forlines, who unabashedly affirms penal satisfaction. Yet Forlines is no Arminian innovator. As we will note below, Forlines is consistent with an Arminian Baptist tradition that reaches back to English General Baptists such as Thomas Helwys, Thomas Monck, and Thomas Grantham, as well as earlier Free Will Baptists and those in North Carolina who affirmed the 1812 Abstract.

Forlines's theology of atonement rests on "five basic assumptions": (1) God is sovereign; (2) God is holy; (3) Man is sinful; (4) God is loving; and (5) God is wise. Forlines also emphasizes that God is a personal God Who has created us as personal beings for communion with Him. Yet as evident from Forlines's second and third assumptions, conflict exists where communion should. This is why the doctrine of atonement is significant since "the atonement is designed to settle a conflict between persons—God and man."[5] The implication of this notion of personhood is that "we must see sovereignty as personally administered by one who thinks, feels, and acts."[6] But as Forlines emphasizes, God's actions—including the way He intends to resolve this cosmic conflict between God and man are always in accordance with His holiness. God's actions are determined by His very nature. As one theologian expressed it, "He [God] is a law unto himself."[7] This will become clear as we examine several facets of Forlines's theology of atonement and justification.

Original Sin and Absolute Righteousness

The Reformed tradition consistently affirms the radical effects of original and actual sin. Original sin (the sin of Adam) corrupts human nature, which includes mankind's ability to think, feel, and act rightly. In addition, all of mankind is rendered guilty before God because of Adam's sin (imputed guilt). We are also all guilty of actual sin that we have personally committed. This makes sinners guilty before God, who in themselves are eternally separated from Him—without hope, without remedy. Right standing before God requires absolute righteousness, which no man has or can achieve by his own merits. As Forlines explains, "The only way any person can ever be justified before God is to have absolute righteousness (or to say it another way, to be considered a doer of the law)."[8] In fact, this is the very essence of Paul's argument in Romans 3. Because of our sin, we are all separated from God since we are unrighteous. Or to use Paul's citation of the Psalms: "None is righteous, no, not one; no one understands; no one seeks for God. All have turned aside; together they have become worthless; no one does good, not even one" (Rom. 3:10-12).

Forlines's theology of atonement, then, is based upon the biblical premise that God is perfectly holy, and demands absolute righteousness from anyone who would stand justified before Him. Furthermore, His holiness demands that sin be punished without exception. Forlines writes, "The justice of God will not tolerate any attempt to set aside or diminish the penalty of the broken law of God. There can be no forgiveness of sin without a full satisfaction of the justice of God in the payment of the penalty."[9] Herein lies the great dilemma: God has made us for Himself. Yet we are separated from Him through our actual sin and the effects of Adam's sin. Consequently we stand in conflict with a holy God, deserving of His judgment. If God demands righteousness as the only means of our justification (right standing before Him), and we do not have absolute righteousness, then God must either act on our behalf, or we forever remain under His righteous condemnation. Forlines puts it succinctly: "We must have absolute righteousness (Rom. 2:6-13). We do not have absolute righteousness (Rom. 3:10). We cannot produce absolute righteousness (3:20). The only hope of justification is to have absolute righteousness provided for us."[10] Jesus is that righteousness.

Active and Passive Obedience

What does it mean that Jesus is our righteousness, or that we can be justified through faith in Him? The two elements that comprise Christ's righteousness are namely, His active and passive obedience. The "active obedience of Christ refers to the idea that He lived a life of absolute obedience to the Father. He lived an absolutely righteous life"; whereas His passive obedience refers particularly to His death by which "He submitted to the wrath of God for our sins."[11] Most preaching and writing focuses primarily on the passive obedience of Christ. For example many believers often speak of His being crucified under Pontius Pilate at the hands of the Jews and Romans, yet we rarely focus on His perfectly righteous life in obedience to the Father's will. John's Gospel emphasizes these two aspects of righteousness as clearly as any other biblical book. John records many of Jesus' words regarding His "hour" (death). But the efficacy of Jesus' death is always predicated upon the fact that He is the divine Son Who perfectly keeps His Father's will (John 4:34; 5:30; 6:38).

In Christ's passive obedience, "the sins of all the world that had ever been committed, were being committed, and ever would be committed were laid on Him."[12] Bearing our sins He took our place, and God's righteous wrath was poured out on Him. As Forlines says, "With our sins upon Him, He took our place as if He were guilty of all the sins of the whole race."[13] If He bore the world's sins, then we must, as Forlines does, conclude that He suffered an "equivalent" penalty.[14] In this way passive obedience and the penalty Jesus paid for sin brings us to the epicenter of Jesus' suffering: the engulfing wrath of God. God's wrath surpassed anything that Roman soldiers could inflict upon Jesus. Forlines writes:

> His own Father inflicted the greatest suffering that was inflicted on Him. He took the place of sinners before God and drank the cup of wrath that was due sinners. He suffered as much on the cross as sinners will suffer in an eternal hell. He experienced separation from the Father. He who had enjoyed unbroken fellowship with the Father in eternity past uttered these words on the cross, 'My God, My God, why have You forsaken Me?' (Mt 27:46). This was a cry of agony rather than a cry from lack of understanding.[15]

His active obedience, or His perfect keeping of the law, is equally essential to the atonement and justification. Whereas we are law-breakers, Jesus is the perfect law-keeper. If we can only be justified by being considered doers of the law, and we are not, then Jesus' perfect law-keeping must be reckoned unto us. Put another way, His obedience must become our obedience; or His righteousness must become our righteousness. As Paul notes in Romans 3:21, "the righteousness of God has been manifested apart from the law" in Jesus. Forlines writes, "This righteousness is a 'God-provided righteousness.' This righteousness is 'without works.'"[16] In no way does this take into account our law-keeping or our law-breaking. Instead it is the righteousness of Christ.

Both active and passive obedience, however, are rooted in a proper understanding of the Incarnation. If Christ were to redeem those who had sinned in the flesh, then coming in the likeness of sinful flesh was necessary. Likewise, if Christ were to pay the penalty for sin, then He must also be God. Christ could atone for sin precisely because He was fully God (perfectly righteous) and fully man (like us, sin excepted). The apostle Paul puts it this way: "For God has done what the law, weakened by the flesh, could not do. By sending His own Son in the likeness of sinful flesh and for sin, He condemned sin in the flesh" (Rom. 8:3). This is exactly what the believers gathered at the Council of Chalcedon (AD 451) were attempting to explain and defend, and Forlines follows their biblical fidelity.

Union and Imputation

The dilemma remains as to how a sinner can be reckoned absolutely righteous by God on the basis of Christ's atonement. How can Christ's righteousness become our righteousness? In two words: union and imputation. More specifically, by being united with Christ and His active and passive obedience being imputed (or reckoned) unto us through faith in Him. This answer needs to be expanded, however. The doctrine of union with Christ is integral to any proper understanding of salvation; it is the basis of our salvation (Rom. 8:12). Paul writes, "Therefore, if anyone is *in* Christ, he is a new creation" (2 Cor. 5:17); and, "There is therefore no condemnation for those who are *in* Christ Jesus" (Rom. 8:1). For Paul union with Christ is at the heart of almost every biblical doctrine and event: salvation, justification, reconciliation, sanctification, suffering, death, and resurrection.

How is a person actually united with Christ? Although this language sounds mystical, believers are united to Christ by the Spirit through faith in Him (Gal. 2:20; Eph. 3:17). Only by being in Christ through faith do believers have any promise or hope of salvation. Arminius likewise understood union with Christ through faith as the basis for salvation: "[God] embraces no one in

Christ, unless he is in Christ. But no one is in Christ, except by faith in Christ, which is the necessary means of our union with Christ."[17] Again, it is only by being in Christ that one partakes in all that belongs to Christ. By being united with Christ by the Spirit, we are also united to the Triune God of Scripture. And as we are in Christ, and Christ in us, Christ is in God (Col. 3:3). Lewis Smedes explains:

> The presence of God in Jesus Christ does, of course, lie at the root of Paul's doctrine of salvation. If God were not immersed in Christ, our being in Christ at all would be inconceivable. For it is God in Christ who enabled the resurrection to take place (Rom. 8:11), God in Christ who at the cross replaced man's assessment of the meaning of life with His own, God in Christ who made justification and reconciliation possible and actual (Rom. 3:23).[18]

Therefore, to be in Christ is to be in God. But what does this mean on a practical level?

First, union with Christ radically changes the believer's identity. Forlines aptly illustrates this:

> Identification by union makes that which was not actually part of a person's experience his by identification. For example, prior to the time that Hawaii became a part of the United States, a citizen of Hawaii could not have said, "We celebrate our day of Independence on July 4." Immediately upon their becoming a state, the same person who formerly could not make the statement could say, "We celebrate our day of Independence on July 4." What happened on July 4, 1776, became a part of their history. The history of the United States became the history of Hawaii, and the history of Hawaii became the history of the United States.

Prior to the union of Christ on the condition of faith, a person could not say, "I died with Christ." Immediately, upon union with Christ a person can say, "I died with Christ." The history of the cross became his history, not in the experiential sense, but by identification so that he received full credit for that death. At the same time, the history of our sins became Jesus' history, not in the sense that His character was affected, but so they would come in contact with the penalty He had already paid for them. He took responsibility for them, but it was a responsibility He had already assumed on the cross.[19]

Second, even before we are united with Christ, a union already exists, common to all humanity: our union with Adam. Reformed Arminians understand that Adam's sin is imputed to us by our union with him as the head of the human race (Rom. 5:12). Each one of us are "in Adam" from birth (1 Cor. 15:22). Therefore, we are both guilty before God and corrupt by nature. By being united with Christ, our sins (both inherited and committed) are imputed to Christ. Fortunately when we are united to Christ, His righteousness is also imputed to us (commonly called double imputation). Sinclair Ferguson helpfully explains, "What the gospel does for us is to take us out of our union with Adam in sin and death and judgment and hell, and to put us into union, and then communion, with our Lord Jesus Christ in righteousness and life and peace and joy and new fruitfulness to God."[20] In Christ a righteousness is imputed to us that is not our own.

Penal Satisfaction Versus Governmental View

As an Arminian one might expect Forlines to spend a significant amount of time in his published work discussing the extent of the atonement, but he does not. Instead, he spends the majority of his time opposing the governmental theory of atonement and advocating penal satisfaction. Forlines focuses on dismantling the governmental view partly because he believes it tends toward theological liberalism, but mainly because he is convinced that it is unbiblical.

Forlines's criticisms of the governmental view stem from its "dangerously close parallels" to the moral influence view, which permeated much of twentieth century liberal theology: "(1) Both views deny that there is any principle in the divine nature that requires satisfaction in atonement. (2) Both deny that it is absolutely necessary to inflict a penalty on sin. (3) Both views consider the value of Christ's death to be revelational [predominately concerned with revealing something about God's character]."[21] Forlines also provides what he believes to be the basic assumptions of the governmental view, in attempt to highlight its differences from penal satisfaction: "(1) God is sovereign. (2) Man is sinful. (3) God is loving. (4) The end of God's sovereignty is the happiness of man."[22]

Forlines summarizes the penal satisfaction and governmental views this way: "If we would be technical in the use of language, the governmental view should speak of 'pardon' and the satisfaction view would speak of 'justification.'"[23] What Forlines means here is that the penal satisfaction view sees God as a "Sovereign Judge" Who must judge sin in accordance with His holiness—no sin can simply be set aside without its penalty being paid. In contrast, the governmental view depicts God as a cosmic Governor Whose interest is to protect the public good. Regarding sin the public good is protected through a public demonstration of God's hatred of sin (Jesus' death); and, through faith in Christ, God sets the punishment for sin aside. Put differently, in the governmental view faith is counted for righteousness, and the punishment for sin is simply removed. However, *no imputation of our sin to Christ or Christ's righteousness to us occurs.*

In the penal satisfaction view, the penalty is not simply pardoned. Christ pays sin's penalty, God's wrath towards sin is appeased through Jesus' sacrifice, and Jesus' righteousness is imputed to the believer through faith. In Forlines's view, the believer is not merely declared righteous because of his faith in Christ. No, the believer truly is righteous since Christ's righteousness has been imputed to him through faith. Forlines's point here is significant: God declaring the believer righteous is not ambiguous or groundless. Instead, God's declaration is rooted in the reality that the believer truly is righteous through union with Christ by faith, and has been imputed with Christ's righteousness in union with Him.

The Extent of the Atonement

Forlines's treatment of the extent of the atonement is remarkably short as he limits his comments to answering a few Calvinist objections to the doctrine. One of those objections, a quite common one throughout the past few centuries, is that a universal atonement necessarily leads to universal salvation. If Jesus died for the sins of every person, so the argument goes, then it must necessarily follow that every person will be saved. Forlines contends this is untrue since Christ's death, even according to Calvinists, is provisional. In other words Jesus died for the sins of the world, but the merits of His death are only applied at the moment of faith, and only those who believe will be saved. Therefore, although the atonement is universal or general (Christ died for the sins of the world), salvation is not since only those who believe are saved. Forlines provides several texts for his position of universal provision and offer of salvation (John 3:16; Acts 17:30; Rom. 10:13; 1 Tim. 2:4, 6, 4:10; Heb. 2:9; 2 Pet. 3:9; 1 John 2:2; Rev. 22:17). One of his more fascinating remarks regarding universal atonement is Scripture so clearly teaches it that even many Calvinists throughout the centuries have willingly embraced it, or occasionally affirmed it. We will return to this insight in the next section.

Reformed Arminianism: A Historical Theology of Atonement and Justification

Forlines's theology of atonement and justification epitomizes what is commonly called Reformed (or Classical) Arminianism. The words "Reformed" and "Classical," as I will use them, mean that Forlines's theology of atonement and justification are, like Arminius's, more akin to the theology of the Reformation than John Wesley's and later developments under the Arminian banner. For example, whereas the Reformers affirmed the corruption of all men and the imputation of Adam's guilt to all of mankind, John Wesley (1703-1791) and John Goodwin (1594-1665) rejected the imputation of Adam's guilt. Whereas the Reformers contended that justification required the imputation of Christ's righteousness to believers, Wesley and Goodwin rejected imputation as unnecessary, unbiblical, and detrimental to holy living. In contrast to Wesley, Goodwin, and later Wesleyans, Forlines follows the Reformed tradition by affirming the imputation of Adam's guilt to all of his posterity, and the necessity of Christ's righteousness being imputed to believers as the necessary grounds for justification. To illustrate we will use Wesley and Goodwin on the one hand, and Thomas Helwys (c.1575-c.1616) and Thomas Grantham (1633/34-1692) on the other, as representatives for these respective traditions.[24]

John Goodwin and John Wesley on Original Sin and Justification

In *Imputatio Fide* Goodwin rejected the imputation of the guilt of Adam's sin to his posterity. For Goodwin although the corruption of Adam's sin is applied to every man's nature and future generations, the guilt of his sin is not. All of mankind does not stand guilty before God from birth because of Adam's sin. Goodwin wrote, "[The] sin of Adam is no where in Scripture said to be imputed to his posterity"[25]; and, "The Scriptures wheresoever they speak of Adam's sin, and the relation of it to his posterity, wholly abstain from the term of imputation, neither do they use any other word or phrase in this argument of like signification."[26] Although man is guilty before God from birth, according to Goodwin, it is not because Adam's guilt has been imputed to him, but because man possesses a sinful nature through the corruption of Adam's sin.

Years later Wesley reiterated Goodwin's emphases on the doctrine of justification. Goodwin and Wesley are significant theologians in the movement we will refer to as "Wesleyan Arminianism." Rather than holding that Christ's righteousness is imputed to man through faith in Christ, Wesley held that faith itself is reckoned unto believers for righteousness. Justification does not consist in the imputation of Christ's righteousness, but in the *non-imputation* of sins. For Wesley Scripture teaches that sins are forgiven on the basis of faith in Christ. Man is not righteous because Christ's righteousness is imputed to him through faith, and God is not pretending that man is righteous when he is actually a sinner. For Wesley justification was the mere pardoning of sin through faith in Christ; imputation is not involved.[27] Wesley was quite militant against the idea that Christ's righteousness was somehow imputed to man through faith. He found it repulsive, because if Christ's righteousness is imputed to man, then man is no longer in need of forgiveness from sin since he is righteous. Furthermore, if we possess Christ's righteousness through faith, then what incentive is there for righteous living? Surely that would encourage all sorts of immoral living, Wesley reasoned.[28]

Thomas Helwys and Thomas Grantham on Original Sin and Justification

Helwys and Grantham differ profoundly from Goodwin and Wesley on original sin and justification, serving as precursors for Forlines's views. Whereas Goodwin and Wesley denied the imputation of guilt to all mankind through Adam's sin, both Helwys and Grantham affirmed the imputation of guilt. In *A Short and Plaine Proof*, Helwys wrote, "The apostle has shown (Romans 5:12–21) that by Adam's sin the fault came upon all to condemnation."[29] There, Helwys inferred that Adam's sin not simply causes man to be sinful by nature, but that Adam's sin actually renders mankind guilty before God. In another place Helwys was even clearer on imputation: "Through whose [Adam's] disobedience, all men sinned. His sin was imputed to all; and so death went over all men."[30]

Grantham also makes similar statements about the imputation of man's sin to Christ and the imputation Christ's righteousness to the believer. For Grantham the great exchange (the believer's sin for Christ's righteousness) is the clear logic of passages like 2 Corinthians 5:21. In his most prolific work, Grantham wrote, "Now certain it is, Christ was made sin for us only by imputation, for he had no sin; and as he was made sin, so we are made the righteousness of God in him, which must needs be the free imputation of his righteousness to us; for there is otherwise none righteous, no not one."[31] There Grantham advocated for what theologians refer to as "alien righteousness." This means the sinner needs a righteousness that is not his own to be imputed to him through faith for him to be right with God. That alien righteousness is Christ's righteousness. Contrary to Wesley and Goodwin, Grantham understands Scripture to teach that Christ's righteousness must be given to man through faith, since no other righteousness exists in the world. Together Helwys and Grantham represent what is often called Reformed Arminianism, and Forlines fits squarely within this tradition.

Arminius on Imputation

Reformed Arminianism is not identical to James Arminius's (1560–1609) theology on every jot and tittle, and Reformed Arminians such as Forlines are aware of this.[32] Yet the doctrine of justification (and imputation specifically) is one area where Reformed Arminianism is more akin to Arminius's theology than Wesley's. On these subjects Arminius wrote,

> The meritorious cause of justification is Christ through His obedience and righteousness, who may, therefore, be justly called the principal or outwardly moving cause. In His obedience and righteousness, Christ is also the material cause of our justification, so far as God bestows Christ on us for righteousness, and imputes His righteousness and obedience to us. In regard to this two-fold cause, that is, the meritorious and the material, we are said to be constituted righteous through the obedience of Christ.[33]

Reformed Arminians believe that this is the theology of Scripture and of the Reformation. Furthermore it is the theology of Helwys, Grantham, and Forlines.

Union and Imputation in An Orthodox Creed

Forlines's insistence on substitutionary atonement and the imputation of Christ's righteousness to believers coheres with the theology of early English General Baptists, the theological forbears of the Free Will Baptists in the

South. They too, as we have already seen with Helwys and Grantham, argued for substitutionary atonement and the imputation of alien righteousness. One example of this is a General Baptist confession of faith entitled An Orthodox Creed (1678). One of the main contributors to the confession was a brilliant, self-taught minister who valiantly defended orthodox theology, Thomas Monck (c. seventeenth century). On the doctrine of justification these General Baptists contended:

> Justification is a Declarative, or Judicial Sentence of God the Father, whereby he of his infinite Love, and most free Grace, for the alone and Mediatorial Righteousness of his own Son, *performed in our Nature and stead*; which Righteousness of the God-Man, the Father *imputing* to us, and *by effectual Faith* received and embraced by us, doth free us by Judicial Sentence from Sin and Death, and accepts us Righteous in Christ our Surety, unto Eternal Life;[34]
>
> The *Active and Passive Obedience of Christ* being the Accomplishment of all that Righteousness and Sufferings the Law, or Justice of God required; and this being perfectly performed by our Mediator, in the very Nature of us Men, and accepted by the Father *in our stead*, according to that eternal Covenant-Transaction, between the Father and Son. And hereby we have a deliverance from the Guilt and Punishment of all our Sins, and are accounted Righteous before God, at the Throne of Grace, by the alone *Righteousness of Christ the Mediator, imputed,* or reckoned *unto us through Faith.*"[35]

The Extent of the Atonement

I have noted several ways in which Forlines's theology and the English General Baptists is unlike Goodwin's. An interesting similarity is that Forlines (like Goodwin 350 years earlier) contends that biblical teaching of universal atonement is so clear that many Calvinists cannot help but embrace it. Good-win cites the Synod of Dort, which condemned Arminius's followers in Holland and whose documents represent what are now commonly called the five points of Calvinism, as affirming a universal atonement.[36] Goodwin notes that even John Calvin affirmed universal atonement with some regularity, though not consistently.[37] Goodwin cited Calvin as saying, "For, though Christ suffered for the sins of the whole world, and through the goodness or bounty of God he offered unto all men, yet all men do not take, or lay hold on him."[38] Forlines writes similarly, "The fact that many Calvinists have accepted the view of unlimited atonement tells us that the biblical case for unlimited atonement must be strong and convincing."[39]

Trajectories: Pastoral and Theological

> let the water and the blood,
> from thy wounded side which flowed,
> be of sin the double cure;
> save from wrath and make me pure.
> —Augustus Toplady

Pastoral Implications

Augustus Toplady's "Rock of Ages, Cleft for Me" demonstrates both the theological riches of these doctrines, as well as their practical application. The final two lines of the first verse reveal the connection between the atonement, justification, and even sanctification (a topic explored further in chapter five). The reasoning goes something like this: Christ died for sinners so they might stand justified through faith in His atoning death before a holy God. Nevertheless, justification, for both Toplady and Forlines, is not the end point of Christ's atonement. Instead, the doctrine of justification signals the starting point of the believer's sanctification. Some, including many Wesleyans, would argue that justification through the imputation of Christ's righteousness might be used as an excuse for sin (One might say: "If I have Christ's righteousness, then why should I live a righteous life?"). Yet "Paul was accused of the same thing (Rom. 3:8; 6:1)," Forlines writes.[40] Against such charges Forlines firmly maintains that the doctrine of "justification is always accompanied by sanctification"[41]; and, "We do not answer the charge by tampering with the doctrine of justification, but by setting forth the doctrine of sanctification."[42]

The doctrines of atonement and justification should take center stage within local church worship. This especially applies to the local church's teaching and singing. The sermons preached, prayers offered, and songs sung should emphasize Christ's substitutionary death. Worshippers should marvel that the Father would send His Son to die willingly for ruined sinners. Believers should be emboldened by the reality that through faith in Christ, they are united with Him, and indwelt by the Spirit. Each of these realities should and must lead to conformity to the image of the Son. Christian worship should embody these truths, making them focal points of Trinitarian worship.

Theological Investigations

Forlines's theology of atonement and justification establish a helpful foundation from which to consider further theological investigation. For example, regarding the extent of the atonement, some Calvinists have argued that penal satisfaction (Forlines's view) necessitates a limited (or "definite") atonement. This is precisely Robert Letham's argument:

> If we wish to maintain that Christ dies for all without exception while rejecting universalism, we will have no alternative but to redefine the nature of the atonement. Christ's death will then have secured the salvation of no-one in particular. It will simply be a provisional suffering, dependent for its effect on a believing response by the sinner. . . . It seems impossible theologically to hold to the penal substitutionary nature of the atonement and at the same time maintain that Christ died provisionally for all without exception.[43]

Letham's argument seems to be based upon the unnecessary logic of other Calvinists that Christ's death accomplishes justification for the elect, almost apart from faith, and thereby relegates faith to an insignificant role in salvation. As Robert Picirilli rightfully notes, justification is no longer by faith in this construct, but by election.[44] Future Reformed Arminian scholarship should assume the task of responding to such objections.

A second development in contemporary theology that relates to our discussion is N. T. Wright's theology of atonement and justification (the so-called "New Perspective" on Paul). According to Forlines, Christ's death should be considered primarily as substitution, but also as identification. Conversely, Wright argues that Pauline substitution is rooted in identification. Wright notes, "*Because* he is Israel's representative, he can be the appropriate substitute, can take on himself the curse of others, so they do not bear it any more."[45] Simon Gathercole, however, has made a fairly convincing case from Romans 5:6-8 and 1 Corinthians 15:3-4 that substitution is at the very heart of Paul's theology of atonement.[46] He does not argue for an either/or scenario whereby Christ's death is either substitution or identification. For him, substitution is at the center, but he also affirms identification and liberation from sin. I am not convinced that the New Perspective on Paul is congruent with the Reformed Arminian understanding of justification, but am concerned that it might appeal to many young Reformed Arminians who, like myself, enjoy some of Wright's work. Therefore, what is needed is not only a Reformed Arminian defense of penal substitution, but a detailed reply to Wright and others that is both scholarly and accessible.[47]

Conclusion

F. Leroy Forlines has rendered a remarkable service by clearly defining how one can be both Reformed and Arminian. There are more options than the way of Wesley or Calvin. Nowhere is this clearer than in Forlines's robust, biblical, Reformed approach to justification and atonement. These doctrines remind Forlines's readers and admirers that he truly is a thoughtful theologian.

The way in which he explains these deep mysteries also reminds us that he is a theologian for the church who desires to lead God's people towards genuine awe and worship. Forlines's theology on these doctrines, I am convinced, will continue to inspire future generations of pastors, missionaries, local church leaders, and congregants to read, reflect on, and proclaim with the apostle Paul: "For our sake he made him to be sin who knew no sin, so that in him we might become the righteousness of God" (2 Cor. 5:21).

---

[1] F. Leroy Forlines, *Classical Arminianism: A Theology of Salvation* (Nashville: Randall House, 2011), 199.

[2] This is not intended to imply that penal substitution is merely a product of Reformation theology. Several scholars have demonstrated that penal substitution was also taught from the early church period to the Reformation period. See Steve Jeffrey, Michael Ovey, Andrew Sach, *Pierced for Our Transgressions: Rediscovering the Glory of Penal Substitution* (Wheaton: Crossway, 2008), 161-204.

[3] Some scholars have argued for a distinction between penal satisfaction and penal substitution, claiming that satisfaction does not necessarily include substitution. Although Forlines articulates atonement in terms of penal satisfaction, it always includes substitution for him.

[4] This is somewhat ironic since some New Divinity Calvinists (followers of Jonathan Edwards) embraced the governmental view of the atonement.

[5] Forlines, 201.

[6] Ibid.

[7] Francis Turretin, *Institutes of Elenctic Theology*, vol. 2 (Philipsburg: P&R, 1994), 425.

[8] Forlines, 204.

[9] Ibid., 202.

[10] Ibid., 205.

[11] Ibid.

[12] Ibid., 206.

[13] Ibid.

[14] Ibid., 208.

[15] Ibid., 206.

[16] Ibid., 209.

[17] James Arminius, *The Writings of James Arminius*, vol. 3, trans. James Nichols and R. Bagnall (Grand Rapids: Baker, 1956), 498.

[18] Lewis B. Smedes, *All Things Made New: A Theology of Man's Union with Christ* (Grand Rapids: Eerdmans, 1970), 79.

[19] Forlines, 216.

[20] Sinclair Ferguson, "Paul on Union with Christ" (address given at the 2010 Basics Conference, Parkside Church, Chagrin Falls, Ohio, May 2010).

[21] Forlines, 227.

[22] Ibid., 221.

[23] Ibid., 227.

[24] J. Matthew Pinson has deeply shaped my understanding of these figures. Pinson has laid a substantial foundation both for English General Baptist studies and Arminian historical theology. Pinson is an important forerunner for my own research and articulation of seventeenth and eighteenth century Arminian theology. See his *Arminian and Baptist: Explorations in a Theological Tradition* (Nashville: Randall House, 2015).

[25] John Goodwin, *Imputatio Fide. Or A Treatise of Justification*, part 2 (London, 1642), 13.

[26] Ibid., 13.

[27] Albert C. Outler, ed., *John Wesley* (New York: Oxford University Press, 1980), 200-02, 206-07, 273.

[28] Wesley also did not believe that Scripture affirmed the imputation of Christ's righteousness. His longest work on imputation was actually just a republishing of John Goodwin's *Imputatio Fide*, thereby showing Wesley's theological alliance with Goodwin on imputation.

[29] Thomas Helwys, *A Short and Plaine Proof By the Word and Works of God That God's Decree Is Not the Cause of Any Man's Sins or Condemnation*, in Joe Early, Jr., *The Life and Writings of Thomas Helwys* (Macon: Mercer University Press, 2009), 82.

[30] Helwys, 68.

[31] Thomas Grantham, *Christianismus Primitivus, Or, The Ancient Christian Religion*, Book 2, Ch. 3, Sect. 7 (London: Printed for Francis Smith, 1678), 68. Even more interesting is that Grantham wholly affirmed the imputation of Christ's active and passive obedience, while the Westminster Assembly was divided over whether imputed righteousness consisted of both Christ's active and passive obedience. See Robert Letham, *The Westminster Assembly: Reading Its Theology in Historical Context* (Phillipsburg: P&R Publishing, 2009), 113-14, 253-64.

[32] One of the clearest examples of this is that Arminius affirmed paedobaptism, whereas most Reformed Arminians affirm credobaptism. Another example is that Arminius never took a definite stance on perseverance; most Reformed Arminians affirm the possibility of apostasy for genuine believers.

[33] Jacob Arminius, "*Disputation XLVIII. On Justification*," in *The Works of Arminius*, trans. James and William Nichols (Grand Rapids: Baker, 1996), 2:406.

[34] Thomas Monck and W. Madison Grace, "Transcriber's Preface to An Orthodox Creed: Unabridged seventeenth century General Baptist Confession," *Southwestern Journal of Theology* (March, 2006), 159.

[35] Ibid; italics added. These General Baptists were also very careful to note that it was Christ's "Mediatorial righteousness" as the God-Man, not His essential or personal righteousness (that which He had from eternity) that is imputed to the believer. See "A Transcriber's Preface to An Orthodox Creed: Unabridged seventeenth century General Baptist Confession," 152-53.

[36] Andrew Fuller also cited the Synod of Dort as affirming the sufficiency of Christ's death for all men. In fact, Fuller's realization that many within the Reformed tradition had utilized the sufficient/efficient distinction was of great comfort to him. See *The Works of Andrew Fuller*, vol. 2 (Harrisonburg: Sprinkle, 1988), 712.

[37] Goodwin is not arguing that Calvin, or any other theologian he has cited in support of general redemption, never taught the opposite doctrine in their other writings. See John Goodwin, *Redemption Redeemed* [London: Printed by Macock, 1651], 561.

[38] Goodwin, *Redemption Redeemed*, 112.

[39] Forlines, 234.

[40] Ibid., 235.

[41] Ibid.

[42] Ibid.

[43] Robert Letham, *The Work of Christ* (Downers Grove: IVP Academic, 1993), 230.

[44] Robert E. Picirilli, *Grace, Faith, and Free Will: Contrasting Views of Salvation; Calvinism and Arminianism* (Nashville: Randall House, 2002), 169.

[45] N. T. Wright, *Paul and the Faithfulness of God* (London: SPCK, 2013), 865.

[46] See Simon Gathercole, *Defending Substitution: An Essay on Atonement in Paul* (Grand Rapids: Baker Academic, 2015).

[47] See Matthew McAffee, "The N. T. Wright Effect: A Free Will Baptist Assessment through the Theology of F. Leroy Forlines" (paper presented at the 2012 National Association of Free Will Baptists, Memphis, Tennessee, July 15-18, 2012).

CHAPTER FIVE

SANCTIFICATION AND SPIRITUALITY

Barry Raper

Twenty-first century American culture can be characterized as extremely "spiritual." In *The Courage to Be Protestant*, David Wells asserts that 78 percent of Americans "say they are spiritual."[1] Postmodernity, after all, is marked by a fascination with spirituality. If a person walks into any major bookstore, he or she will encounter hundreds of titles on the subject. However, with so many competing worldviews and religions converging together, spirituality becomes a mixture for most people—a blended, smorgasbord spirituality, a buffet of beliefs and practices. Spirituality is what you make it, both in terms of your personal beliefs and spiritual practices. To quote Wells's assessment of the "spiritual" scene, "There are as many spiritualities as there are spiritual seekers."[2]

In this religious environment, Christians and churches must display a distinctly biblical spirituality. To do this they must also embrace a scriptural understanding and practice of the doctrine of sanctification. Thankfully F. Leroy Forlines has provided Free Will Baptists with clear and reliable teaching on sanctification and spirituality. This chapter's purpose is to examine these topics in select Forlines writings, particularly *The Quest for Truth*. Due to his expansive ministry and writing career, this chapter will only scratch the surface of the wealth of material available on these topics. We will examine four major areas in Forlines's view of sanctification: (1) the meaning of sanctification; (2) the goal of sanctification; (3) the means for sanctification; and (4) the role of self in sanctification.

The Meaning of Sanctification

In considering the subject of sanctification, we must first take into account the doctrine of justification (discussed in the previous chapter). An inseparable connection exists between the two. Forlines provides this chart to illustrate the relationship between the two doctrines, while also highlighting some differences:[3]

JUSTIFICATION	SANTIFICATION
(1) Positional (Standing)	(1) Experiential (State)
(2) Objective	(2) Subjective
(3) Right Standing with God	(3) Conformity to the Image of
(4) Always Full and Complete	Christ
(5) Christ's Righteousness	(4) Moving Toward Completion
(6) Absolute Righteousness	(5) Personal Righteousness
	(6) Relative Righteousness Now—
	Absolute in the Life to Come

Forlines asserts that justification "makes both a negative and a positive contribution to sanctification."[4] He explains,

On the negative side, the power of sin is broken. Paul says, "For sin shall not have dominion over you, for you are not under law but under grace (Rom. 6:14)." As we observed in Romans 6:7 [the text] should be translated, "For he that died is justified from sin." The death referred to is the penal death of Christ which belongs to the believer by union with Christ.

Justification based on the identification of the believer with the penal death of Christ is given by Paul as the grounds for his statement, "that henceforth we should not serve sin" (verse 6, KJV).[5]

The positive contribution of justification is demonstrated by "open[ing] the way for the entrance of God's sanctifying grace," and providing the believer with the ability to "live a life of triumphant power over sin."[6] Putting both doctrines together, Forlines states, "The likeness of Christ's death (justification) opens the way for likeness of Christ's resurrection (sanctification)."[7] Joel Beeke sums up the relationship between the two doctrines similarly: "Sanctification is the inevitable fruit of justification (1 Cor. 6:11). The two may be distinguished, but never separated; God himself has married them."[8] Forlines would also make this claim. "Justification is organically linked to sanctification; new birth infallibly issues in new life," Beeke continues. "The justified will walk in 'the King's highway of holiness.' In and through Christ, justification gives God's child the *title* for heaven and the boldness to enter; sanctification gives him the *fitness* for heaven and the preparation necessary to enjoy it."[9]

What, then, is sanctification? The New Testament frequently uses the Greek word *hagiazo*, which carries the idea of declaring or making something holy or sacred for special use.[10] The concept itself is rooted in the Old Testament where God set apart articles for use in the tabernacle and later in temple worship. Theologically speaking, God directs sanctification primarily toward believers. In the unfolding plan of redemption, God's purpose is to save a people for Himself and make them holy. This purpose found in Scripture reveals two dimensions of personal sanctification: positional and experiential.

Positional sanctification has also been described as *definitive* sanctification. Believers experience this definitive act at conversion; this entails God setting the believer apart from sin and unto Himself. Definitive sanctification is based on Christ's finished work—by Whom we are declared righteous and holy. The apostle Paul reminds the Corinthians, "And because of him you are in Christ Jesus, who became to us wisdom from God, righteousness and sanctification and redemption" (1 Cor. 1:30). Through union with Christ by faith, Christ followers enjoy the present status of righteousness and are declared "sanctified" in Him. Similarly Hebrews states, "And by that will we have been sanctified through the offering of the body of Jesus Christ once for all" (Heb. 10:10).

Experiential sanctification, on the other hand, is an ongoing process. This dimension of sanctification is the Holy Spirit's progressive work in the believer's life through which he or she grows in holiness. While Hebrews 10:10 highlights a sanctification that has already been accomplished and declared because of Christ's finished work, Hebrews 10:14 points to both the positional sanctification believers enjoy and the progressive sanctification still taking place: "For by a single offering he has perfected for all time [positional/definitive sanctification] those who are being sanctified [progressive/experiential sanctification]." In this chapter, we give primary consideration to the experiential/progressive aspect of sanctification.

Most historic statements and confessions of faith speak to the progressive nature of sanctification. For example, the influential Reformed document the Westminster Confession of Faith (WCF), first issued in 1643, outlines sanctification in three articles. While some of it reflects the positional dimension of sanctification, its overall thrust is the progressive nature of God's work in believers. True believers are "further sanctified."[11] "Several lusts are more and more weakened and mortified" and are "more and more quickened and strengthened in saving graces, to practice true holiness."[12] WCF also notes the incompletion of sanctification in this life, since indwelling sin is still present in the believer. However, the regenerating work of Christ in believers overcomes this and so "the saints grow in grace, perfecting holiness in the fear of God."[13] As we will see, Forlines emphasizes many of these themes, albeit from a Reformed Arminian perspective.

Free Will Baptists can trace their theological views on sanctification at least back to the General Baptists' An Orthodox Creed, drawn up in 1678, several decades after WCF.[14] Containing fifty different articles of faith, its thirty-sixth article is entitled, "Of Sanctification, and good Works." Though lengthy, we will cite it in full:

> Those that are United unto Christ by Effectual Faith, are Regenerated, and have a new Heart and Spirit created in them, through the virtue of Christ his Death, Resurrection, and Intercession, and by the Efficacy of the Holy Spirit, received by Faith; and are Sanctified by the Word and Spirit of Truth dwelling in them, by destroying, or pulling down the strong Holds, or Dominion of Sin and Lust, and more and more quickened and strengthened in all saving Graces, in the practice of Holiness; without which no Man shall see the Lord. And this Sanctification is throughout the whole Man though imperfect in this Life, there abiding still in the best Saints, some to the remnants of Corruption, which occasions a continual War in the Soul; the Flesh lusting against the Spirit, and the Spirit against the Flesh. Yet through the continual supply of strength from Christ, which flows from him to Believers by means of the Covenant of Grace, or Hypostatical Union with our Nature, the Regenerate part doth overcome, pressing after a Heavenly Life, in Evangelical obedience to all the Commands that Christ, their King and Lawgiver, hath commanded them in his Word, or holy Scriptures, which are the only Rule, and square of our Sanctification and Obedience in all good Works, and Piety. And since our only assistance to good Works (such as God hath commanded) is of God, who worketh in us both to will and to do, we have no cause to boast, nor ground to conclude, we merit any thing thereby, we receiving all of free and undeserved Grace, and when we have done the most, yet we are unprofitable Servants, and do abundantly fall short; and the best duties that we can now perform, will not abide the Judgment of God: Neither do any

> good Works whatsoever, that are done by Unregenerate Men,
> or without Faith in, and Love to Christ, please God, or are ac-
> cepted of him. Yet good Works are of great advantage, being
> done in Faith, and Love, and wrought by the Holy Spirit, and
> are to be done by us, to shew our thankfulness to God, for the
> Grace of the New Covenant by Christ, and to fit us more and
> more for Glory: And in this sense, the Ten Commandments,
> as handed forth by Christ the Mediator, are a Rule of Life to a
> Believer, and shew us our Duty to God and Man, as also our
> need of the Grace of God, and Merit of Christ.[15]

The believer's sanctification is rooted in Christ's person and work. The Christian is united to Him by grace through faith and is sanctified "through the virtue of Christ in His death, Resurrection, and Intercession, and by the efficacy
of the Holy Spirit." Even as progress in holiness is made, "we have no cause to
boast nor ground to conclude, we merit anything thereby, we receiving all of
free and undeserved grace." Sanctification is described as "a continual war in
the soul." This war is present because of the remnants of sin, which are found
in "even the best of saints." Therefore, the Holy Spirit is needed to mortify the
body's deeds. Divine assistance is necessary to advance "in all saving graces."
This ongoing transformation occurs throughout the "whole man"—no aspect
of an individual is untouched by sanctification's work.

Proceed to the *Treatise of the Faith and Practices of the National Association of
Free Will Baptists* on sanctification: "Sanctification is the continuing of God's
grace by which the Christian may constantly grow in grace and in the knowledge of our Lord Jesus Christ."[16] More recently Millard Erickson, a theologian
from a different Baptist tradition, defined sanctification as "a process by which
one's moral condition is brought into conformity with one's legal status before
God. . . . Sanctification is the Holy Spirit's applying to the life of the believer
the work done by Jesus Christ."[17] Wayne Grudem, another contemporary Reformed theologian, describes sanctification as "a progressive work of God and
man that makes us more and more free from sin and like Christ in our actual

lives."[18] Forlines operates squarely within this tradition of Reformed thought on the doctrine of sanctification.

The Goal of Sanctification:
Restoration of the Image of God in Man

When God created Adam and Eve, He made them both in His image and likeness. Scripture reads, "So God created man in his own image, in the image of God he created him; male and female he created them" (Gen. 1:27). But what does the "image of God" actually mean? According to Forlines, the *imago Dei* is summed up in the term "personal": "The basic thrust of the idea of being created in the image of God is that *man is a personal being. A person is one who thinks, feels, and acts.*"[19] Furthermore, God's image in man possesses two aspects. Forlines first comments on the constitutional likeness, "What has been said about man as a personal, rational, moral creature is frequently referred to as the formal likeness of God in man. I prefer to speak of it as the *constitutional* likeness of God in man."[20] Second, he discusses functional likeness, which "means that man, as created, thought, felt, and acted in a way that was pleasing to God."[21]

Humanity possesses a constitutional likeness to God, which finds expression in the functions of thinking, feeling, and acting. However, humanity's fall into sin has affected every aspect of his being. Scripture teaches that man is totally depraved and unable to free himself from sin's power. Though God's image in man has been distorted, it is still there nonetheless (constitutional likeness). Therefore, God's goal in redemption is to restore the functional image of God in man by transforming the personality so an individual thinks, feels, and acts according to God's will. Forlines maintains, "The ultimate concern of God in redemption is to restore fallen human beings to favor and to a functional relationship with God."[22]

THE PROMISE OF ARMINIAN THEOLOGY

Forlines's "ultimate concern" is seen in many New Testament passages. Romans 8:29 states, "For those whom he foreknew he also predestined to be conformed to the image of his Son, in order that he might be the firstborn among many brothers." The restoration to favor with God occurs instantaneously; the restoration to functional relationship with God continues throughout one's life and is fully realized when we see Christ (1 John 3:2). At the same time, perfectionism, the notion that a fully realized sanctification can be attained in this life, is not a feature of historical, Free Will Baptist teaching. Instead, Forlines argues that the New Testament points toward a maturation process, "When we are challenged to be perfect in the New Testament, we are challenged to be mature, complete, and equipped. Certainly, this would call for moral concern and progress, but it does not entangle us with the depressing goal of moral perfection."[23]

While God does not expect us to reach moral perfection in this life, sanctification does extend into every aspect of life. Sanctification's scope entails our four basic relationships and points toward total personal transformation. Our basic relationships with God, self, others, and the created order are inevitably impacted (see chapter eight). As our inner man experiences transformation, it affects our total experience. "The influence of sanctification is to manifest itself in our total experience," writes Forlines.[24] "It embraces our experiences both as a member of the church and as a member of society. To believe in a unified view of knowledge, we must believe that our belief in God and Christian values have implications for the whole of life."[25] Yet if sanctification is a progressive work of God's grace in man, then what does God use to accomplish it? For this we will consider a third important theme.

The Means of Sanctification

Having considered sanctification's meaning and goal, we turn now to its means and implications for spirituality. A survey of the Forlinesean corpus will yield comments on prayer, the church's preaching ministry, local church involvement, and others. In prayer, for example, Forlines reminds us, "We are invited to come boldly to the throne of grace. There we will find a compassionate High Priest who can be touched by the feeling of our infirmities. He faced temptation in the real encounters of life."[26] He explains further, "He understands and cares. He is able to help (Heb. 4:14-16). When we come to Him with a desire to overcome sin and a desire to be holy, we can be sure that that is the kind of prayer He wants to answer."[27] Growth in Christ is both an individual and communal project, Forlines stresses, "In the New Testament, the sanctification of the members was not only the responsibility of the leadership of the church but the whole body."[28]

While lengthier treatments from Forlines's pen on prayer and other means of sanctification would be have been helpful, he focuses primarily on the Holy Spirit and Scripture.

The Holy Spirit

The Spirit's work in the believer's life is two-fold. Forlines explains, "Stated negatively, the Holy Spirit is working in us to give us victory over sin. Stated positively, the Holy Spirit works in us to produce virtue that is expressive of Christian values."[29] This two-dimensional work of the Holy Spirit is seen in the familiar Pauline expression of putting off the old man and putting on the new (Eph. 4:22-24). Additionally, Forlines reminds us that the Spirit is accomplishing redemption's overall purpose: "The Christian virtues mentioned as the fruit of the Spirit are constituent elements in the functional likeness of Christ in us."[30]

As God's Spirit establishes Christ's functional likeness in us, He does so by influencing us to make real and personal choices that impact our progression in holiness. Forlines writes, "The relationship of the Holy Spirit and the Christian is a relationship between persons. This means we are talking about influence and response, not mechanical cause and effect."[31] Forlines couches God's work in salvation in terms of influence and response over and against the typical Reformed view of cause and effect. This influence and response view manifests itself in God's work in sanctification—growing into Christ's image. At least two parties are engaged in sanctification. The Holy Spirit is influencing and empowering sanctification, but the believer possesses the real choice to respond to the Spirit's gracious influence.

Several passages support this view. For example, "But by the grace of God I am what I am, and his grace toward me was not in vain. On the contrary, I worked harder than any of them, though it was not I, but the grace of God that is with me" (1 Cor. 15:10). Paul highlights God's grace as the empowerment for His kingdom work. However, the grace at work in Paul's life propelled him to work "harder than any of them." We find a similar picture in Philippians: "Therefore, my beloved, as you have always obeyed, so now, not only as in my presence but much more in my absence, work out your own salvation with fear and trembling, for it is God who works in you, both to will and to work for his good pleasure" (Phil. 2:12-13). Paul also demonstrates the dynamic relationship between the Spirit's work and his work in the church in Colossians 1:29: "For this I toil, struggling with all his energy that he powerfully works within me."

The Word

The Holy Spirit always works in concert with God's Word. Any spirituality divorced from God's Word and its truth is devoid of true spiritual power. Forlines frequently stresses the absolute necessity of truth in the Christian life: "Truth is experienced as knowledge. Truth is grasped and understood by the mind, experienced or felt in the heart, and acted upon by the will. Truth must be grasped and understood in order for there to be growth and stability in the Christian life."[32] Here sanctification's work is seen as truth restores the functional likeness of God in man. Forlines explores this connection further: "When we truly believe an idea, that idea produces the appropriate attitude in our heart. What we know and feel is what guides our behavior. Our will is influenced by our ideas and attitudes."[33] Emphasis is placed on man's nature—on his mind, heart, and will. All three aspects are involved in the growth process. William Yount provides a helpful illustration of what he terms "the Christian teacher's triad."[34] The three dimensions of mind, heart, and will are reflected below:

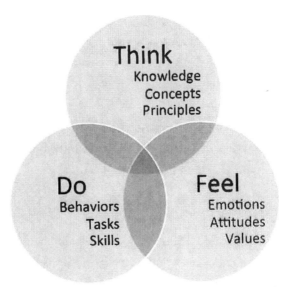

This shows the connection between each aspect of the human person. An inseparable relationship exists between what we think, feel, and do.

As we give ourselves over to deep thinking upon God's Word, God uses it to produce change in the mind, which produces change in our affections and results in changed behavior. Forlines states,

> Why meditate? In meditation, ideas take on depth and become richer, but the main purpose of meditation is for ideas to produce proper attitudes in the heart. In meditation our subconscious mind becomes programmed with ideas and attitudes. This programming of the subconscious mind changes our basic inner nature. The actions that arise out of this programming are expressions of the real self. Our subconscious mind needs to be programmed with the Word of God. It is then that it [the Word] will become a sanctifying influence

in our life to transform our personality into the likeness of Christ.[35]

Forlines prescribes biblical meditation—wherein the believer ponders and internalizes God's objective Word—as a primary means for change. Biblical mediation is the consistent thinking upon the truths of God's Word so that one might commune with, understand His will, and obey Him.[36] This deep and consistent thinking upon God's truth then sanctifies us and allows our "subconscious mind to be programmed with ideas and attitudes."[37] Mere acquaintance with the truth does not sanctify; truth must be understood by the mind, embraced by the heart, and obeyed in life.

Self and Sanctification

Another major contribution of Forlines is his emphasis on the self and sanctification.[38] This too has important implications for spirituality. Often unbiblical and therefore unhealthy views of self develop as persons seek to grow in holiness.[39] Following Jesus is costly. Becoming more like Him inevitably involves denying oneself. We cannot grow as disciples without discipline. Jesus said, "'If anyone would come after me, let him deny himself and take up his cross daily and follow me'" (Luke 9:23). In an extended discussion of this verse, Forlines observes,

> Self-denial is necessary to the extent that it requires us to set aside all plans and personal interests that would interfere with following Jesus. When self-denial causes us to set aside all of our desires and plans that would interfere with following Jesus, it has fulfilled its purpose. Self-denial is a tough assignment, but it does not call on a person to grind himself or herself into the dust of nothingness. A person who is truly following Jesus has practiced and is practicing self-denial, but this kind of self-denial is not an obsession. . . . Self is not some aspect of our being that gives us trouble. Self is the real

you—the real person. Selfhood embraces our personhood and personality. A person does not need to crucify the self. He needs to surrender self and develop self. He or she needs self-improvement, not self-crucifixion.[40]

The caution not to allow self-denial to become an obsession is appropriate. Both the Bible and church history demonstrate that the self has often become the focus, instead of the Lord, as people pursue spirituality. Paul dealt with this very issue in many churches. Perhaps the most instructive passage is Colossians 2, where Paul reminds believers that true spirituality is rooted in the person and work of Christ. Near the end of his discussion, he asks, "If with Christ you died to the elemental spirits of the world, why, as if you were still alive in the world, do you submit to regulations—'Do not handle, Do not taste, Do not touch' (referring to things that all perish as they are used)—according to human precepts and teachings?" (2:20-22). He then writes, "These have indeed an appearance of wisdom in promoting self-made religion and asceticism and severity to the body, but they are of no value in stopping the indulgence of the flesh" (2:23). Forlines thus offers this balancing statement, "We need to be Christ-centered, not self-centered. The focus of the verse [Luke 9:23] is on Jesus' words 'follow me,' not on 'deny himself.'"[41] In light of these principles, Forlines offers at least two important implications for the self and sanctification: self-involvement and self-worth.

Self-involvement in Sanctification

Author Jerry Bridges reminds us that grace is not against self-effort, but against attempts to earn salvation.[42] Salvation and thus the outworking of sanctification is all by grace. However, every believer must fully engage himself or herself in the work, which itself occurs in Christian community. We have already noted that two parties are primarily involved in sanctification: God and man. Believers, then, can never be passive in spirituality if they desire to grow in Christlikeness. In the following paragraph, Forlines talks about the relationship between believers' dependence and independence in spiritual growth. He also speaks of the limitations of cliché phrases that believers often use to describe their roles:

> Dependence is seen in that the various virtues listed are called
> the fruit of the Spirit. But when we talk about love, joy, peace,
> longsuffering, etc., we are not simply talking about divine ac-
> tivity in which we are used as channels. It may sound good
> to talk about God loving through us, but what about God
> having joy through us, or God having peace through us, and
> so on through the list? The Holy Spirit is helping us to be the
> kind of person who loves, experiences joy, peace, longsuffer-
> ing, etc. . . . In this work of the Holy Spirit, we are both active
> and passive. He is working in us as active persons, not as pas-
> sive puppets.[43]

Forlines thus provides a useful critique of the view that sanctification means we should "let go and let God." The self is not lost in the sanctification pro-cess, but is actively involved and growing.

Closely related to a let-go-and-let-God theology, another mistake believers often make is to compare themselves with others. This temptation is especially common when we hear testimonies of spiritual victory, which come on the heels of a defining or crisis moment. Occasionally this type of experience is even referred to as a "second work of grace." In a very personal and transpar-ent fashion, Forlines recounts the following about his own spiritual struggle in this regard,

> I deeply desired such a transforming and empowering by the
> Holy Spirit for myself. This was the beginning of a long pe-
> riod of frustration. I did not share very much of my struggles
> with anyone else, but for a long period of time I tried to have
> an experience like these men had related. During this time,
> I became highly introspective. I figured that if I confessed all

of my sins, that would help me have the experiences these men spoke of. I went over my life with a microscope trying to confess all my sins, I tried everything I knew to try, but it was all in vain.[44]

This tension would be resolved later in life as Forlines learned over time from experience and study:

> As a rule, there is a background of events that lead up to a crisis experience, when they are made into a doctrine. We are expected to tune in on about the last five minutes of that person's experience and have the same experience. It just does not work that way. As I said above, my experience has not been characterized by a lot of crises experiences. The great moments in my life have come when a great truth became clear to me. That is why my favorite Scripture verse is, "And ye shall know the truth, and the truth shall make you free (John 8:32)." For example, it was a great moment for me when as a result of studying the Bible, I arrived at the conclusion that there is no such thing as a once-for-all, transforming experience that comes after conversion and is available for all Christians.[45]

This personal example from Forlines's spiritual pilgrimage is instructive. First, it reminds us that we should not examine our spirituality by comparing ourselves with others. More importantly, it reinforces the need to test all spiritual experience by Scripture.

Forlines strings together a series of Scripture passages that underscore true self-involvement in the sanctification process. One of the most insightful comments he makes regards Philippians 4:11b: "I have learned in whatever situation I am to be content." "Paul did not say, 'I used to have this problem with discontentment. I got tired of it. One day I asked God with sincerity and faith and He took it away,'" writes Forlines.[46] "No, he said, 'I have learned to be content.' God did not simply deal with the problem by a single stroke of Divine power. Rather, there was a learning experience and Paul was genuinely involved in it."[47]

On a personal note, after being exposed to some "let-go-and-let God" theology shortly before entering Welch College, Forlines's explanation on this subject in class was a breath of fresh air. Before transferring to Welch, I went through a long period of intense and painful introspection related to my own shortcomings in the Christian life. I actually bought a little booklet entitled, "Let Go and Let God," but after reading it, could not seem to reach the place the author described. One of the greatest takeaways from my Systematic Theology course was when Mr. Forlines delivered those two sentences described above: "God did not simply deal with the problem by a single stroke of Divine power. Rather, there was a learning experience, and Paul was genuinely involved in it."

Self-worth and Sanctification

Before leaving the discussion of self and sanctification, one final area should be noted. A proper view of sanctification and spirituality helps a person with self-worth. Though fallen, man is still created in God's image. Not only is the Christian made in God's image, but he or she has been redeemed. Believers, therefore, should develop biblical and healthy views of themselves. Forlines cautions us not to downgrade God's handiwork, "It is no compliment to God for a Christian to grind himself or herself into the dust of nothingness so he can claim no credit for what he is and so he can give all glory to God. It is no compliment to God for us to thank Him for making us 'nothing.'"[48] Instead, we should possess a proper self-worth, one which recognizes our limitations and weaknesses, but also our progress and worth in God's sight. An individual who possesses biblical self-worth will find that "this recognition gives rise to gratitude and humility."[49]

Conclusion: Application for the Twenty-first Century

Forlines's emphasis on total personality change and inner transformation is vital for each Christian and local church. Ministering in the type of "spiritual, but not religious" climate described earlier means we must hold unswervingly to this truth: The whole gospel is for the whole man. Surface level change is not the gospel's goal. Christ makes real and lasting change where genuine repentance and faith are present in an individual. Church leaders must continue to insist that "forgiveness and change always go together."[50]

Spiritual growth takes time. Individual and corporate growth depends on the simple, God-ordained means of growth: God's Spirit, God's Word, meditation, and prayer. Our focus must be Christ, even as we commit ourselves to the disciplines commanded and modeled in Scripture. These means are not an end—they are means to an end—of knowing Christ and becoming more like Him. We dare not invent new ways of approaching God and spirituality, but instead must hold to the time-tested, God-approved ways of pursuing holiness.

F. Leroy Forlines has provided us with a theologically grounded way forward in the area of sanctification and spirituality. He firmly believes that God's design in redemption is to restore man to favor with God and to have a functional relationship with Him. God accomplishes sanctification's end through simple and timeless means, as believers respond to His divine initiative and influence. Brother Forlines's ability and willingness to interact honestly with the Bible and its intersection with real life issues is one of his greatest gifts to Free Will Baptists. He has not only taught us in the classroom and through his writings, but has also proven to be a faithful model of spirituality. As Hebrews 13:7-8 reminds us, "Remember your leaders, those who spoke to you the word of God. Consider the outcome of their way of life, and imitate their faith. Jesus Christ is the same yesterday and today and forever."

[1] David Wells, *The Courage to Be Protestant: Truth Lovers, Marketers, and Emergents in the Postmodern World* (Grand Rapids: Eerdmans, 2008), 179.

[2] Ibid., 182.

[3] F. Leroy Forlines, *The Quest for Truth: Answering Life's Inescapable Questions* (Nashville: Randall House, 1995), 217; hereafter *Quest*.

[4] F. Leroy Forlines, *Classical Arminianism: A Theology of Salvation* (Nashville: Randall House, 2011), 278.

[5] Ibid., 278.

[6] Ibid., 279.

[7] Ibid.

[8] Joel Beeke, *Overcoming the World: Grace to Win the Daily Battle* (Phillipsburg: P&R, 2005), 95-96.

[9] Ibid.

[10] Walter Bauer, *A Greek-English Lexicon of the New Testament and Other Early Christian Literature*, trans. and eds., William F. Arndt and F. Wilbur Gingrich (Chicago: The University of Chicago Press, 1979), "hagiazo."

[11] "The Westminster Confession of Faith," Center for Reformed Theology and Apologetics; http://www.reformed.org/documents/wcf_with_proofs/; accessed on May 11, 2015; Internet. In addition, this historic confession, and others, may be found in books on doctrine and/or systematic theology, such as Wayne Grudem, *Systematic Theology: An Introduction to Biblical Doctrine* (Grand Rapids: Zondervan, 1994), 1179-1196.

[12] "The Westminster Confession of Faith."

[13] Ibid.

[14] Free Will Baptists can trace their heritage to the English General Baptists of the 1600s. An Orthodox Creed is one example of General Baptist documents, influential in forming Free Will Baptist doctrine. For a detailed discussion of Free Will Baptist heritage, see J. Matthew Pinson's *A Free Will Baptist Handbook* (Nashville: Randall House, 1998), chapter 1.

[15] A transcription of the original document can be found at Southwestern Baptist Theological Seminary's Center for Theological Research. Madison Grace completed this transcription work. The full text may be found at http://baptiststudiesonline.com/wp-content/uploads/2007/02/orthodox-creed.pdf.

[16] *A Treatise of the Faith and Practices of the National Association of Free Will Baptists.* (Nashville: Executive Office, National Association of Free Will Baptists, 2008), 12. An online version of this document may be viewed at http://www.nafwb.org/files/images/treatise09.pdf.

[17] Millard Erickson, *Christian Theology* (Grand Rapids: Baker, 1986), 968.

[18] Grudem, 746.

[19] Forlines, *Quest*, 138.

20 Ibid., 139; italics added.

21 Ibid.

22 Ibid., 218.

23 Ibid., *Classical Arminianism*, 300; see also Forlines, *Biblical Ethics*.

24 Forlines, *Classical Arminianism*, 292.

25 Ibid.

26 Forlines, *Quest*, 240.

27 Ibid.

28 Ibid.

29 Ibid., 238.

30 Ibid.

31 Ibid.

32 Ibid., 239.

33 Ibid.

34 William Yount, *Created to Learn* (Nashville: Broadman and Holman, 1996), 249ff.

35 Forlines, *Quest*, 239.

36 See Donald S. Whitney, *Spiritual Disciplines for the Christian Life* (Colorado Springs: NavPress, 1991), 48.

37 Forlines, *Quest*, 239.

38 Though Forlines gives no specific definition, he seems to equate self and person. Thus, the personhood (constitutional likeness) and personality (functional likeness) are bound up in the term "self." In a personal correspondence with Brother Forlines he stated, "Whatever you can attribute to person or personality, you can also attribute to self."

39 One might think, for instance, of asceticism. While it does not currently plague the Western church, it has created problems in past periods of church history. Any form of self-denial that becomes the obsession and focus misses the point of sanctification and true biblical spirituality.

40 Forlines, *Quest*, 228.

41 Ibid.

42 See Jerry Bridges, *The Discipline of Grace: God's Role and Our Role in the Pursuit of Holiness* (Colorado Springs: NavPress, 2006), in which Bridges provides a helpful treatment of sanctification.

43 Forlines, *Classical Arminianism*, 287.

44 F. Leroy Forlines and Harold Harrison, *The Charismatic Movement: A Survey of Its Development and Doctrine* (Nashville: Free Will Baptist Commission for Theological Integrity, 1989), 16.

45 Ibid., 38.

[46] Leroy Forlines, "Understanding Yourself and Others: A Biblical, Theological, and Practical Approach to Personality" (unpublished manuscript, 1994), 72.

[47] Ibid.

[48] Forlines, *Classical Arminianism*, 288.

[49] Ibid.

[50] Forlines, *Quest*, 219.

CHAPTER SIX

LEAVING JESUS: FORLINES'S VIEW OF CONDITIONAL PERSEVERANCE

David Outlaw

As a boy I spent many off-school hours on the Welch College campus. Most of my fondest memories are painted on a mental canvas owning Richland Avenue as its background. Since my father was a college professor, I wandered through the nooks and hallways of Welch, searching for anything that might interest a boy with a healthy imagination. Too often confined to my father's office and forced to endure the drudgery of homework, I listened to the sounds of whispers and footsteps that would announce my father's arrival and the merciful end of an academically boring day.

I remember the creak of the stairway door spilling its echo into the hollow chamber of steps. My ears perked, and I listened for the footsteps. Rather than my father's long stride, I often heard the sound of shorter steps. Sometimes they were the quick steps of someone urgent to write down a thought or resume reading a deep theological tome filled with truths I could not yet pronounce. Other times they were the slow, contemplative steps of one whose thoughts were in a distant place. The pace was different, but the source was the same: Mr. F. Leroy Forlines. Was he reading, deep in thought? My curiosity was overwhelmed so I quietly cracked the door to see what he was doing.

I do not remember a time when I did not know Mr. Forlines, or consider him with respect, taking my cue from those around me. Catching me in the act of spying, he would sometimes invite me into the hollowed chambers of his office. His conversation would center on life or theology, and strange words slid from his mouth, which I assumed communicated ideas that I should already know. While engaged in conversation my eyes were fixed on any number of interesting office toys and trinkets. My two favorites were a bird that would dip down into water seeming to drink repeatedly, and a domino clock.

Even then I knew I should leave his office saturated with Bible knowledge and wisdom for life. I can still taste the disappointment in myself for leaving his office more confused than when I had entered. Perhaps these visits curbed my worldly appetites from amusements that would have spelled my downfall, but soon I had to return to my homework. Unfortunately, I do not remember Mr. Forlines's advice or teaching from those formative years. What I do remember, however, is that a man of intelligence, importance, and dignity was willing to spend time with a little boy struggling to do his homework. For these reasons and more, I am honored to write on a Forlinesean view of conditional perseverance.

What Did Forlines Teach?

Within the Arminian community, approaches vary widely with regard to grasping, formulating, and communicating the doctrine of perseverance. However, Forlines offers reason, passion, and clarity to this topic. Pertinent to this study are his views as expressed in *Biblical Systematics*, *The Quest for Truth* (hereafter *Quest*), and several booklets.

Conditional Perseverance: An Introduction

With classic Forlines clarity, he explains his view in his discussion of his chapter titles too:

> I have chosen to entitle this chapter "Continuance in Salvation" for three reasons: (1) As a subject it embraces both the Divine and the human side. (2) To speak of continuance in salvation speaks of continuance in both justification and sanctification, not simply justification. (3) It is a way of speaking of the subject by a title that is appropriate whether a person believes in conditional continuance or unconditional continuance.[1]

Each reason illuminates a corresponding characteristic of Forlines's approach. First, he displays balance between divine sovereignty and human responsibility in soteriology. Second, he demonstrates the appropriate nuance to account for the relationship between justification and sanctification. Third, he seeks clarity when communicating his view.

Forlines explains his position on conditional security in the opening paragraph of his chapter "Perseverance" in *Quest*. He is straightforward in defining his view: "I am going to take the position that it is possible for a person who has been saved to commit apostasy and become once again lost and under the wrath of God."[2] Forlines stresses that the person under consideration was actually saved, and not just appearing to be saved. Forlines develops his argument in three phases. First, he begins with a theological assertion to lay the foundation for his understanding of conditional perseverance. Second, he proceeds to expound numerous conditional security passages. Third, after considering the biblical argument, he turns to demonstrating the consistency of his views with other major doctrines. Like testing a puzzle piece, he hopes to show that conditional perseverance fits with other pieces to form a coherent picture.

The Theological Foundation

When laying the doctrinal foundation of his case, Forlines appeals to man's creation in God's image as a personal being. Interestingly, his guiding argument is one that many would consider anthropological rather than soteriological: "The theological foundation that supports the possibility of becoming lost again after a person is saved is found in what it means to be made in the image of God. Being made in the image of God means that we are personal beings. We think, feel, and act."[3] Man's personhood as a facet of God's image is a recurring theme throughout Forlines's writing. Christian doctrines do not exist in isolation, but bleed into one another. Christian thought defies the kind of demarcation that would allow a thinker to sequester himself in a single area of Christian doctrine without acknowledging other doctrinal truths. No one builds theology in a laboratory, but they do so recognizing that Christian theology functions as a comprehensive worldview.

Forlines further argues that people make choices and decisions for which they must take responsibility. No matter how much influence is applied, the person must make a choice, and resistance is always possible. Forlines proposes that God does not violate man's personal nature while dealing with him. Stephen Ashby echoes these concerns, "If God did not consider Christians to be persons who make choices (both good and bad), which are truly and significantly their own choices, then the volume of paraenetic and hortatory writings that deal with Christian behavior would not be needed."[4] Scriptural warnings only make sense if those receiving them can and must make choices. This reflects the personhood that Forlines considers an integral part of God's image created in man. Concluding the doctrinal foundation of his argument, Forlines comments, "Freedom of will is involved in what it means to be a person."[5] Since Forlines is a Free Will Baptist, we would not expect him to have trouble with the phrase "free will." His emphasis, however, is not so much on the demand that people have the autonomy implied in free will, but that people are free, moral agents. This agency is important primarily because it reflects personhood as a necessary component to the image of God.

Personhood is also a controlling idea for Forlines in his approach to sote-riology as a whole, and conditional perseverance in particular. "The one word that sums up the idea of rationality and morality is the word 'person,'" he writes.[6] "God is personal. Man is personal. The basic thrust of the idea of be-ing created in the image of God is that *man is a personal being*. A person is one who thinks, feels and acts."[7] For Forlines, man does not simply have the right to be personal; rather, man is personal. Personhood is not one among several options for people; people are personal because they were created in God's im-age. This personhood involves reason, by which man makes moral choices and has the capacity for a relationship with God. Forlines reasons that God's offer of salvation deals with man as a personal being, which can be accepted or re-jected. Why would the same ability not exist after salvation? Ashby follows the same line of thought, "If divine grace is resistible prior to conversion, it is also resistible after conversion. God does not take away our free will at the moment of conversion."[8] This singular idea continually informs and directs Forlines's presentation of conditional perseverance. Equipped with the assurance that God deals with man as a personal being, Forlines moves to the exegetical phase of his argument.

The Biblical Argument

Forlines's methodology necessarily leads him to Scripture. He builds his argument primarily on the strength of three, major passages that he believes irrefutably teach conditional perseverance: Hebrews 6, Colossians 1, and John 15, with three questions guiding his exposition of each passage. Though word-ed to fit each passage's context and content, the questions follow the same general pattern: (1) had these people been saved; (2) what had they done; and (3) what is their condition?[9] By answering these questions, we should uncover the New Testament writers' views regarding perseverance. Forlines considers the biblical argument to be of primary importance, given his high views of scriptural inspiration, inerrancy, and authority (see chapter one). In studying his teaching we will highlight the broad answers to his three questions gleaned across the study of each major passage.

When asking if these people had been saved, Hebrews 6:4-6 employs six characteristics of the person under consideration: having once been enlightened; having tasted the heavenly gift; having been made partakers of the Holy Ghost; having tasted the good word of God; having tasted the powers of the world to come; and having repented. After listing these characteristics, Forlines comments, "It would certainly seem obvious that the characteristics given above are descriptive of a saved person."[10] Against his critics, Forlines demonstrates that a plain reading of the text, not to mention the way these terms are understood elsewhere, leaves one with the impression that the person in mind is indeed saved. To a large degree, one's answer to this question determines the direction of the larger theological question of apostasy.

Moving to the second question, "What had these people done?" Forlines focuses on a phrase found in Hebrews 6:6 (KJV): "they crucify to themselves the Son of God afresh." Again, revisiting the first question, Forlines comments, "A person could not crucify to himself the Son of God afresh unless he were in a living relationship to Him; therefore, such could be committed only by a saved person."[11] Moving onto the second question and determined to elucidate the author's meaning, Forlines compares Hebrews 6:6 with 10:29, where he says that the person had "counted the blood of the covenant, wherewith he was sacrificed, an unholy thing":

> When a person came to this point, he denounced his faith in Christ; he drove Christ out of his life; in relationship Christ became a dead Christ; thus, he had crucified Christ to himself. When this person denounced his former faith in Christ, he was saying that there was nothing to the experience he thought he had had with Christ. In so doing, he put Him to an open shame.[12]

Note the force of these actions; it is not simply that sins have been committed, but that the person has severed their relationship with Christ. Second Peter further demonstrates their rejection of the knowledge of Christ. The combined actions observed in these three passages imply a total rejection of God's work in Christ.

The final piece to the interpretive puzzle deals with the result of rejecting Christ and His work by those who had once been saved. Forlines explains that the biblical writers consider this falling away or rejection of Christ irremediable. While examining Hebrews 6:4-6, Forlines states,

> The writer of Hebrews says that it is impossible to renew such a person again unto repentance. It is my understanding that this means that he cannot be restored to faith. He cannot be saved again. Not everyone who interprets this passage to teach that loss of salvation is possible accepts the position that it is impossible for such a person to be saved again. It seems to me that "For it is impossible . . . to renew them again unto repentance" admits no other interpretation than that it is impossible for such a person to be saved again.[13]

This is a key conclusion for three reasons. First, he concludes that the person who commits the sin of apostasy cannot be restored to salvation; this represents one of the unique features of the Reformed Arminian view. Second, he draws this conclusion directly from Scripture; any interpreter who differs from this interpretation must deal not only with Forlines as an interpreter, but also with Scripture's exact words. Third, he concedes that not everyone accepts this conclusion, other Arminians included.

While Forlines would contend that many other passages support his view, he points to two in particular. In consideration of Colossians 1:21-23, verse 23, "if indeed you continue in the faith," gives Forlines special concern: "Here it is definitely implied that to fail to continue in the faith would mean loss of salvation."[14] This continuation does not only mean that a believer should continue to obey Christ's teachings, but also that he should not be lured away by false teachers.

Forlines also addresses John 15:2, 6. While conscious of the danger of overworked analogies, he focuses on the branch and compares it with the metaphors in Hebrews 6, 1 John 2:24, and 2 John 9:

> Upon considering these references, it seems clear that for a person not to abide in Christ, as in John 15:6, would mean that he forsook the true teachings of Christ. Is it not also taught in other references mentioned that to fail to continue in the true doctrine of Christ would mean rejection by God, which John 15:6 describes as being cast forth as a branch? The result of being cast forth is to be withered and burned. The same thing happens to the apostate of Hebrews 6 as is seen in the figure set forth in verse 8.[15]

Thus "not abiding" equates with forsaking Christ's teachings, both relationally and intellectually. Additionally, Forlines identifies the imagery of being "cast out" as God's judgment. Finally, he links the images found in John 15 and Hebrews 6.

By interpreting these various passages in the manner that he has, Forlines's position begins to crystalize: Scripture teaches that a saved person may forsake their relationship with Christ and forfeit their salvation. Salvation is conditioned upon faith in Christ, but when a person forsakes that faith, the result is forfeiture of salvation. This salvation cannot be regained.

Broad Theological Consistency

Forlines also maintains balance as a theologian, always analyzing his interpretations in perspective of the broader theological landscape to ensure biblical accuracy and theological consistency. If his analysis is correct, it should fit with the broader picture; and if his view of the broader picture is correct, it should fit the detailed analysis.

One of the most frequent criticisms voiced against the Arminian view of conditional perseverance is that it violates God's sovereignty. Forlines convincingly counters this accusation, arguing that God deals with man based on an influence and response relationship over against the cause and effect relationship advanced by Calvinism (see chapter three). He resists the notion to define or conceptualize sovereignty in solely cause and effect terms. Rather, he insists that the question should revolve around God's description of the administration of His sovereignty as revealed in Scripture. Scripture does not require the interpreter to approach it with the presupposition of determinism, or the belief that divine sovereignty demands a guaranteed effect.

Forlines clarifies his belief in God's sovereignty this way:

> I believe God accomplishes *all of His purposes.* He achieves *all of His goals.* The choice to create human beings as personal beings was His own choice. That choice meant He would deal with us as persons. He would work with us in the framework of *influence* and *response.* This meant man's responses could include both *obedience* and *disobedience.* God does not lose His sovereignty when man disobeys. We are not to assume that God desires man's disobedience. We should assume however that God desires that disobedience would be a real option for man, created as he is with personality. In the *cause* and *effect* relationship approach to sovereignty, it is rather difficult to see how disobedience ever entered the universe without either destroying God's sovereignty, if He disapproves of sin, or corrupting His holiness if He does not. It does not help very much to say that God's ways are inscrutable to us.[16]

This is a deeply important statement when relating the Reformed Arminian position to those of other evangelicals. He clearly affirms God's sovereignty. God chose in His sovereignty to deal with man as a personal being in the context of an influence and response framework. Within that framework, disobedience does not violate God's sovereignty. Finally, in no way is the discussion aided by an appeal to the inscrutability of God's ways. In fact, there is no place to discuss these ideas at all if God's ways are ultimately inscrutable. Instead, God's ways are mysterious to us in that they are greater than we have the ability to understand. The fact that we cannot fully understand them does not mean that we cannot have some understanding of them.

Forlines also shows theological consistency by showing how conditional perseverance relates to the satisfaction view of the atonement. Atonement is not merely the fulfillment of arbitrary regulations; God's very nature demands it and is satisfied by it. Atonement does not simply acquire God's desired approval, but satisfies something within God. If this is the case, the rejection of Christ's atonement amounts to a rejection of God's character and attributes. Connected with this is the imputation of Christ's death and righteousness, and the believer's union with Christ. Through the atonement, Christ's active and passive obedience are credited to the believer (see chapter four). More than simply a courtroom verdict, this transaction occurs within the context of an intimate relationship with Christ. In reference to conditional perseverance, then, apostasy can take place only if and when that union with Christ is severed.

Believing that salvation is only by God's grace and through faith in Jesus Christ, Forlines demonstrates how his view of conditional perseverance is consistent with this view of salvation. At issue is the fact that salvation is not by works. If salvation is not by works, then the belief that salvation can be lost by works, or by the failure to perform the right works, is logically inconsistent. In response to this, Forlines holds that faith does not contribute to the grounds of our justification; it is not a work. Instead, it is the recognition of Jesus as Lord and Savior. It is the beginning of the believer's relationship or union with Christ, through which the necessary price for sin is paid, and the righteousness demanded by God is realized. In apostasy that relationship is discontinued and salvation is lost.

Forlines's approach is three-fold. First, he holds views of sovereignty and the atonement that, while not foreign to other Arminian theologians, are historically consonant with views held by Reformed theologians. For this reason,

Forlinesean theology is called Reformed Arminianism. Second, he recognizes the need for consistency with other major doctrines and judges the validity of his view against that demand. Third, he carefully articulates his view in sight of salvation by grace. He seeks to avoid any hint that salvation relies on man's work, or that apostasy is the result of works on the believer's part.

Sins of Ignorance and Sins of Presumption

In 1995 at the Southeastern Region meeting of the Evangelical Theological Society, Forlines presented a paper in which he discussed the results of a study he conducted on sins of ignorance and presumptuous sins. Numbers 15:27-30 was the paper's focus and provided the grid for understanding these two types of sins. A study of the tables provided at the end of the paper reveal that sins of ignorance include those meaning "to sin through ignorance," "to err," and "to go astray." Sins of ignorance can also be termed sins of weakness. On the other hand, presumptuous sins are daring, defiant, and self-willed. Forlines links presumptuous sins with the blasphemy of the Holy Spirit spoken of by Jesus, and the sin leading to death referred to by John. He and others also strongly connect these words, phrases, and pictures to the willful sin (Heb. 10:26-39). Forlines clarifies:

> When it comes to presumptuous sins (or willful sins), it is very important that we understand that not all sins that involve a conscious choice of the will are presumptuous sins. The vast majority of conscious sins are sins of ignorance, not presumptuous sins. Presumptuous sins are only committed by informed people who do so with a presumptuous, willful, defiant, arrogant, attitude toward God.[17]

Clarification that all willful sins are not presumptuous is necessary here since many people read about "sinning willfully" and assume that it means any sin a person consciously commits. Additionally, sins committed by Christians normally fall under the "sins of ignorance" category. This does not imply that these sins are not serious and do not demand repentance, but they do not constitute apostasy or presumptuous sins.

Evaluation

When characterizing Forlines's teaching on conditional perseverance, the word "balance" materializes. Even if the reader does not agree with Forlines, he must admit that Forlines approaches the subject from several angles. His writing entails biblical support, theological consistency, and pastoral practicality. He does not ignore those who hold opposing views, but does his best to acknowledge their teaching, and respond to their criticisms and concerns in a clear and honest manner.

If anything is missing from Forlines's presentation of conditional perseverance, it is strangely, a historical argument. Forlines's writings usually drip with awareness of his theological predecessors, especially Jacobus Arminius. While this may have ultimately have been tangential to his systematic presentation, perhaps even detracting from the desired clarity, some historical discussion would have been helpful.[18]

Other Answers to the Question of Perseverance

One of the greatest lessons I have learned from Forlines is to deal with others with integrity. Once when assigned the task of reporting on a movement held in suspicion by some in his denomination, Forlines's report was not as harsh as some wanted. When questioned he responded, "I'm not going to make the Devil out to be worse than he really is." Those with different views of perseverance, whose writings we will now consider, are certainly not the Devil, but are instead our Christian brothers. Any representations of their views are written with care and fear, but must be done with some level of summation and generalization.

Other Arminians

Through the centuries many have used the term "Arminian" in such a broad manner that the term has lost much value. Rather than identifying a particular person as closely associated with Arminius's beliefs, many times the label simply means "not a Calvinist." Regarding conditional perseverance, Forlines stands at odds with many who use the Arminian moniker. Wesleyans represent the largest contingent of organized Arminians. Forlines's view of conditional perseverance bears mere superficial similarities with Wesley and his followers.

Forlines differs from Wesleyans with regard to the extent of depravity, the nature of the atonement, and the imputation of Christ's righteousness in salvation (see chapter four). With these differences in mind before the conversation on conditional perseverance begins, there is little hope that the two sides would agree at that point. Not surprisingly, then, Forlines also differs from Wesleyans with regard to how forfeiture of salvation occurs, and on the question of the remedial nature of apostasy. Steven Harper explains Wesley's view:

> The loss of salvation is much more related to experiences that are profound and prolonged. Wesley saw two primary pathways that could result in a permanent fall from grace: unconfessed sin and the actual expression of apostasy. As we will see, even these two avenues are not without restorative recourse, but they are surely to be guarded against as we grow in the grace and knowledge of our Lord and Savior Jesus Christ. To discount the possibility of either is to make us even more vulnerable to their occurrence.[19]

At least two areas deviate from Forlines's teachings. First, whereas Harper presents two paths for loss of salvation, Forlines acknowledges only one. Second, while Wesleyans see "restorative recourse" available for either path, Forlines believes that renewal is impossible for the apostate.

Though a Baptist, Robert Shank shares the Wesleyan hope of restoration for the apostate. In view of Peter's persistent denial of Jesus on the night before the crucifixion, Shank remarks,

And yet, Peter found forgiveness. Is that not encouraging for
us all, as we think of the many times and ways we have so
shamefully denied our Holy Savior? Have we not sworn by
deed and life, if not in word, "I know not the man"? Have we
no need to go out and weep bitterly with Peter? But still He
comes—the Man of Sorrows, forever scarred—and gently asks,
"Lovest thou me?"[20]

Forlines is sympathetic to Shank's appeal, but is still unconvinced, especially
concerning the link between Hebrews 10 and Numbers 15, and the belief that
there is no sacrifice for presumptuous sins. He writes, "Surely, we cannot keep
Numbers 15:30, 31; Hebrews 6:4-6; 10:26-29; and the teachings of Jesus on the
unpardonable sin in mind and still sustain the position that there is no sin for
which there is no remedy."[21]

Modified Calvinists

Many within the evangelical community accept Arminian doctrine on
points such as conditional election, the extent of the atonement, and the resistible nature of God's offer for saving grace. When approaching the conditional-
ity of perseverance, however, these same interpreters balk; we might call them
"modified Calvinists." We should recognize and compare Forlines's teaching
to at least two types of modified Calvinists.

Some believe in eternal security such that no matter what happens after
the expression of saving faith, the person will be in heaven. Forlines calls this
the "popular view of 'once saved always saved,'" or eternal security.[22] He mentions the popular preacher Charles Stanley while dealing with this form of
eternal security. Well-known scholars like Charles Ryrie and Zane Hodges also
hold this view. In *The Gospel under Siege*, Hodges concludes that though Hebrews teaches the possibility of a believer committing apostasy, this does not
result in the loss of salvation: "It is widely held in modern Christendom that
the faith of a genuine Christian cannot fail. But this is not an assertion that
can be verified in the New Testament."[23]

In 1975, Forlines wrote a booklet entitled "Cheap-Easy Believism." In it he combats the view that saving grace does not lead to a life of holiness: "It is absurd to think about salvation delivering us from hell without doing something about the sin in our lives. . . . If salvation is designed to do something about sin and to make us new creatures, it is inconceivable that a person could be saved and not have his experience with sin changed."[24] Forlines's disagreement here was not about the means to salvation, but about the very nature of saving faith. While not believing in perfectionism, Forlines believes that the saved person experiences change. No change means there is no evidence of salvation.

Classical Calvinists

A growing number within evangelical churches are holding a fuller form of Calvinism. They understand Scripture to teach that God's unconditional election of individuals for salvation implies that the elect will persevere in the faith. Pastor, professor, and Enjoying God Ministries founder Sam Storms summarizes his position that anyone who believes at any point in the past will continue in that belief. "That doesn't mean they will remain secure in their salvation simply because of that past belief," he explains. "It means they are secure because the God in whom they put their trust, preserves them in that faith, apart from which there is no hope or eternal life."[25] This is an important distinction from the modified Calvinist position. Classical Calvinists do not support an antinomian position, but insist that the truly saved will necessarily persevere in that faith. John Piper, R.C. Sproul, and others stand as current representatives of this line, which flow from the Reformed tradition, most notably John Calvin and Jonathan Edwards.

Forlines shares many similarities with these Reformed thinkers. He agrees with them on matters such as the nature of God, the atonement, and the role of Christ's imputed righteousness in our justification. Concerning the doctrines discussed in the Canons of Dort, however, he expresses strong disagreement. His dispute with the Calvinists centers in two major areas. First, he remains unconvinced that election is unconditional. He maintains that Scripture offers faith as the condition demanded for salvation, and is prior to regeneration. Second, he claims that God's offer of saving grace is resistible. Here the real implications of "free will" come into view.

Implications of Conditional Perseverance for Christian Life and Ministry

If the Reformed Arminian position on conditional perseverance and the biblical teaching on assurance of salvation is correct, these truths should change the way the church ministers. What follows are some suggestions on how an understanding of conditional perseverance might provide clarity and instruction.

Evangelistic Methodology

Sharing the gospel demands clarity and simplicity. Salvation involves both justification and sanctification. When we separate these aspects of salvation, we may cloud the gospel's demands through evangelistic approaches that truncate Christ's demands and misrepresent the nature of saving faith. A person does not become a believer simply because they repeat a prayer, raise their hands, or come forward at the end of a service. Jesus' call to salvation is the invitation to follow Him with all that we are. Our evangelistic strategies should be realistic about the nature of saving faith. We cannot simply offer words that, if repeated, will open heaven's gates like a magic mantra.

The Grounds for Assurance

Scripture gives people markers for knowing they belong to God. These may be counterfeited for a period of time, but God's people live in a manner characterized by these signs. Among the indicators are love for God, love for God's people, righteous lives, repentance of sin, and submission to God's authority. What is not among the markers, however, is a baptismal certificate or the ability to recall the place and time where we came forward to pray. Above all, these events may be fabricated. I am not suggesting that these things are wrong or devoid of value. However, a life that continues in sin screams louder than the testimony of a date and event. The church must teach its members to evaluate their salvation in terms of growth in Christ, rather than stagnating that growth with false assurances.

Discipleship

If conditional perseverance is correct, the church has no excuse for laziness with regard to discipleship. Many pastors and other church leaders divide evangelism and discipleship in an unhealthy way. Forlines reminds us that justification and sanctification exist together. If a saved person may commit apostasy and be eternally lost, how can the church do anything but ground that person in the fertile soil of the faith? A kind of godly fear must exist for walking in holiness. A love for the things of God and a hatred for sin are essential for growth in Christ.

Church Discipline

Another area for improvement is that the body of Christ must address sin corporately. If the church refuses to confront sinful behavior, its people slide into danger without the restraint of God's people. While there is always the danger of judgmental people in the church, there is also a danger when the church winks at sin. Church discipline serves two goods. First, it purifies the body. If church members live in public sin, the community learns to despise the church and its message. When the community sees love and holiness in harmony, they know that something special is before them. Second, with discipline, we hope to provoke the person to repentance and restoration. Confronted with their sin, some will respond defensively and even angrily. As God's Spirit deals with them, however, full repentance and restoration are real possibilities. With this second point the experience of both forgiveness and the desire for holiness are maintained.

Relating to the World

The Christian who does not see their need to pursue holiness forgets caution in relating to the world and its temptations. When we do not fear or hate sin we are inclined to follow its path. While the world cannot take our salvation from us, it can lure us into sin. Sin may callous our hearts in our relationship with God. We must separate ourselves from worldliness, while loving the people in the world. Life in Christ, however, makes us different from the world. We do not share the same goals, traits, power, or methods as the world. Perhaps believers should be concerned if they feel too comfortable in the world.

Conclusion

Since boyhood, I have learned how to pursue the truth of God with passion and integrity from Leroy Forlines. His teaching on conditional perseverance is an extraordinary example of his willingness to follow the biblical teachings wherever they lead, while testing his conclusions in light of other interpreters. His biblical faithfulness and balanced reason combine with a heart that longs for God and aches for the fallen world around him. In his teaching, not only does Forlines see the possibility that a believer may leave the faith, but he also believes in a glorious Savior in Whom all who come find both the reason and power to persevere in love and faithfulness.

---

[1] F. Leroy Forlines, *Biblical Systematics: A Study of the Christian System of Life and Thought* (Nashville: Randall House, 1975), 207.

[2] F. Leroy Forlines, *The Quest for Truth: Theology for Postmodern Times* (Nashville: Randall House, 2001), 269; hereafter *Quest*.

[3] Ibid., 276.

[4] Stephen Ashby, "A Reformed Arminian View," in *Four Views on Eternal Security*, ed. J. Matthew Pinson (Grand Rapids: Zondervan, 2002), 170.

[5] Forlines, *Quest*, 277.

[6] Ibid., 138.

[7] Ibid.

[8] Ashby, 170.

[9] Forlines, *Quest*, 277-80.

[10] Ibid., 277.

[11] Ibid., 279.

[12] Ibid., 279-80.

[13] Ibid., 280.

[14] Ibid., 288.

[15] Ibid., 289.

[16] Ibid., 290.

[17] Ibid., 481.

[18] Similar treatments, such as Robert E. Picirilli, *Grace, Faith, and Free Will. Contrasting Views of Salvation; Calvinism and Arminianism* (Nashville: Randall House, 2002), spend more time demonstrating the direct connection with Arminius's thought. Another treatment that delves deeper into this historical connection is Ashby, "A Reformed Arminian View," in *Four Views on Eternal Security*, 137-196.

[19] Steven Harper, "A Wesleyan Arminian View" in *Four Views on Eternal Security*, ed. J. Matthew Pinson (Grand Rapids: Zondervan, 2002), 239.

[20] Robert Shank, *Life in the Son* (Minneapolis: Bethany House, 1960), 329.

[21] Forlines, *Quest*, 282.

[22] Ibid., 272.

[23] Zane Hodges, *The Gospel Under Siege* (Dallas: Redencion Viva, 1981), 68.

[24] Leroy Forlines, *Cheap-Easy Believism* (Nashville: Randall House, 1975), 5.

[25] Sam Storms, *Kept for Jesus: What the New Testament Really Teaches about Assurance of Salvation and Eternal Security* (Wheaton: Crossway, 2015), 190.

CHAPTER SEVEN

FORLINESEAN ESCHATOLOGY: A PROGRESSIVE COVENANTAL APPROACH

Matthew McAffee

It is my distinct privilege to write the eschatology chapter for this volume honoring F. Leroy Forlines. His thought on this subject has made a deep impression upon me over the past several years—as a student, colleague, and friend. Our conversations on the topic of covenant and eschatology have been extremely fruitful and helpful during these formative years. I consider Forlines a mentor in the faith, and I am thankful for his investment in me these past seventeen years.

My first exposure to Forlinesean eschatology occurred when I took his course on the subject as a Welch College student in the spring semester of 1999. Students routinely bemoaned the fact that he never got around to the "end times" until the last week or two of the semester. Instead, he devoted the bulk of his teaching time to the biblical covenants as he traced their development from Genesis 3:15 onward. A second decisive event in my interaction with Forlines and eschatology was when we co-taught that same course at Welch in the spring of 2005. What was remarkable about this experience was that he and I held different interpretations of the millennial reign, which made for stimulating classroom exchanges. Forlines's willingness to engage a topic in this way authenticates his earlier call to a civil and genuine exchange of ideas relating to eschatology.[1]

This chapter sketches the major contributions of Forlinesean eschatology. It is an ambitious task for a single chapter, but doable nonetheless. Front and center to his eschatological framework is his understanding of covenant. At the end of this discussion I will try to locate Forlines's millennial interpretation, though it is not a defining feature of his eschatology. Before tackling his understanding of covenant, however, I must define his approach to eschatology and its overall importance.

Defining Forlinesean Eschatology

Eschatology is more than an investigation into history's summative events; it is the study of the whole Bible and how it fits together. Forlines observes a connection between what he calls "the abridgment of Christian thought" and the tendency for some to dismiss eschatology. Some believe we can entirely omit eschatology from our theology, since we can still be Christians even when our eschatology is wrong; in fact, doing so is sometimes thought to promote unity.[2] Much is at stake when we do this, however. Forlines explains,

> When we are silent on eschatology, illiteracy prevails in the development of the drama of redemption. Abraham, Isaac, Jacob, Moses, and David are usually used for character studies without showing the important place that they had in the unfolding of the drama of redemption. Illiteracy reigns when it comes to Israel and the redemptive covenants. The price that is paid for leaving off the treatment of eschatology is that people have no real grasp of their spiritual ancestry. This leaves an unfulfilled void in their hearts.[3]

This assessment echoes his earlier charge that an interest in eschatology is essentially an interest in interpreting the Bible and developing an understanding of God's redemptive program.[4] Eschatology is therefore "whole-Bible theology." It should not be restricted to the doctrine of "last things," but encompasses the overall pattern of God's redemptive work in the world throughout history, even if it focuses on its summation.[5] For an eschatology thus defined, we begin with the progression of covenant.

Covenant and Eschatology

God's covenant with Israel is central to Forlines's eschatological framework; covenant is the Bible's organizing principle.[6] In this way Forlinesean eschatology stands within the tradition of Reformed covenant theology, which understands God's relationship with humanity in terms of three covenants: (1) the covenant of redemption: relationship between the Godhead prior to creation; (2) the covenant of works: God's covenant with Adam prior to the Fall; and (3) the covenant of grace: God's covenant with believers through Christ.[7] Forlines articulates a Reformed eschatology by seeing the covenant of grace (though he does not utilize this terminology) as a single plan of redemption developed throughout biblical revelation.

Therefore, we must consider the progressive unfolding of God's redemptive program, which was His purpose before the world's foundation, and which began its implementation in Genesis 3:15—sometimes called the proto-*euangelion*, or first redemptive hope: "I will set enmity between you and the woman, between your seed and her seed; he will bruise you on the head, and you will bruise him on the heel."[8] This statement signals not only a conflict between the seeds of the woman and serpent, but also the ultimate triumph of the woman's seed. It reveals God's desire to redeem, fulfilled ultimately in Christ's defeat of sin, death, and the devil on the cross.[9]

God's disposition to redeem is therefore couched in terms of a struggle. Within the confines of a given redemptive narrative, divine victory is not always readily apparent. Take, for example, two epochs in redemption history that seemed detrimental to the divine plan: the flood (Gen. 6-9) and the Tower of Babel (Gen. 11). Forlines calls these two developments "negative divine interventions" whereby God intervened in history in a negative way to preserve humanity. The flood, he suggests, gave an opportunity for "the people of God to get a new start" in preventing their extinction. The Tower of Babel incident threatened to expunge God's redemptive revelation in the world, so that His negative intervention likewise preserved both His people and redemptive revelation.[10]

These two negative interventions set the stage for the Abrahamic covenant first articulated in Genesis 12, the first redemptive covenant. Genesis 1-11, especially 3:15, is preparatory for God's covenant with Abraham, the central covenant for the divine redemptive program.[11] Forlines thus defines this revelatory progression of redemption through the covenants:

> When we speak of progressive revelation, we are referring to the progressive unfolding of the message of redemption through Jesus Christ. This message came in installments. The first installment was Genesis 3:15. At various times in the Old Testament, God revealed more about the plan of redemption through covenants, prophecies, and types. This revelation reached its high point in the coming of Jesus Christ and in the establishment of the New Covenant.[12]

The single thread of God's redemptive work can be traced throughout the Bible, beginning with Genesis 3:15 and culminating in Revelation 21 with the new heavens and earth; these demonstrate a single program of restoring fallen humanity to fellowship with the Creator.

Identifying the singularity of this redemptive program, however, does not require a monolithic development throughout the Bible. For instance, Paul speaks of the 'covenants' that belong to Israel in Romans 9:4. Forlines believes that these 'covenants' must refer to all the covenants that God made with Israel, beginning with the Abrahamic covenant, the "basic redemptive covenant."[13]

His formulation of the relationship between the Abrahamic covenant and subsequent covenants is extremely helpful: "Later covenants serve to broaden the understanding of the Abrahamic Covenant by enlarging our understanding of what was already inherent in it. Or they help in the implementation of it."[14]

This is a much more robust way of articulating the relationship between these covenants than what is advanced by other varieties of covenantalism (or even dispensationalism), which drive a wedge between the Abrahamic and Mosaic covenants;[15] I find no basis for that interpretation, but instead find much to commend the view that each successive covenant builds upon and expands the former. One of the major ways this can be seen is in those places where the promises to the patriarchs are reinterpreted in Exodus through Deuteronomy as being ratified through Israel. This aspect is never clearer than when the threefold reference to the patriarchs—the God of Abraham, Isaac, and Jacob—is repeated throughout the book of Deuteronomy.[16]

Abraham as "Heir of the World"

Abraham's seed becoming the heir of the earth has stimulated Forlines's thinking concerning the Abrahamic covenant's broader significance. He makes a strong case for the Abrahamic promise of land having its ultimate realization in the eschatological future.[17] He argues that God's promise to Abraham of inheriting the land forever requires a fulfillment after the body's resurrection—since Abraham did not inherit the land during his lifetime (Acts 7:5), it must refer to a future inheritance post-resurrection. Romans 4:13 is of utmost importance because Paul does not speak of Abraham being an "heir of the land," as we might expect, but an "heir of the world." What is the basis for such an expansionistic view of Abraham's inheritance? Forlines rightly observes that this interpretation of Abraham's land inheritance is attested elsewhere in the Bible.[18] The Psalter, for instance, envisions it as the eternal reward of the righteous in contrast with the judgment of the wicked.[19] In His Sermon on the Mount, Jesus quotes from Psalm 37:11, "the meek shall inherit the earth," relating its possession to the kingdom of heaven (Matt. 5:5).

Hebrews' author understands the Abrahamic land promise in terms of a heavenly reality. Abraham went out "to a place which he was about to receive for an inheritance" by faith, though he went not knowing where he was going (Heb. 11:8). He lived in the land of promise as an alien in a foreign place, with Isaac and Jacob being fellow heirs of the same promise (11:9). Yet Abraham "was expecting a city having foundations whose architect and builder is God" (11:10). As the writer summarizes the faithful saints thus far mentioned in the chapter, he states, "They desired a better country, that is, a heavenly one" (11:16). The mention of the city and heavenly country envisions new creation in the eternal state, or as John describes in Revelation: "And I saw a new heaven and a new earth; for the first earth passed away, and there is no longer any sea. And I saw the new Jerusalem, coming down out of heaven from God, made ready as a bride adorned for her husband" (Rev. 21:1-2; cf. 21:10). Does John's 'new earth' require a total annihilation of the world as we now know it, or total renovation?[20] Forlines insists that the Abrahamic covenant demands a renewed earth, since anything less would annul God's promise to Abraham.[21] From Hebrews we understand that Abraham died without having received the promise (Heb. 11:13), meaning that it is still to come in the "heavenly" reality of the new creation.[22]

Abraham and his seed will therefore possess the land of promise for eternity. Gentiles inherit the promise by becoming Abraham's seed by faith (Rom. 4; Gal. 3). Ethnic Israelites maintain their status as his seed by faith. Forlines sees all of this as coming to fruition in the Messiah's redemptive work:

> The promise of the Messiah is involved also. The Messiah, by His redemptive work, provides the basis for the fulfillment of the eschatological promise of Gen. 13:15 and 17:8. A number of other promises were made to Israel, but these promises are involved in the outworking and the implementation of the promise of the eschatological future and the Messianic promises.[23]

Israel and the Church

Also related to covenant is the relationship between Israel and the church. Forlines distinguishes between ethnic Israel and believing Israel, which accords with what has been dubbed 'remnant theology.' Paul clarifies that "they are not all Israel which are of Israel" (Rom. 9:6). Romans 9 constitutes his defense of God's justice if not all Jews are saved, instead demonstrating that this is a misunderstanding of God's covenant promises to Israel. Forlines suggests two meanings for the term "Israel" in Paul's discussion: (1) all who have descended from Abraham through Jacob; and (2) an Israel within Israel consisting of those who will actually inherit the promise of the Abrahamic covenant. The latter group's condition is faith. Forlines observes:

> The Covenant promise is made to all of the descendants of Abraham. But it is made on the condition of faith. It is no violation of the Covenant promise made to the seed of Abraham if unbelievers do not inherit the promise. Abraham "believed in the LORD; and he counted it to him for righteousness" (Gen. 15:6).[24]

How do believing Israelites and believing Gentiles relate? This takes us to Paul's olive tree metaphor in Romans 11, which Forlines thinks is "one of the most important statements in the book."[25] It is a metaphor for Israel—Israelites who continue in faith will remain as branches of the olive tree; unbelieving branches, Paul says, are broken off (11:17, 20). Believing Gentiles are represented as wild olive branches, who, because of faith in Christ, are grafted into the olive tree as individual branches. As Forlines notes, the imagery of Paul's metaphor denotes a "conjunctive" relationship between Israel and the church, much more so than a "disjunctive" one.[26] He thus distinguishes his interpretation from that of amillennialists and dispensationalists. The former tend to view the church as replacing Israel,[27] while the latter overwhelmingly understand Israel as having been cast aside during the church age until a time in the eschatological future when it will return to God and govern His kingdom during the millennial reign.[28] To be fair these two broad approaches are not uniform, so a number of distinctions could be drawn from each. Forlines's approach generally falls outside either view, at least as they are broadly conceived.

Another important passage in this discussion is Ephesians 2. Paul describes Christ as having obliterated the wall of partition between Jew and Gentile, and calls this new creation reality of their union in Christ "the one new man" (Eph. 2:15). The overall thrust of this passage is that those who were once alienated from the covenant promises (Eph. 2:12-13) have now been granted the potential for full participation in the same body, namely, Israel. In this sense we must be clear that God has never made a covenant with Gentiles at any point in history, but only with Israel. However, the new creation reality inaugurated in Christ's death, resurrection, and ascension has made a way for non-Israelites to be grafted into the olive tree of God's people. Undoubtedly this is what Jesus means when He tells the Samaritan woman, "Salvation is of the Jews" (John 4:22). "By being grafted into the olive tree, Gentile believers partake of the salvation that God promised to the seed of Abraham," Forlines remarks, "in fact, they become the seed of Abraham. Since the olive tree is Israel, Gentile believers become members of Israel. It is better to say that Gentiles are saved the same way the Jews are than to say the Jews are saved the same way Gentiles are."[29] In response to those who might counter that the church is never actually called Israel, he reiterates:

> Let me say, first of all, that in identifying the Church with Israel, I am not robbing Israel of its identification as the seed of Abraham that descended through Jacob. If we take that identification away from Israel, we have destroyed it. There is no redemptive covenant with an Israel that did not descend from Abraham through Jacob. . . . If God had cast away Israel, it would be the termination of redemption. There is no redemptive covenant with anyone else.[30]

Essentially Israel functions as God's covenant vehicle for redemption, which is why Forlines believes that "Israel is the church" is better than "the church is Israel."[31] In this way he sees his understanding of the relationship between Israel and the church as distinct from amillennialism, dispensationalism, and even historic premillennialism. Because his view of the millennial kingdom is similar to the latter approach, this particular point needs additional clarification.

According to historic premillennialism, God has cast off Israel for their unbelief, the result being the salvation of Gentiles by faith. In continuing to affirm a certain level of distinction between Israel and the church, George Eldon Ladd argued that the church age is not the last event in God's story of redemption because two further things must happen: "the fullness of literal Israel must come in, and by her salvation greater riches be brought to the Gentile world."[32] This distinction is given further expression in Douglas J. Moo's careful differentiation between those prophecies applicable to "Israel *as a nation* (and which must be fulfilled in a national Israel) versus those for Israel *as the people of God* (which can be fulfilled in the people of God—*a people that includes the church!*)."[33] Forlines is unwilling to admit that Israel itself has been cast away, but only the unbelieving branches and not Israel as a whole—and I think he is right.[34] He sees a "conjunctive" relationship between Old Testament Israel and the New Testament church, not a "disjunctive" one, so that both identify "with the spiritual history of the Old Covenant."[35]

This approach to Israel and the church is largely founded upon his exegesis of Romans 11:25-27, which appears to speak of a future ingathering of Israel. Since Forlines is careful to maintain that the true Israel (the church) consists of believing Jews and Gentiles, he therefore believes that Paul is speaking about a time in the eschatological future when ethnic Israelites will exercise faith in Jesus *en masse* and thus be grafted into the olive tree. On this point two important phrases in Romans 11 deserve special attention: (1) "the fullness of the Gentiles" (11:25); and (2) "so all Israel will be saved" (11:26). Forlines takes the fullness of the Gentiles to refer to the age from Christ's ascension up to the point of His return. As such Paul is speaking about the completion of

Gentile dominance in the program of God's redemption, at which point ethnic Israelites will demonstrate a massive movement of faith.[36] Before Christ's coming, the Jewish nation dominated the scene of God's redemptive work, but afterwards Gentile believers have largely dominated this work. Accordingly, "all Israel" (11:26) must refer to a massive ingathering of believing Jews in the eschatological future who have been provoked by the faith of believing Gentiles.[37]

Although some theologians would place this future engrafting of Jewish converts in a future millennial kingdom, I suggest that this is less likely exegetically. The Forlinesean interpretation is extremely useful in not requiring a particular strand of millennialism, instead allowing flexibility on this question. Even though Forlines cautiously adopts the chronology of historic premillennialism, he does not affirm its understanding of the Israel-church relationship, as already observed. In fact, his formulation of the Jew-Gentile relationship brings to mind the nuance of Frank Thielman's interpretation of "the Israel of God" in Galatians 6:16, defining the new covenant community as an "eschatologically restored" community. He writes that Paul is claiming "the Galatian believers, although Gentiles, have joined believing Jews to constitute the eschatologically restored Israel. The 'new creation' is a newly defined Israel—the Israel of God."[38]

The Progression of Covenants and the Paidagōgos in Galatians 3:23-4:7

The relationship between the old and new covenants is of major importance in the development of one's eschatology. This is clear when one considers the place of the law in the new covenant. The prophecy in Jeremiah 31 about the new covenant is instructive. Remarkably, this text affirms that the problem of Israel's hardened heart will finally be remedied in this new covenant, since God will actually write His law upon His people's hearts (Jer. 31:33; Heb. 8:10). We should not miss Jeremiah's point: It is "my Torah," not a new Torah. At the very least this statement requires that the law must have continued significance for the new covenant people.

Nevertheless, how does this point correlate with the New Testament's apparent denial of the law's ongoing validity for the new covenant community? Thielman and others distinguish between the Law of Moses and the law of Christ, the latter being something entirely new as the ethical standard for God's "eschatologically restored" people. Disobedience to the Law of Moses enacted the Deuteronomistic curse of exile upon His people, from which the new covenant people needed deliverance and restoration.[39]

Forlines believes that the relationship of the law to the old and new covenants is best understood in Paul's use of the *paidagōgos* metaphor in Galatians 3:23–4:7.[40] In 3:24 Paul utilizes this motif to describe the law and its relationship to the old covenant people from the time of Moses until the time of Christ: "Before the faith came, we were kept in custody under the law, being shut up to faith which was later to be revealed."[41] Forlines takes "the faith" as a reference to the new covenant (i.e., "the faith later to be revealed") in contrast to the time of the Mosaic Law under the old covenant (i.e., "before the faith came").[42] The Greek term *paidagōgos* (lit. 'child-leader') originally referred to a person charged to conduct a boy or youth to and from school and to oversee his conduct. After the young boy matured to adulthood, the *paidagōgos* was no longer needed.[43] This metaphor's significance in relation to the old covenant saints is that they were immature, thus being "kept/guarded" and "shut up/enclosed" under the law as their *paidagōgos*. These two notions—being kept and shut up—are not necessarily negative, the former appropriately connoting protection[44] and the latter limitation for the sake of preservation.[45] This protector and preserver of God's people functioned to lead old covenant Jewish believers to Christ so they might "be justified by faith." Forlines understands this reference to justification to refer to the Old Testament saints, who, under the law's tutelage, were being led to Christ's future justification work in the scheme of redemption.[46]

A second term that deserves special attention in this passage is *ta stoicheia*, or 'the elements' (4:3).[47] Paul states, "So also we, while we were children, were held in bondage under the elemental things of the world." What are the 'elemental things of the world'? Originally a *stoicheion* referred to a simple sound of speech (e.g., the first component of a syllable), and eventually to letters that are pronounced,[48] which constitute the rudimentary components of language and expression, the building blocks of communicative speech.[49] It also developed a physical meaning, occurring in 2 Peter 3:10 of the world's natural elements that will be consumed by fire on the Day of the Lord. This usage is instructive because it connects the meaning of *stoicheia* to the fundamental elements of the natural world with which Jewish and Gentile religion was so familiar. Thus *stoicheia* often denotes the elementary principles of religious knowledge, and this appears to be the concern of the other four New Testament passages where it occurs (Gal. 4:3-9; Col. 2:8, 20-22; Heb. 5:12; 6:1-2).[50]

These passages deal with some manifestation of Jewish religious practice. In Galatians and Colossians, Paul is concerned that some believers are being led to believe that they must submit to the external (elementary) forms of Jewish law in order to adhere to the gospel. This aspect may have appealed to Gentile believers who were all too familiar with the elementary nature of their own pre-conversion religion. But we must be clear in stressing that Paul does not intend to collapse pagan and Jewish religion into the same thing; this would be out of step with God's unique design for the law delivered to Israel at Sinai. On the contrary Paul intends to emphasize the law's preparatory role in leading God's people throughout childhood until the time of adulthood in Christ. According to the meaning of *stoicheia*, the multiple applications of the law in its ancient Near Eastern context are the rudimentary components of God's revelation. They are incomplete in the scheme of God's progressive revelation, and are 'filled up' in Christ, the climax of redemptive revelation (Matt. 5:17). For Hebrews' author a rejection of Christ in an attempt to go back to the "elementary principles of the beginning of the oracles of God" (Heb. 5:12) is tantamount to apostasy, since doing so is rejecting God and His fuller and final revelation in Christ.[51]

One of the important contributions of the Hebrews passage regarding the *stoicheia* ('elements') is that it associates the concept with the status of immaturity, which correlates with the context of Galatians 4. In Hebrews 5–6, focus on these elementary aspects of the beginning of God's revelation is a sign of immaturity—"leaving aside the word of the beginning of Christ, let us move on to maturity" (Heb. 6:1)—and requires one to embrace, not only the things that God had spoken to the fathers through the prophets, but also the things God has spoken in His Son during these last days (Heb. 1:1). The aspects that characterized these elementary components listed in Hebrews 6:1-2 are characteristic of Jewish religious observance, which can no longer be practiced to the exclusion of God's fuller revelation in Christ. This seems to be a similar argument to Paul's in Galatians 4 where he associates the law as *paidagōgos* with the elementary things of the world.

Theologians have not adequately explored the theological significance of this discussion, even though the exegesis is well established.[52] Paul's use of the *paidagōgos* metaphor as a means of explaining the relationship of the law to the old and new covenants offers both continuity and discontinuity. Forlines has long thought this metaphor is key to anyone's articulation of the relationship between the old covenant redemptive program and the new.[53] Part of the problem theologians have in developing Paul's understanding of the law's function in the redemptive covenants may lie in the fact that it poses serious problems for both dispensationalism and covenantalism alike.

Such a framework challenges the sharp distinction that classical dispensationalists make between God's covenant with His "earthly people," Israel, and the New Testament saints.[54] For classic dispensationalism even the new covenant of Jeremiah 31 must be viewed as entirely distinct from God's work in the church, since Jeremiah states it is a new covenant with "Israel and Judah,"[55] despite the fact that Hebrews 8 affirms otherwise. If, as Paul seems to be arguing in Galatians 3-4, God's people were led under the *paidagōgos'* guardianship throughout childhood until the time of full adulthood in Christ, we should expect he understands this as a progression from one stage of life to another—immaturity to maturity. The implication is that we are not dealing with two separate "dispensations" (i.e., the earthly dispensation of Israel and the spiritual dispensation of the church), but successive developments within God's redemptive work among His people.

Covenantalists have traditionally rejected such distinctions in favor of more continuity in God's redemption through covenant, but only between the Abrahamic and new covenants. Like Forlines, covenantalists believe the Abrahamic covenant is the foundational covenant upon which all other covenants are founded, but some also argue the Mosaic covenant is formally distinct.[56] For example, Michael Horton, following the work of George E. Mendenhall, Delbert Hillers, and Meredith Kline, suggests the Abrahamic covenant was formally a royal grant, while the Mosaic covenant was construed as a suzerain-vassal treaty.[57] They argue that the distinguishing feature of these two covenant types is unconditional versus conditional: as a grant treaty, the promises of the Abrahamic covenant are enacted unconditionally; as a suzerain-vassal treaty, the promises of the Mosaic covenant are conditioned upon obedience to the covenant stipulations.[58] Horton thus calls the Mosaic or Sinaitic covenant a "parenthesis" to God's redemptive work through Abraham, which functioned to bring "life to the whole world."[59] Because of its conditional nature, the Mosaic covenant has been annulled by the mere fact that the nation of Israel broke the terms of the suzerain-vassal agreement. They are under the covenant curses.

Admittedly, this interpretation of the Sinaitic covenant is a minority view in Reformed covenant theology, whereas Forlines's understanding is much more in line with the Reformed tradition. I mention it here to highlight a more recent discussion within covenantalism and show its inconsistency with a broadly covenantal framework, which tends to understand more continuity in the redemption plan throughout the ages.[60] It is therefore beyond my purposes at this juncture to offer an extended criticism of the assumption that the biblical covenants formally corresponded to their ancient Near Eastern counterparts in every way; that is for another discussion. In short, I believe the biblical documents represent an amalgam of ancient literary forms and therefore cannot be straightjacketed into any one corresponding mold.[61] What is important to stress, however, is that Forlines's application of the *paidagōgos* metaphor to the old covenant's relationship to the new raises additional problems for Horton and other like-minded covenantalists. According to Paul's line of reasoning, the relationship is one of transition from one stage of development to the next: from childhood to adulthood. The law provides a unifying link between them.

The law of God as expressed in the Decalogue and applied in the judgments, statutes, and ordinances of Exodus-Deuteronomy, is now written upon His people's hearts (Jer. 31:33; Heb. 8:10). Forlines differentiates between the form and substance of the law: the form (or application) of the law in the old and new covenants is different, but its substance remains the same.[62] It is important to maintain these two aspects—form and substance—because Jeremiah's vision of the new covenant is one in which "my law," not another, will be written on covenant members' hearts. This tempers those who attempt to argue that the law of Christ in the new covenant is also a new law.[63] It is much simpler to understand the distinction to be one of application: God's law applied in two distinct redemptive contexts. The law's form in the old covenant context specifically relates to God's people living in the ancient Near East at an earlier stage of progressive revelation. This context contrasts with its formal application in the new covenant, which is characterized by the inauguration of a heavenly reality among the mature people of God (Heb. 9:23-28).

God's covenant with Israel at Sinai therefore served an important revelatory function in the divine redemptive program. Forlines summarizes its overall significance with the following five observations:

(1) It was designed to serve a temporary need and purpose (Gal. 3:19).

(2) The blessings accompanying its obedience would have taken place during its administration, which was from the giving of the law to Christ's death.

(3) Through its laws and ceremonies it taught the people moral and redemptive truth and gave guidance and discipline.

(4) In no way did it alter the Abrahamic covenant (Gal. 3:14-18), but served toward its implementation.

(5) A study of Galatians 3:19–4:10 helps us get a perspective on how the Mosaic Law fit into God's plan.[64]

The new covenant's establishment in Christ is both the final implementation of the Abrahamic covenant and the replacement of the Mosaic covenant. But again, Forlines is careful to explain such replacement in light of Galatians' *paidagōgos* motif: "The replacing is not to be thought of in the sense of one system replacing another where enmity exists between the systems," he writes; "Rather it is to be compared with that difference of treatment between the way one deals with children and adults. The difference is not a difference in basic goals and of objectives, but a difference in method."[65]

Covenant and Cultural Transformation

The Forlinesean interpretation of the canonical progression of covenants yields an important implication regarding the relationship between church and culture. The way in which Forlines understands the progression of God's redemption, from the Fall to the flood, from Abraham to Moses, from David to Jesus, and from new covenant community to the eternal state, indicates a transformational trajectory. In H. Richard Niebuhr's typology of Christ and culture, Forlinesean covenantalism favors the Christ transforming culture model. It likewise rejects a two kingdoms view (Niebuhr: Christ and culture in paradox).[66] The basic notion of the Lutheran two kingdoms model is that the kingdom of this world and the kingdom of Christ are two separate entities that operate according to a different set of standards. As Luther explains, "There are two kingdoms, one the kingdom of God, the other the kingdom of the world. . . . God's kingdom is a kingdom of grace and mercy . . . but the kingdom of the world is a kingdom of wrath and severity."[67]

In describing the dualism of this perspective, Niebuhr says that "man is a great amphibian who lives in two realms, and must avoid using in one the ideas and methods appropriate to the other."[68] Gene Edward Veith, a two kingdoms advocate, terms this approach "God's double sovereignty," whereby God rules over both the church and secular culture, but with different rules respective to each sphere. The Christian must maintain this distinction in understanding that he is a citizen of both the heavenly and earthly kingdoms at the same time, even though God is sovereign over both.[69] Horton explains well how his particular brand of covenantalism coincides with his adoption of the two kingdoms position, writing that when one "distinguishes the covenant of creation from the covenant of grace, law covenant from promise covenant, Moses and Israel as a theocratic fusion of religion and culture from Abraham and his faith in a heavenly city, one will be likely to distinguish also the kingdom of God from the kingdoms of this world."[70]

Forlines puts things together into a comprehensive framework much akin to the Reformed creation-fall-redemption-new creation rubric. His treatment of the Mosaic covenant as a further "implementation" of the Abrahamic covenant rejects Horton's formulation of the former as a "fusion of religion and culture." He is much more in line with Christopher J. H. Wright who similarly asserts that the Sinai covenant should not be separate from or superior to the Abrahamic, but "was the consolidation of what God had promised to Abraham now that one part of the promise had been fulfilled—namely, his descendants had now become a great nation."[71] The covenants are a sequential progression culminating in the new creation of the *eschaton*.[72] The Bible's coherent redemptive plot, from creation to the Fall to redemption to new creation, means that salvation encompasses all of creation. Wright explains, "God's plan of salvation includes bringing the whole of creation to a new, restored unity in Christ (Eph. 1:9-10). This is God's cosmic mission. And at the cross God accomplished this, in anticipation, even though we do not yet see it finally completed."[73]

Rather than distinguishing two separate kingdoms under God's rule with distinct rules of governance, the Bible tells the story of a cosmic rebellion against God's rule under which the whole creation has been subjected, groaning for its deliverance (Rom. 8:22). This world's kingdom is an illegitimate one that will be judged on the last and final day. God's single plan of redemption is an answer to this tyrannous rebellion, providing a means of escaping its fateful destruction in the end. The story of redemption offers hope that all which was lost will be once again made new. Christ's resurrection is the guarantee.

The Millennial Kingdom

The millennial reign is often the first thing that comes to mind when thinking about eschatology. Although this interpretive challenge has its rightful place in eschatology, it is not necessarily of central importance. Eschatology is more broadly concerned with the summation of redemptive revelation and therefore requires that we devote considerable attention to how all of that revelation both begins and progresses in the Bible. This may be why many of Forlines's students were regularly frustrated by his eschatology course: they had a much narrower definition limited to one's view of the millennium, and whether the church would experience a secret rapture.

Because Forlines had devoted so much of his efforts in eschatology to explaining the development of redemptive revelation through the biblical covenants, it is unsurprising that millennial views were left for the last week or two of the course. He does not believe the biblical covenants address the issue, even though he adopts a future millennial kingdom. In fact, his covenantal interpretive framework remains unaffected by this question: "I believe that there will be such a reign of Christ on earth. But I do not believe that any of the covenants promise such. The Abrahamic, the Davidic, and the New Covenants could all be fulfilled without a 1000 year reign by Christ."[74] The millennial reign has been an ancillary development in Forlinesean eschatology, and is not a driving component of his approach.

Much of the discussion about the millennial kingdom among evangelical scholars has focused attention on Revelation 20. Ladd, a major spokesman for historic premillennialism, went so far as to say that it is "the only place in the Bible that speaks about an actual millennium," eschewing all attempts to ground this doctrine in the Old Testament.[75] He believed that any support for a future millennial kingdom would have to be based upon "the most natural exegesis of this passage."[76] Others disagree. Craig Blaising, a progressive dispensational premillennialist, catalogues a number of Old Testament passages in support of a future millennial kingdom occurring prior to the eternal state. These Old Testament prophecies purportedly indicate "a future kingdom that God will set up on this earth and which will be everlasting in duration."[77] Forlines similarly believes that the prophets describe conditions favorable for a future 1,000-year reign of Christ.

Forlines posits a series of questions concerning a given passage: Are the conditions described being fulfilled in the present? Will the conditions described be fulfilled in the eternal state? Do the conditions described prohibit being fulfilled in either the present or the eternal state? According to this rubric, if a passage neither reflects our present world's reality, nor that to come (that is, it is too good for the now, but not good enough for the not yet), it must refer to an intermediate period of time. This intermediate stage of redemptive history would therefore be the 1,000-year reign depicted in Revelation 20. The passages that he believes are too good for our current world, but not good enough for the eternal state include Isaiah 2:2-5; 11:1-9; 59:20; 60:11-12; 65:17-25; Zechariah 14:9.

For example, Isaiah 2:2-5 depicts the nations streaming to the mountain of YHWH's house, where they are taught in His ways and receive just judgments; God's law goes forth from Zion, all of which Forlines considers too good for the present reality, but not good enough for the eternal state. Likewise, Isaiah 11:1-5 seems to depict the struggle of good and evil wherein good prevails—this despite the fact that the wolf dwells with the lamb, and the child plays with the cobra without harm (11:6-9). These conditions are true of neither the now, nor the not yet. Also, Isaiah 65:17-25 mentions death, old age, and the unconverted, leading Forlines to conclude that it must refer to an intermediary period of redemptive history. Another important passage is Ezekiel 40—48 and its detailed measurements of the newly constructed temple in the midst of the land of Israel, which has been newly apportioned to the twelve tribes. Though many commentators argue for a figurative reading of these chapters, Forlines is drawn to a more literal interpretation that would require fulfillment in an intermediate millennial reign.[78]

However, we should clarify what Forlines is not suggesting. He is certainly not overly dogmatic on his millennial view, mainly because he does not believe it to be the defining aspect of his eschatology. Furthermore, the fulfillment of the land promises given under the Abrahamic covenant cannot find their ultimate fulfillment during the posited intermediate millennial reign because Scripture states that Abraham and his seed will possess the land forever (Gen. 13:15; 17:8). As he has rightly cautioned, a literal 1,000-year reign is not forever.[79] Besides, one major problem for dispensationalists who wish to see the millennial reign as the final fulfillment of the covenant promises to Abraham and Israel, as Blaising and others suggest, is that the final judgment seems to divide the millennium and the eternal state into two distinct periods of redemptive history.[80] Revelation 20:11-15 presents the judgment as the closing chapter of this millennial reign, after which the new heavens and earth are established forever. Nonetheless, premillennialists of all types would counter that there are actually two judgments (and two resurrections): the judgment seat of Christ for believers (2 Cor. 5:10), and the great white throne judgment for the damned (Rev. 20:11).[81] Even so, the New Testament elsewhere presents the judgment as a single event, especially in Matthew 25:31-46 where the sheep (believers) and goats (unbelievers) are separated. Dispensational premillennialism therefore represents a rather complicated interpretation of the millennial reign that is difficult to reconcile with the New Testament teaching on the singular Day of the Lord and its culmination in divine judgment.

So what purpose does the millennial kingdom serve? Again, if Forlines accepts an intermediate millennial reign like other premillennialists, it does not constitute the fulfillment of any covenantal promises. Rather, it is much akin to the historic premillennial understanding, which sees this period of redemptive history as a more visible manifestation of Christ's rule in the world whereby He brings all enemies to subjection under His feet.[82] This "millennial" reign would contrast the nature of His inaugural reign during the "last days" (the time between His resurrection and second coming) and thus bring the kingdom one step closer to its full implementation in the new heavens and earth.[83] In other words, the millennial kingdom is the last and final step in the ultimate establishment of God's kingdom on earth. This idea is not that far removed from the amillennial perspective in interpreting the millennial kingdom as Christ's inaugurated reign, although placing its beginning at the time of Christ's resurrection and its end at His return when the kingdom is finally established.[84] Such a purpose is irreconcilable with the dispensational premillennialist approach, whether classic or progressive, which insists the millennium is a time in which ethnic Israel features prominently.[85]

As noted above, Forlines's view that the salvation of "all Israel" in Romans 11:26 constitutes a future ingathering of believing ethnic Jews is not necessarily tied to a millennial kingdom, but would in fact precede it. Even when considering the dispensational framework, the importance of believing Jews is not their turning to the faith (which is the purpose of the seven year tribulation), but their dominant role in the economy of God's reign upon the earth. For all premillennialists the millennial kingdom is not the time when "all Israel" is saved, but is characterized by the nations streaming to Zion. This is one reason why amillennialists have been critical of the premillennial interpretation of the Old Testament texts just mentioned, arguing instead that the nations coming to Zion is characteristic of Christ's first coming, and sets in motion the mass of Gentile conversions to follow Jesus' teachings, the Jewish Messiah.

Summary Observations

As I conclude this sketch of Forlinesean eschatology, a few observations remain yet to be made. Of first importance, we should extend our gratitude to Forlines for the groundwork he has laid for Free Will Baptists (and evangelicals in general) in formulating a full-orbed, whole-Bible eschatology. Although he has never published a book-length treatment on eschatology, his work on Romans, the development of a systematic theology, and his years of teaching eschatology at Welch College have established foundational work in this area for Free Will Baptists.[86]

One of the major contributions of Forlines's thinking about eschatology is that it offers a means of avoiding a major impasse typical of the conversation: What is your millennial view? As I have mentioned, this question may not be entirely inconsequential, but it is not definitive for Forlinesean eschatology, and I believe that is a good thing. The place where any valid eschatology begins must be the place where scriptural revelation begins: creation and the first redemptive hope. Once we start there we are immediately faced with God's ultimate solution to the problem of sin: covenant. Covenant is the thread that ties Scripture's grand metanarrative together into a cohesive whole. The high points along the way—Genesis 3:15, Noah, Abraham, Moses and Israel, David, and the prophets who speak of a future new covenant—all find their resolution and ultimate meaning in Christ's cross. Paul's description of the Day of the Lord and the resurrection, or John's magnificent revelation of the new heavens and earth, can only be comprehended in light of the covenant story of divine redemption. True biblical eschatology must first look backward before looking forward, and the means for doing so is covenant.

That is not to say, however, that Forlines's work addresses all the pertinent questions in formulating a mature eschatology. Such requires time and multiple generations of inquiry. I believe his contribution to a distinctly Free Will Baptist eschatology is a major step forward. What he has established is a broad framework within which more biblical exegesis and theological formulation need to occur. Also, I would add that this framework is neither dispensational (of any variety), nor Reformed covenantal, nor amillennial, nor historic premillennial, or whatever. It captures the spirit of other theologians who have recently called for a middle way, but in a distinctively Reformed Arminian way.[87] One area that needs further development, for instance, is a fresh exegesis and systematization of key passages in the Old Testament. This work would exegetically anchor the Forlinesean eschatological framework envisioned here.

No doubt much of this kind of effort has been the impetus of Forlines's escha-tology, but it needs to be given fuller expression and development.

In the end, I am grateful for what Free Will Baptists have been given in Forlines's insistence that eschatology serves a crucial and integral role in bibli-cal and systematic theology. The task now remains for our movement to em-brace his vision for the proper place of eschatology in Free Will Baptist theol-ogy and renew our concern for articulating faithfully the redemption story for the church.

---

[1] See F. Leroy Forlines, "The Doctrine of Last Things," *Contact* (August 1971): 12, where he urges that "there should be a degree of liberty and tolerance" in non-fundamental matters to Free Will Baptist doctrine.

[2] F. Leroy Forlines, "A Plea for Unabridged Christianity," *Integrity* 2 (2003): 88-89.

[3] Ibid., 92.

[4] Forlines, "Doctrine of Last Things," 12.

[5] See F. F. Bruce: "Eschatology may therefore denote the consummation of God's purpose whether it coincides with the end of the world (or of history) or not, whether the consummation is totally final or marks a stage in the unfolding pattern of his purpose" ("Eschatology," in *Evangelical Dictionary of Theology*, ed. Walter A. Elwell [Grand Rapids: Zondervan, 1984], 362).

[6] Forlines shares much in common with Peter J. Gentry and Stephen J. Wellum who likewise agree that "correctly 'putting together' the biblical covenants is central to the doing of biblical and systematic theology" (*Kingdom through Covenant: A Biblical-Theological Understanding of the Covenants* [Wheaton: Crossway, 2012], 23).

[7] For more on covenant theology, see Geerhardus Vos, "The Doctrine of the Cov-enant in Reformed Theology," in *Redemptive History and Biblical Interpretation: The Shorter Writings of Geerhardus Vos*, ed. Richard B. Gaffin, Jr. (Phillipsburg: P&R, 1979), 234-67; John Murray, "Covenant Theology," in *Studies in Theology: Colleced Writings of John Murray*, vol. 4 (Carlisle: Banner of Truth, 1982), 216-40; and Vern Poythress, *Understanding Dispensationalists* (Phillipsburg: P&R, 1993), 39-51.

[8] Unless otherwise indicated, all Bible translations are my own.

[9] F. Leroy Forlines, "TH 403 Eschatology: Class Notes" (Nashville: Welch College, Spring 2012), 6.

[10] Ibid.

[11] Forlines clarifies the Abrahamic covenant's significance in light of God's overall re-demptive plan as follows: (1) in comparison with Genesis 3:15, which is preparatory

to the Abrahamic covenant, it is more specific in what it entails; (2) in comparison to the law given at Sinai, which is temporary (at least in form [see below]), it is permanent; (3) believers are heirs of its promises (Gal. 3:29); and (4) later covenants serve to broaden its understanding and implement it ("TH 403 Eschatology: Class Notes," 10).

[12] Ibid., 1.

[13] F. Leroy Forlines, *Romans*, The Randall House Bible Commentary, gen. ed. Robert E. Picirilli (Nashville: Randall House, 1987), 252.

[14] Ibid.

[15] E.g., Michael Horton, who believes the Mosaic covenant has been annulled by Israel's rebellion, thereby claiming that all subsequent covenants revert back to the Abrahamic promises (*Introducing Covenant Theology* [Grand Rapids: Baker, 2006], 35-50). This interpretive move is similar to what we see in classic dispensationalism, which more broadly sees discontinuity between old and new covenants.

[16] E.g., 6:10; 9:5, 27; 29:13.

[17] Forlines, *Romans*, 113.

[18] See Forlines's discussion in *Romans*, 111-13. He adds, however, that the basis of this move from the 'land' as Canaan and the 'land' as the whole world is the fact Abraham was the father of many nations, not just the Jews. This is certainly one way of rationalizing such a development, but I do not think it is necessary, since the land boundaries promised in Genesis 15 conceivably spanned the entire ancient Near Eastern world.

[19] See Psalms 25:12; 37:9, 11 (quoted by Jesus in Matt. 5:5), 22, 28-29, 34; see also Forlines, *Romans*, 111.

[20] We should caution that the reference to the destruction of heaven and earth at the final judgment in 2 Peter 3:10-12 does not necessarily assume its total annihilation. In Matthew 24:36-39 Jesus appeals to the Genesis flood as the proper analogy, which, although bringing destruction, does not annihilate the earth itself. The burning up of the elements may indicate refinement through purification rather than total annihilation. Furthermore, the meaning of *aperkomai*, "to pass away," in Revelation 21:1 does not indicate annihilation of the heavens and earth either. Rather, it means "to discontinue as a condition or state," like the healing of leprosy in Mark 1:42 (Walter Bauer et al, *A Greek-English Lexicon of the New Testament and other Early Christian Literature*, 3rd ed. BDAG [Chicago: The University of Chicago Press, 2000], 102). In other words, the currently fallen state of the heavens and earth has come to an end.

[21] This aspect of Forlinesean eschatology offers a much-needed corrective to an overly spiritualized view of the eternal state. Popular theology often envisions heaven as a disembodied state of mystical bliss forever, with the physical world ultimately destroyed at the judgment. Much like earlier Gnosticism, this perspective results in an unnecessary dichotomy between the physical and spiritual: The physical will one day be destroyed and all that will remain will be the spiritual. This idea violates Scripture's clear teachings, which speak of new heavens and a new earth. If we

maintain God's promise to Abraham that he would possess the land forever, we must conclude it will be fulfilled when the earth has been renewed. Therefore, it is more theologically accurate to understand "new earth" as "renewed earth."

[22] As Forlines correctly emphasizes, we should not think of Hebrews' use of the term "heavenly" to describe the country Abraham was looking for in 11:16 as a reference to location (i.e., 'in heaven'), but to quality (i.e., 'heavenly reality'). This language speaks of the realm of God's new creation, which indicates the earth's restoration to its Edenic state with the divine presence once again in its midst (see Forlines, *Romans*, 112).

[23] Forlines, *Romans*, 253.

[24] Ibid., 256.

[25] Ibid., 306.

[26] Ibid., 307.

[27] See Louis Berkhof, *Systematic Theology* (Grand Rapids: Eerdmans, 1953), 570-71. For a recent example, see Kim Riddlebarger, *A Case for Amillennialism: Understanding the End Times* (Grand Rapids: Baker, 2003), 120, where he states: "Although the church and Israel occupy different roles and stages in redemptive history, that does not constitute an argument for distinctive plans for each group. . . . In Christ, God takes the two peoples and makes them one." Riddlebarger is fairly nuanced in his treatment of this relationship, but I still think he downplays Israel's redemptive-historical significance. For a critical evaluation of this view (i.e., supersessionism), see Michael J. Vlach, *Has the Church Replaced Israel? A Theological Evaluation* (Grand Rapids: B&H Academic, 2010).

[28] See Charles C. Ryrie, *Dispensationalism Today* (Chicago: Moody, 1965), 132-55; William F. Kerr, "Tribulation for the Church—But Not *The Tribulation*," in *Understanding the Times*, eds. William Culbertson and Herman B. Centz (Grand Rapids: Zondervan, 1952), 102-03. Note, however, that progressive dispensationalists have moved away from such distinctions, which allows Craig A. Blaising to qualify that although the church is "new in the progress of revelation, it is not wholly different, not a secondary, parallel plan of God" (Craig A. Blaising and Darrell L. Bock, *Progressive Dispensationalism* [Grand Rapids: Baker, 1993], 262). Although they understand that God's grace through the church is "in keeping with the promises of the Old Testament," progressive dispensationalists still maintain, "The church should be distinguished from the next dispensation in which all of the blessings will not just be inaugurated, but completely fulfilled" (Blaising and Bock, 49).

[29] Forlines, *Romans*, 308.

[30] Ibid.

[31] Forlines, "TH 403 Eschatology: Class Notes," 16; idem, *Romans*, 309.

[32] George E. Ladd, *A Theology of the New Testament* (Grand Rapids: Eerdmans, 1974), 561.

[33] Douglas J. Moo, "The Posttribulational Rapture Position," in *The Rapture: Pre-, Mid-, or Post-tribulational*, Contemporary Evangelical Perspectives: Eschatology, ed. Glea-

son L. Archer et al. (Grand Rapids: Zondervan, 1984), 207 (also referenced in Stanley J. Grenz, *The Millennial Maze: Sorting Out Evangelical Options* [Downers Grove: InterVarsity, 1992], 139).

[34] Forlines, *Romans*, 309.

[35] F. Leroy Forlines, *The Quest for Truth: Theology for Postmodern Times* (Nashville: Randall House, 2001), 491; hereafter *Quest*.

[36] Ibid., *Romans*, 313.

[37] Forlines is careful to insist that this verse's "all" does not necessitate every single Jewish person coming to the faith, but rather refers to the mass of them coming to Christ at that particular time in the history of God's redemption work (*Romans*, 313). Similarly, James D.G. Dunn, *Romans 9-16*, Word Biblical Commentary 38B (Dallas: Word, 1988), 681; Douglas Moo, *Epistle to the Romans*, New International Commentary on the Old Testament (Grand Rapids: Eerdmans, 1996), 722-26; Thomas R. Schreiner, *Romans*, Baker Exegetical Commentary on the New Testament (Grand Rapids: Baker, 1998), 618-22; Ben Witherington III, *Paul's Letter to the Romans: A Socio-Rhetorical Commentary* (Grand Rapids: Eerdmans, 2004), 275. Colin G. Kruse outlines six different interpretations for this reference to all Israel being saved: (1) all Israelites from every age; (2) all the elect of Israel of all times; (3) all Israelites alive at the end of the age; (4) Israel as a whole alive at the end of the age, but not every single Israelite; (5) a large number of Israelites at the end of the age; and (6) Israel redefined to include all Jews and Gentiles believing in Jesus Christ (*Paul's Letter to the Romans*, Pillar New Testament Commentary [Grand Rapids: Eerdmans, 2012], 448-51). Kruse rejects the views that place this salvation of Jews at the end of the age, favoring that it refers to the elect of Israel of all times (see Ben L. Merkle, "Romans 11 and the Future of Ethnic Israel," *Journal of the Evangelical Theological Society* 43 [2000], 717, 721). For a defense of this salvation as God's true people who exercise faith in Christ, Jew and Gentile alike, see Joseph A. Fitzmyer, *Romans: A New Translation and Commentary*, Anchor Bible 33 (New York: Doubleday, 1993), 619-20.

[38] Frank Thielman, *Paul and the Law: A Contextual Approach* (Downers Grove: IVP Academic, 1994), 138.

[39] Ibid., 135, 141.

[40] See Forlines, "Understanding Yourself and Others: A Biblical, Theological, and Practical Approach to Personality" (unpublished manuscript, 1994), 89-102 (later presented as a paper under the title, "Stewardship and the Exercise of Christian Liberty," at the Theological Symposium Sponsored by the Commission on Theological Integrity of the National Association of Free Will Baptists, held in Nashville, TN, October 2010); idem, *Quest*, 489-98. Especially important in the development of Forlines's thought on this concept are Patrick Fairbairn, *The Revelation of Law in Scripture* (Edinburgh: T&T Clark, 1869; repr., Grand Rapids: Zondervan, 1957), 385-405; and Ernest D. Burton, *The Epistle to the Galatians*, International Critical Commentary (Edinburgh: T&T Clark, 1921; repr., 1959).

[41] This idea also informs his interpretation of the law in Romans 7:6 (see *Romans*, 165-66).

[42] Forlines, *Quest*, 490.

[43] BDAG, 748.

[44] See especially Philippians 4:7 where *phroureō* describes God's peace guarding His peoples' hearts. See also BDAG, 1066-67.

[45] For a positive sense, see Luke 5:6 where *sugkleiō* refers to a net full of fish. See also BDAG, 952.

[46] Forlines, *Quest*, 492.

[47] The following treatment of *stoicheia* is my own development of Forlines's discussion of the *paidagōgos*, though it is partly informed by our private conversation as well.

[48] H. G. Liddell and R. Scott, *Greek-English Lexicon*, 9th ed. with revised supplement (Oxford; Oxford University Press: 1996), 1647.

[49] See Fairbairn, 401-02.

[50] See the helpful discussion in Burton, 510-18; and Linda L. Belleville, "'Under Law': Structural Analysis and the Pauline Concept of Law in Galatians 3:23–4:11," *Journal for the Study of the New Testament* 26 (1986): 64-69.

[51] Belleville comes to a similar conclusion in identifying these elements with "the pre-Christian life of the Jew" and that Paul's warning in Galatians 4:8-11 is clear: "to place themselves 'under law,' that is, to subject every aspect of their lives to strict regulation and close supervision, is in effect to return to serving that which is by nature 'not gods'" (68-69). She continues, "These elementary principles are not, however, suitable for an age of majority which is characterized by the receipt of the Spirit as an inward power and controlling principle and not by an external, regulatory code" (69).

[52] See Belleville, 57-63; Hans Dieter Betz, *Galatians*, Hermeneia (Philadelphia: Fortress, 1979), 178-79; F. F. Bruce, *Epistle to the Galatians: A Commentary on the Greek Text*, New International Greek Testament Commentary (Grand Rapids: Eerdmans, 1982), 182-83; Burton, 200-01; Timothy George, *Galatians: An Exegetical and Theological Exposition of the Holy Scripture*, New American Commentary 30 (Nashville: Broadman & Holman, 1994), 265-70; David T. Gordon, "A Note on ΠΑΙΔΑΓΩΓΟΣ in Galatians 3.24-25," *New Testament Studies* 35 (1989): 150-54; Ladd, *A Theology of the New Testament*, 507; J. B. Lightfoot, *The Epistle of St. Paul to the Galatians* (Grand Rapids: Zondervan, 1957), 148-49; Richard N. Longenecker, "The Pedagogical Nature of the Law in Galatian 3:19-4:7," *Journal of the Evangelical Theological Society* 25 (1982): 53-61; David J. Lull, "'The Law was our Pedagogue': A Study in Galatians 3:19-25," *Journal of Biblical Literature* 105 (1986): 487-96; Thomas R. Schreiner, *Galatians*, Exegetical Commentary on the New Testament (Grand Rapids: Zondervan, 2010), 248-52; Michael J. Smith, "The Role of Pedagogue in Galatians," *Bibliotheca Sacra* 163 (2006): 197-214; and Ben Witherington III, *Grace in Galatia: A Commentary on Paul's Letter to the Galatians* (Grand Rapids: Eerdmans, 1998), 262-67. Of these studies listed, I find Belleville's the most helpful and in general agreement with Forlines. Many of these studies focus on the negative aspects of the *paidagōgos*

(see, however, Lull, 481) and its temporary nature. Belleville, however, emphasizes that it is neither negative nor positive but necessary (60), and furthermore stresses it does not so much focus on the passing of one age to another, but points "to the realization at the coming of Christ of what under law is merely nominal" (63).

[53] Belleville dubs Galatians 3:21-4:11 "a *crux interpretum* for the Pauline concept of the law" (54).

[54] This dualism has been cast as one of the definitive features of classical dispensationalism (see Blaising, "The Extent and Varieties of Dispensationalism," in Blaising and Bock, 23).

[55] Blaising, "Varieties of Dispensationalism," 28-29.

[56] Note that progressive dispensationalists are remarkably similar on this point. See Blaising, "The Structure of the Biblical Covenants," in Blaising and Bock, 142-51, 155. Blaising also distinguishes the form of the Mosaic covenant from that of the Abrahamic and new covenants, insisting that "the Mosaic dispensation marked a change from the way God related to the patriarchs" (151).

[57] George E. Mendenhall, *Law and Covenant in Israel and the Ancient Near East* (Pittsburgh: The Biblical Colloquium, 1955); Delbert R. Hillers, *Covenant: The History of a Biblical Idea* (Baltimore: Johns Hopkins University Press, 1969); Meredith G. Kline, *The Treaty of the Great King* (Grand Rapids: Eerdmans, 1963); idem, *The Structure of Biblical Authority* (Grand Rapids: Eerdmans, 1975).

[58] See also Moshe Weinfeld, "The Covenant of Grant in the Old Testament and in the Ancient Near East," *Journal of the American Oriental Society* 90 (1970): 185.

[59] Horton, 69-70.

[60] For example, Vern Poythress emphasizes that the covenant of grace is still essentially one covenant, though it may be administered in diverse ways throughout biblical history (40).

[61] For instance, scholars have noted the similarities between the form of Deuteronomy and that of the Hittite treaties from the second millennium B.C. Yet much of Deuteronomy's content resembles that of Hammurapi's laws. I think K. A. Kitchen is right in his assessment that the biblical materials represent a "confluence" of both law and treaty literary forms (*On the Reliability of the Old Testament* [Grand Rapids: Eerdmans, 2003], 289; see also Gentry in Gentry and Wellum, 134, 362).

[62] Forlines (personal communication).

[63] E.g., Thielman states that in "Galatians, as in 1 Corinthians, the law of Christ is something new" (*Paul & the Law*, 141).

[64] Forlines, "TH 403 Eschatology: Class Notes," 12.

[65] Ibid., 14.

[66] See H. Richard Niebuhr, *Christ and Culture* (New York: Harper & Row, 1951). I am aware of D. A. Carson's criticisms of Niebuhr's broad categories: (1) Christ against culture, (2) the Christ of culture, (3) Christ above culture, (4) Christ and culture in paradox, and (5) Christ the transformer of culture. Essentially, he thinks they are too broadly defined with not enough nuance, asserting that "some, and perhaps

all, of Niebuhr's five patterns need to be trimmed in some way, by reflection on the broader realities of biblical-theological developments" (*Christ and Culture Revisited* [Grand Rapids: Eerdmans, 2008], 60). I am sympathetic toward and generally agree with his concern that we should think about this matter of the church's relationship to culture in a "biblical-theological" way. At the same time, however, I also think Carson is too rigid in his rejection of Niebuhr's categories (see especially 59-65), since they are still a helpful means of understanding broadly how the relationship between the church and its cultural context has been articulated throughout its history. Alister E. McGrath agrees (see *Christian Theology: An Introduction*, 5th ed. [West Sussex, UK: Wiley-Blackwell, 2011], 118).

[67] *Works of Martin Luther*, vol. 4 (Philadelphia: United Lutheran, 1915-1932), 265; cited in Niebuhr, 171.

[68] Niebuhr, 183.

[69] See Gene Edward Veith, "Christianity and Culture: God's Double Sovereignty," *Modern Reformation* (January/February 1997); www.mtio.com/articles/aissar26. htm; accessed May 15, 2015; Internet. For a handy critique of Veith's overall approach, see John M. Frame, "Christianity and Culture" (Lectures given at Pensacola Theological Institute, July 23-27, 2001), 17-19; accessed May 15, 2015; http://www. thirdmill.org/newfiles/joh_frame/Frame.Apologetics2004.ChristandCulture.pdf; accessed May 15, 2015; Internet.

[70] Horton, 124.

[71] Christopher J. H. Wright, *Salvation Belongs to Our God: Celebrating the Bible's Central Story*, Christian Doctrine in Global Perspective (Downers Grove: IVP Academic, 2007), 90.

[72] Ibid., 88-96.

[73] Ibid., 186.

[74] Forlines, "TH 403 Eschatology: Class Notes," 18.

[75] George E. Ladd, "Historic Premillennialism," in *The Meaning of the Millennium: Four Views*, ed. R. G. Clouse (Downers Grove: InterVarsity, 1977), 32. Rather emphatically he asserts, "[A] millennial doctrine cannot be based on Old Testament prophecies but should be based on the New Testament alone."

[76] Ladd, "Historic Premillennialism," 32.

[77] Craig A. Blaising, "Premillennialism," in *Three Views on the Millennium and Beyond*, ed. Darrell L. Bock (Grand Rapids: Zondervan, 1999), 193, listing the following Old Testament passages: Daniel 2:34-35, 44; Isaiah 2:2-4; Micah 4:1-8.

[78] This observation comes from both an earlier version of his course notes for TH 403 Eschatology, taught during the spring semester of 1999 (9), and personal conversation (April 2015). Most recently, he observed that he still needs to work through this issue more thoroughly, and that he is still open to alternative interpretations of Ezekiel 40—48 (personal communication).

[79] Forlines (personal communication).

[80] See progressive dispensationalist Blaising, "Premillennialism," 200-04. As he states, "My argument for premillennialism is that the millennial kingdom revealed to John, while new in its specific content, is compatible with this earlier revelation concerning the eschatological kingdom and the manner of its coming. Not only that, but now that we have the revelation of a future millennial kingdom, that revelation harmonizes with and clarifies earlier revelation that spoke of the coming eschatological kingdom in a more general manner" (200).

[81] See Grenz, 143.

[82] Ladd, "Historic Premillennialism," 39.

[83] We should note that Forlines has always been adamant that the "last days" as are described in the New Testament always refer to the time from Christ's ascension to His return (see esp. 2 Tim. 3:1 and Heb. 1:2) (personal communication).

[84] To be fair, then, the label *amillennial* (no millennium) is somewhat of a misnomer, since advocates of this view do not actually deny a millennial reign of Christ, but instead interpret its beginning point at an earlier stage of redemptive history than premillennialists. Riddlebarger alternatively calls this view "present" or "realized" millennialism (*A Case of Amillennialism*, 31). See also G. K. Beale, *The Book of Revelation: A Commentary on the Greek Text*, The New International Greek Testament Commentary (Grand Rapids: Eerdmans, 1999), 972, who suggests "inaugurated millennialism."

[85] Blaising, "The Kingdom of God in the New Testament," in Blaising and Bock, 267-70.

[86] I must qualify this assessment with the fact that Forlines intends to turn his full attention to this subject very shortly, once his current writing project has been completed.

[87] I think particularly of Gentry and Wellum who call for a *via media* ("middle way") between the covenantalism of the Reformed tradition and dispensationalism (23-26), though their concerns are not entirely unique.

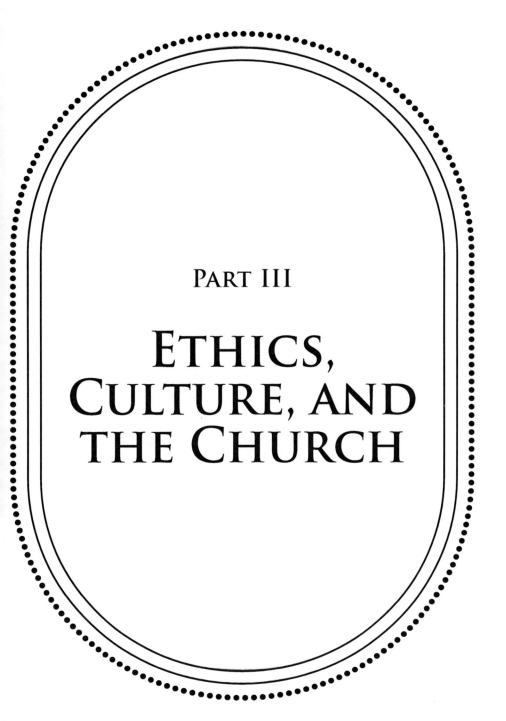

PART III

ETHICS, CULTURE, AND THE CHURCH

CHAPTER EIGHT

BUILDING A FORLINESEAN ETHIC

W. Jackson Watts

Foundations are essential to any structure. If a homeowner notices cracks in his home's foundation, he will eventually hear unpleasant news from a contractor. Therefore, during early construction, careful attention must be given to the foundation. Yet the blueprint's remaining sketches must also take shape. Walls, plumbing, wiring, and other elements must come together. Even when a structure is technically a house, more work is still required for the house to become a *home*. Furnishings must be purchased, walls painted, pictures hung, and more. Homemaking is a life-long project. Still, most who imagine this home taking shape assume one important detail: *People* are making the home. A house requires brick and mortar, but a home requires people. To have a dwelling place is to be a creature. But to make a home is to be human. We could even extend the metaphor further: to have a beautiful home in which to raise a family is to be a happy person. However, what happens without blueprints, or a skilled architect? What if the building materials are second-rate? Building a home requires more than opinions about architecture. One must possess sound blueprints, quality materials, and the right builder.

With some imagination Christians can envision this metaphor as a way of thinking about the moral life, or what is generally known as "ethics." Though the Greek word for ethics (*ethos/ethikos*) usually means custom or character, the word *anastrophe* better captures F. Leroy Forlines's perspective: an entire manner or way of life.[1] While ethics and morals are often used interchangeably, the former usually entails a wider belief system about morality and ideals, whereas the latter tends to focus on the rightness or wrongness of specific acts. More specifically, ideals pertain to something's goodness or badness. Ethics, then, is a discipline that attempts to assess right and wrong (morals), and good and bad (ideals) in all of human life.[2] Christian ethics specifically includes the mind, heart, and will surrendered to God as the evidence of saving faith. It demands we properly understand the gospel, as well as basic relationships and values. Without God as our architect, His Word as the blueprints, and His grace as the building material, our lives are certain to crumble. As Jesus taught, the wise man considers the ground upon which he builds; the foolish man does not, causing his home to tumble when inclement weather comes (Matt. 7:24-27).

The Moral Enterprise: Why Ethics?

Why is ethics necessary? Why do we find ourselves thinking about right and wrong, and good and bad? Is it because of our need for order in a chaotic world, or some deeper reason? Fundamentally ethics matters because of the human condition. In Genesis 1 God created human beings in His image and likeness (Gen. 1:26). Much historical-theological commentary has been written concerning this verse's significance. Not only do theologians and biblical scholars weigh into this discussion, but even politicians.[3] While theological accounts differ regarding what this doctrine entails,[4] Forlines argues that morality and rationality are its essential components.[5] These are not only taught in Scripture (Eph. 4:23-24; Col. 3:10), but are presupposed and confirmed by our capacity for relationships, communication, work, imagination, creativity, and more. After creating humans God gave them responsibilities: "Be fruitful and multiply," "Subdue it and have dominion," and "work it and keep it [the

Garden of Eden]" (Gen. 1:28; 2:15). Additionally, God prohibited Adam and Eve from eating from the tree of the knowledge of good and evil, lest they die (Gen. 2:16-17). While the text does not make the philosophical claim that human beings are morally responsible creatures, these passages assume it. God's command for humans to act in a certain way implies the freedom to respond accordingly. That we can keep or break laws makes us moral creatures; that we have broken them, and that we ourselves are broken requires the construction of a biblical ethic.

This side of Eden, biblical ethics is non-negotiable if we want to honor God and enjoy the blessedness (or happiness) only He gives. Forlines's subtitle for *Biblical Ethics*, his signature work in ethics, indicates his approach is for "happier living." While he does not discuss happiness at length, he assumes that living within the morality of God's Word will produce the happiness that so often eludes people. Though ethics in antiquity was often linked to happiness, many modern Christians distinguish joy from happiness, understanding the former to be a spiritual fruit, and the latter to be a momentary feeling.[6] This distinction is understandable given the widespread misunderstanding on the subject. However, Forlines believes those who seek God will experience happiness this world cannot offer:

> We cannot ignore morals and ideals. They are woven into every yard of the fabric of life. We may violate our standards, but only at a price. We may fall short of our ideals, but not without concern. It is as if we have an ethical nerve system that responds to every life situation. Anyone who wishes to be happy must take these factors into account.[7]

Challenges in Studying Ethics and Living Morally

Certain challenges accompany our reflection on ethics and morality; some even impinge on our ability to live morally upright lives. For these reasons we will consider three basic challenges: (1) the diversity within Christian ethical literature; (2) the unique context of Forlines's contributions; and (3) the total depravity of man, which grounds the need for ethics, and influences our effort to live morally.

Diverse Approaches

Christian ethicists primarily operate in one of four lanes: (1) they relate scriptural truth to moral reasoning, and use the Ten Commandments or other key biblical texts to advance a particular ethical framework;[8] (2) they advance the basic ethical framework and moral principles by which Christians should operate based on Scripture's storyline and cardinal doctrines;[9] (3) they address specific topics individually from a biblical perspective, such as warfare, sexuality, or ecology;[10] or (4) they synthesize these elements into a more holistic presentation.[11] Ethicists vary in how they use Scripture and philosophical tools, as well as the extent to which contemporary problems dictate the questions being asked. Questions even arise about which methods for moral reasoning are congenial to the Christian worldview.[12] Context therefore is important.

Several influential, twentieth century figures loom over the Christian ethical landscape. No study can neglect the contributions of Paul Ramsey (1913-1988), long-time Princeton University professor. His work has contributed especially to the renewal of interest in Just War Theory in the late-twentieth century. Others working within a Protestant background are Oliver O'Donovan (b. 1945) and Stanley Hauerwas (b. 1940). O'Donovan taught most of his career in the United Kingdom, though his books have significantly influenced Christian ethics in America.[13] Hauerwas taught theological ethics primarily at Duke Divinity School and published prolifically during his career.[14] Best-known for his critiques of Constantinianism and arguments for nonviolence, the Christian ethical landscape of the late-twentieth century is unintelligible apart from understanding Hauerwas.

Within the evangelical fold, several figures have exerted significant influence in the twentieth century. Scottish-born Presbyterian theologian John Murray (1898-1975) was a household name due to his *Principles of Conduct*. Murray was one of Forlines's many Calvinist conversation partners in his published work due to his period of scholarly influence. More recently, John (b. 1946) and Paul Feinberg (1938-2004) made a significant contribution with their widely-used *Ethics for a Brave New World*.[15] Norman Geisler (b. 1932), perhaps more often associated with apologetics, has also contributed several works in this area. His *Christian Ethics: Options and Issues* has been in print for over 25 years.[16] However, Scott Rae (b. 1954) has authored maybe the most widely used Christian ethics textbook today.[17] Theologian and biblical scholar Wayne Grudem (b. 1948) has also increasingly moved into this scholarly lane with works on gender, politics, and economics.[18] The final figure of extensive contemporary influence is Russell Moore (b. 1971), President of the Southern Baptist Convention's Ethics and Religious Liberties Commission. Moore has become a trusted voice on many issues for conservative evangelicals.

Where does Forlines fit within this brief sketch of modern Christian ethics? For Free Will Baptists, he has been the central voice for most of his career.

Forlines's Unique Contribution

Ethics has not been a significant domain for Free Will Baptist scholarship. Even most of what has been considered "moral challenges or dilemmas" have been treated within the arenas of pastoral care, discipleship, systematic theology, or even denominational polity.[19] Thus Forlines's *Biblical Ethics* is the only book of its kind published by Free Will Baptists in modern times. Forlines wrote one smaller treatise that could be considered "moral theology,"[20] and also edited a volume addressing several ethical issues facing the church.[21] Teaching ethics courses at Welch College (beginning in 1968) provided a context to advance some of his trademarks, such as the "four basic relationships" and "two forms of legalism." Of course ministering within a smaller movement, among other factors, did not provide quite the audience others had.[22]

Forlines's worldview emphasis bears similarities to Carl F. H. Henry's, whose influence in evangelicalism contributed to greater discussion of modernism and postmodernism. Such themes are significant in Forlines's work (see chapter two). Still, Forlines demonstrates some caution with the early neo-evangelical project. In evaluating Henry's call for fundamentalists to have a "world program" concerning social problems, Forlines finds much with which to agree.[23] Yet he expresses concerns about the church-state relationship that Henry's proposal may require, as well as the extent of cooperation one may have with non-evangelicals. Though Henry was certainly one influence on Forlines's ethical perspective, Forlines had his own unique context from which to operate.[24]

A Tainted Image

The greatest challenge inherent in Christian ethics is the reason for its very existence: human sinfulness. Humanity, made in God's image and likeness, is completely fallen. As opposed to representing God in his total personality—in his thinking, feeling, and acting—man's personality is no longer compatible with His.[25] Forlines explains, "God looks at anything that is incompatible with His holy nature as sin."[26] Sometimes we knowingly violate God's will; other times we act ignorantly and fail to live in conformity with God's holiness. In other situations, an action's rightness or wrongness is built into the very nature of things.[27] Regardless of the circumstance, all sin somehow arises from unbelief, selfishness, or ignorance. We often justify our sin, calling it something other than wrong or evil.[28] To paraphrase Forlines, we're "label-switchers."[29]

As an extension of the self-deception and selfishness behind sin, immorality arises from what is momentarily comfortable, pleasurable, and desirable, as opposed to what is ultimately good, loving, just, and wise.[30] Sin manifests itself in three main forms: (1) ungodliness, or lack of reverence; (2) unrighteousness, or the failure to conform to God's moral standards; and (3) opposition to the truth, meaning the suppression and distortion of truth, and the promotion of error.[31] These manifestations of sin confirm our two-fold problem of guilt and depravity. Sinners are truly guilty, and the penalty for their sin is death (Rom. 6:23). Furthermore, depravity as "the power of sin that brings the person under its grip" reveals why ethics is a challenge for the Christian.[32] We should make sound moral decisions, but our depraved nature makes this difficult. As Forlines explains, our tainted image makes it impossible for us to answer adequately life's inescapable questions: "Is there a God? If so, what is He like?

How can I know Him? Who am I? How can I tell right from wrong? Is there life after death? What should I and what can I do about guilt? How can I deal with my inner pain?"[33] The biblical response is that ethics require spiritual transformation, rather than a list of rules devised by fallen man.

This account departs from how ethics is framed in secular discourse. In conventional moral philosophy (non-religious, ethical discussion), an optimistic anthropology is espoused: Human beings are essentially good. Sometimes they do act in self-interest, but we should expect this due to our "evolutionary heritage" (biological and social). However, what if a different narrative shows Christian ethics to be a more coherent and desirable approach to human life?

God, Morality, and the Gospel

Contemporary ethical literature is commonly aimed at the whole world. Authors attempt to present a universally applicable ethic that is also multi-cultural.[34] Strangely, they advance an absolutist moral framework while being relativists about all morality! (As Forlines says, people are interested in questions of right and wrong, even if for the wrong reasons).[35] Such people would impose their values on the world around them, hoping to make it the way they think it should be. While we may try to deny universal moral norms in structuring an ethical outlook, absolute moral claims cannot be escaped. Philosophers have long debated whether such a pattern points to God's existence.[36] They ask, "Can we be good without God?"[37] However, the more practical question is what does *biblical* ethics require of free, moral agents? Is it being in basic moral agreement with the Judeo-Christian tradition, or a spiritual orientation of the heart and mind? Can we truly live morally without making certain spiritual commitments?

Many social commentators today root public policy arguments simply in what has been traditionally believed in American society, as opposed to orthodox, theological claims. Yet O'Donovan, for instance, argues that Jesus' resurrection (not some return to past values) fundamentally grounds the way we approach ethics.[38] This is not mere assent to the resurrection event, but to having been buried and raised with Jesus (Rom. 6:4-5). Forlines concurs, "Redemption is the work of God that delivers man from the wrath of God and reclaims and restores him from the destructive power of sin."[39] Consequently, "the matter of atonement is ethical to the core."[40] Having paid sin's penalty, Christ solves the guilt problem in justification. The Holy Spirit's ongoing, sanctifying work in people's lives addresses depravity's effects. Living morally now flows from God's power, as opposed to being as an attempt to earn God's gracious salvation. Christ's righteousness becomes ours by faith, just as our unrighteousness is taken upon Him (2 Cor. 5:21; Gal. 3:13; Phil. 3:9). We become righteous in standing (justification) and experience (sanctification). However, while the former is an event, the latter is a process. As redeemed persons in an influence-response relationship with God (see chapter three), obedience occurs in time and space.[41] Sanctification, then, is unavoidably a temporal process because we are temporal beings.[42] To summarize, Christian ethics is grounded in justification, which leads to sanctification; and growth in moral conformity to God's will is an ongoing process until we see Him as He is (1 John 3:2). Ethics is thus built into our journey through the sanctification experience.[43]

While we may long for moral perfection, this is different from establishing legalistic standards with the assumption that moral perfection is possible in this life. These observations are why Forlines confronts the errors of perfectionism, showing that maturity does not require flawlessness (which is impossible), but wholeness or completion (properly understood from Matthew 5:48).[44] This perspective is not only useful for Christians tempted by works-righteousness, but also for public life. We recognize that no perfect political solution exists in a broken, fallen world. Yet a gracious God Who saves and helps us, despite our inability to solve all of our contemporary problems, works through our feeble efforts. Our efforts—even in a democratic republic with enumerated rights—often do not result in morally ideal outcomes. But as Christians transformed by the gospel, we continue to consider its implications and the opportunities we have to reflect its truths in public life. We are then able to act with freedom, courage, and moral imagination on the basis of Christ's finished work.

Forming Moral Judgments

As we will see later, wisdom is an essential value to ethics. But this requires placing wisdom, and specifically reason, in a biblical perspective. When assessing the nature of sin, Forlines initially demonstrates a type of moral realism common in twentieth century Protestant thought. Reinhold Niebuhr often cited G. K. Chesterton's observation that original sin is the most empirically verifiable and validated Christian doctrine in human history.[45] Forlines speaks similarly: "Sin is too obvious for anyone to deny its existence,"[46] and, "Anyone can tell that righteousness pays in the long run."[47]

Naming sin and assessing its moral status is important because it demonstrates how rationality is involved in moral discernment. Some theologians have challenged the perspective that we can understand what sin is apart from Christ's work. To paraphrase Hauerwas, "original sin" is not a description of something called "the human condition."[48] We could say we are worthless, morally inconsistent creatures. But from a Christian perspective, this is not the same thing as saying we are sinners. We cannot have "sin without the Christian understanding of God, or the Jewish understanding of God."[49] Consider New York Times' columnist David Brooks's recent remarks in *The Road to Character*. Brooks laments the loss of "sin" from society's moral vocabulary, and then offers what initially appears to be a substantial account of sin:

> Sin is a necessary piece of our mental furniture because it reminds us that life is a moral affair. No matter how hard we try to reduce everything to deterministic brain chemistry, no matter how hard we try to reduce behavior to the sort of herd instinct that is captured in big data, no matter how hard we strive to replace sin with nonmoral words, like 'mistake' or 'error' or 'weakness,' the most essential parts of life are matters of individual responsibility and moral choice: whether

to be brave or cowardly, honest or deceitful, compassionate or callous, faithful or disloyal. When modern culture tries to replace sin with ideas like error or insensitivity, or tries to banish words like 'virtue,' 'character,' 'evil,' and 'vice' altogether, that doesn't make life any less moral; it just means we have obscured the inescapable moral core of life with shallow language.[50]

Much of Brooks's definition sounds like traditional, theological reflection on contemporary society. Yet when examined closely, the vertical dimension of sin is missing. Brooks's account acknowledges sin against a neighbor, but not against a Creator. Forlines correctly observes, "It is not enough to see sin as a mistake, or to just see it as wrong. It must be seen as against a holy God. It must be seen as rightly incurring eternal punishment. It must be seen as the cause of suffering, misery, shame, disgrace, and ruin."[51] So Forlines actually helps us understand sin theologically, and thus proceed to explain the tools of moral reasoning.

The Tools of Moral Reasoning

Forlines stresses the importance of an inspired, infallible, and inerrant Bible, which is "our authoritative source for answers concerning God, man, and morals."[52] With this affirmation also comes a commitment to the personal, sovereign, holy, loving, and wise God Who reveals Himself in Scripture. We are morally accountable to Him since righteousness and justice flow from His holy character and standards. This helps us understand the dilemma of being under God's judgment, and His commitment to deal with sin at the cross. These become building blocks that form "an essential part of the theological foundation for a system of Christian ethics."[53] Encountering these doctrinal emphases is not surprising because of the mutually-reinforcing relationship between belief (orthodoxy) and practice (morals).[54] When we alter our beliefs on certain issues, it also tends to influence our conduct. Conversely, when we tolerate certain behavior, whether in others or ourselves, it gradually alters what is believed. Sound theological convictions—especially about God and Scripture—are essential for moral reasoning.

Alongside cardinal theological convictions, liberty and freedom accompany the Christian experience (including moral decision-making).[55] This flexibility does not minimize the importance of adhering to biblical principles or moral laws. We guard against potential abuses to Christian liberty, while also cultivating a godly testimony and positive moral influence (Matt. 5:16; Rom. 14:16).[56] But a new covenant perspective emphasizes stewardship and maturity,[57] and it helps us avoid seeing ethics as glorified rule-keeping. Christians are certainly able to grow in moral discernment through practicing the Scriptures (Heb. 5:11-14). However, the Holy Spirit begins to orient us toward the liberty found in the gospel, freeing us from legalism and antinomianism. As Paul explains in Galatians, the freedom in which we are to stand (5:1) entails walking by the Spirit (5:25) and not the flesh (5:16).

Rationality is also an important tool in moral reasoning. Because rationality is part of God's image in man, it is expressed (even in its fallenness) by all humans. As moral, rational beings, people have a "sense of oughtness and obligation."[58] Many secular writers believe that living a good life is a spiritual matter; yet they locate spirituality in a humanistic framework, which privileges unaided reason.[59] However, even for orthodox Christians, reason is important. For Forlines "the development of this rationality is a divine obligation. Reason came not as a product of the fall, but as a product of creation."[60] This observation does not privilege reason over revelation because God has designed us to discern (with His Spirit's help) spiritual truth found in biblical revelation. This includes the ability to form moral judgments. Our reason must be redeemed, but it is still a part of God's image in us. As Forlines writes, "We must *think* if we are to understand the application of right and wrong, or good and bad, to the various situations of life."[61]

To summarize, Scripture operates as an authoritative guide, bearing witness to the Holy Spirit Who "guides us in our pursuit of ethical truth" (John 16:8).[62] Forlines shows that reason, Scripture, and the Spirit work together in helping Christians make godly decisions.[63] While this does not exhaust all the principles in moral reasoning, they are the central tools necessary to pursuing ethical truth. However, in addition to considering, "With what tools are such decisions made?" we must also consider, "Unto Whom are such decisions being made?" This question requires exploring the realm of relationships.

Four Basic Relationships:
The Lived Environment of Ethics

Morality is not exercised in a vacuum; it concerns ways of thinking, acting, and feeling *in the context of relationships*. There is no truly meaningful way to discuss what one should do without reference at least to one (and often more) of four basic relationships.

The first and most important relationship is with God, providing direction to all other relationships. Scripture teaches that God is a personal being, and that humans are made in His image. Despite the vast difference between God and man, we have been made with the capacity for fellowship with Him. Moreover, a relationship with a personal God is different than relating to a code of laws. Because our personhood consists of the mind, heart, and will, God cares about our entire self. Like every relationship, justification and sanctification restores and sustains this relationship. We love God, and thus that which is holy or consistent with His character (1 John 2:15). Our love "involves affectionate concern that leads to action" because "sound ethical judgments can be rendered only by an involved and interested person."[64] Detachment from God is not possible for those interested in Christian ethics. Scripture commands us to love God with all our heart, soul, mind, and strength (Mark 12:30).

The second great commandment is to love our neighbors as ourselves; this is also the second basic relationship. While we tend to think of interpersonal relationships as a pleasant but optional part of life, we cannot purely see ourselves in individual terms. Concern for neighbor is not simply a command; "it is built into who we are."[65] People are not puppets or machines, but social creatures. And though we are different in our social characteristics (sin certainly influences interpersonal relationships), we were made for community. We need fellowship with others. The New Testament's "one-another" language calls significant attention to the relevance of these relationships.[66] Certainly not all relationships are equal. Forlines distinguishes between the believer's obligations to his neighbor, other Christians, and his enemies. Murray summarizes this relationship well: "The biblical ethic takes account, not only of individuals as individuals and of their behavior as such, but of individuals in their corporate relationships. There is corporate responsibility and there is corporate action."[67] "Corporate" (derived from the Latin *corpus* meaning "body") usefully connects this relationship to the biblical metaphor of the church as a body.

The third basic relationship is perhaps the most overlooked by believers, though this is changing due to growing environmental concerns.[68] This relationship is the one we have with the created order, or the "material universe and its animal inhabitants."[69] This relationship is expressed in the stewardship and exercise of dominion over creation. Many are giving increased attention to this relationship, including those working within Christian ethics today. Forlines's principal emphasis is that Christians should avoid developing a negative view toward materiality—both with respect to the created order and material goods such as wealth.[70] After all, Psalms 8 and 19 promote delight in God's good creation. Writing in the early 1970s, some environmentally conscious Christians may be surprised to read Forlines mention drilling for oil, cutting timber, mining, and other practices. Many of these concerns are shaped by larger cultural beliefs about climate change and scientific theories that were not as fully developed during Forlines's earlier career; even many today (Christians or not) still debate the extent of these problems. However, if one adopts the grateful, delightful attitude in Scripture toward God's handiwork, it should foster the right approach to animal and plant life, material goods, labor, and creation in general. Christians cannot help but recognize their embeddedness in a world designed by the Creator, and thus respond as discerning stewards engaged in "creation care."[71]

The final relationship is the one that exists between a person and himself. Because this relationship is largely manifested through what psychologists call one's "self-concept," it is often not seen in relational terms. Yet Forlines explains that a person's attitude toward himself is a significant part of moral health. Moral decisions arise from *within* (Prov. 4:23). For this reason, the themes of personal development and personality are found throughout Forlines's work.[72] The cultivation of honesty, humility, self-denial, self-esteem, self-respect, and self-confidence all influence this relationship. Of course, this also has profound implications for the other basic relationships. An inflated view of self marginalizes other relationships; but a diminished self-concept hinders one from embracing the courage and virtue necessary for participation in these other relationships. All four relationships then are each profoundly interrelated and interdependent.

To think of relationships as the "lived environment of ethics" is simply to say that believers cannot conceive of morals and ideals without considering their involvement in each basic relationship. As Forlines explains, "It is not only possible for us to be rational and moral and to have functioning relationships, but we need to function rationally and morally, and properly in the context of the four basic relationships. Failure in any of these areas means loss."[73] Even when understanding the connections between a specific decision and its relational impact is difficult, the wise Christian remembers their reality. Forlines is careful to remind us that everything is not reducible to clear-cut moral rules under the new covenant. We must reject long-list legalism (works-righteousness) and short-list legalism (licentiousness).

Next, we must consider the building materials that fill out this lived environment. After all, one does not simply sit on a finished foundation. The remaining building materials are the four basic values.

Four Basic Values: The Building Materials

In the last several decades, there has been a resurgence of Christian reflection on virtue.[74] Though these discussions have not necessarily taken root in much evangelical discourse (with a few notable examples), "values" is sometimes used analogously. Forlines's four basic values are perhaps as close as any account in emphasizing the relevance of virtue or character to morality. He sets these values in a hierarchical order: holiness, love, wisdom, and ideals. While he is careful not to pit any of these virtues against each other, he demonstrates that certain theological convictions order and prioritize them because they are derived from God's character.[75]

Holiness, God's fundamental attribute according to Forlines, serves as our starting point.[76] This is more than simply morality, but is "separation from sin, conformity to righteousness, and dedication to God."[77] Holiness is a matter of moral set-apartness in the heart; it is about Who God is, and our conformity thereunto in what we do (1 Peter 1:15-16). It is equally true, however, that God is love. Thus we are called to love. Love is said to be superior to faith and hope (1 Cor. 13:13); it is not optional for the Christian. Working from his exegesis of 1 John, Forlines argues, "John leaves no doubt that love for our Christian brothers must be a part of a person's experience if he is to be considered a Christian."[78] Love then involves both affection and action. It not only feels; it acts. Love gives of itself, and patiently seeks others' well-being. It flows from God's love manifested in Jesus Christ. This act of love also expresses how God's holiness can be maintained, while sin is dealt with. It is not surprising that Forlines advocates the penal satisfaction view of the atonement as it embodies a robust understanding of how holiness and love function together (see chapter four).

The third and fourth basic values are wisdom and ideals. Forlines defines wisdom as "sanctified common sense."[79] It is good, sound judgment exercised in light of eternal values. More broadly, it is the translation of doctrinal, moral, and spiritual truth into "practical truth for real life situations."[80] In a complex world, the ability to apply biblical principles to imperfect situations is essential. By extension ideals concern excellence, or that which is dignified, beautiful, and in good taste. In this arena good and bad are more appropriate descriptions than right and wrong. Drawing on Philippians 4:8, Forlines contends that while we may not be disobeying God by certain judgments about ideals, His perfections lead Christians to pursue excellence in all of life. New Testament scholar Andreas Köstenberger writes, "God is the grounds of all true excellence. . . . It stands to reason that as beings created in God's image, creatures who are called to exercise representative rule over his creation, we must do so with excellence."[81] The common thread behind these two values is their influence upon practical judgment that functions more along the axis of good and bad, and better and best, instead of right and wrong. Because this distinction is uniquely developed in Forlines, it offers some opportunities for further theological reflection on how they operate in everyday life.

One of the critical areas of Forlines's ethics is the way he relates these values to one another. Grounding them in a biblical understanding of God and the gospel provides a foundation to prioritize certain values based on the arc of salvation. For instance, in the atonement Forlines explains, "Love bowed to the demands of holiness and fulfilled its demands."[82] Such statements illustrate how God's attributes relate, and thus how these inform our moral values. Writing on the same subject, David F. Wells offers additional insight into the relationship between these two:

> There is only one character in God. . . . He is simultaneously loving and holy in such a way that we never encounter his love without his holiness or his holiness without his love. Indeed, his love is an expression of his holiness, and we never know his love except in the context of what is eternally right.[83]

Making a decision driven more by holiness instead of love does not mean we choose one aspect of God over another, as if the holy thing is not loving. Instead we remember their relationship to one another within the economy of salvation. God's character forms the basis for the values that are relevant to our decision-making. He is also supremely powerful, just, wise, and excellent. These are not in competition. But His communicable attributes are those that most directly forge our value system, guiding what we do and who we are.[84]

When we speak of virtue (or values in the Forlinesean sense), we are discussing who we are as much as what we do.

As mentioned earlier, God cares about the whole self, and not just outward conduct (Matt. 5:27-28). That said, while Forlines is more Augustinian than Aristotelian in his understanding of morality and ethics, his work does encourage particular moral habits. Believers' outward engagement with the world reflects the moral transformation that God is working within their hearts, and thus further sanctifies them in the grace of Jesus Christ (Tit. 2:11-14).

The Future of Forlinesean Ethics

Because the ethical program presented by Forlines is biblically and theologically coherent, it holds great promise for future generations who will study ethics seriously and live morally. By no means is his work comprehensive on every important ethical question. But this is understandable since most ethicists and theologians writing prior to *Roe v. Wade* (1973) were not as "issues-focused" as today. Indeed, the moral climate of the social context in which we live shapes the questions we ask, and how we answer them. What we gain from Forlines's contribution is a framework of timeless biblical truths that inform contemporary life, no matter which basic relationship is in view. Anecdotally, some of Forlines's formulations—namely the two forms of legalism—have been unknowingly appropriated by several popular, contemporary evangelical authors.[85] No doubt an ethical framework driven by careful, biblical study—such as Forlines's—will never be out of vogue if the church still believes the Bible is essential for Christian ethics!

Forlines's ethics provides a helpful outline for life in the home, church, academy, and world at large. An earlier chapter noted that Forlines's view of cultural engagement would most comfortably fit within the "Christ the Transformer of Culture" category found in H. Richard Niebuhr's famous typology.[86] I think this is indeed the case, with some qualifications. First, his approach could be considered transformational because of the many areas of life he believed the Christian moral vision addressed. In *Biblical Ethics* alone we find discussion not only of godly relationships and values, but also of personality development, gender roles,[87] economic concerns like labor and poverty, creation care,[88] entertainment, and personal appearance. While some might relegate these latter two areas to a past era of fundamentalism, such persons ignore that Forlines's approach to ethics requires an account of ideals. To think wisely in matters of entertainment and leisure, dress, and so forth has some basis if one believes that all of life is lived under Christ's lordship. We may rightfully debate the appropriate framework or context for discussing such matters. We could even say these would be useful horizons for future reflection and development. But denying the relevance of such topics to Christian inquiry succumbs to a form of dualism that separates the spiritual and material, a dichotomy that Forlines roundly rejects.

A second reason why Forlines's ethical vision is congenial to the transformational category is that his approach requires and indeed emphasizes the transformation of the self in salvation, which must be the basis for any cultural engagement. Anytime the English word "transform" (or a derivative) appears in the New Testament with respect to believers, it refers to some aspect of moral change or spiritual growth (Rom. 12:2; 2 Cor. 3:18; Phil. 3:21). In one instance, it even speaks of *eschatological* change (readers will note the early chapters of *Biblical Ethics* emphasize this foundation also). Recognizing the exegetical data is not meant to imply Christians cannot or should not influence the world in which they live. The same epistles that speak of spiritual transformation also refer to Christian influence and witness in the social sphere (Rom. 13:1-7). Yet this is grounded in the ongoing transformation of the total personality, which then enables us to fulfill our "responsibilities" (a term Forlines uses frequently) to the world around us. In fact, phrases like "influence upon" or "responsibility to" society may be preferable to "transform," which tends to connote an unclear outcome that cannot be guaranteed by even the most transformed Christian. Someone or something is transformed into *something*, which will look different in different social and political contexts.[89] Nevertheless, Forlines's work encourages us to think in terms of responsibility, duty, and faithful Christian obedience, remembering that ultimate outcomes are in the Lord's hands.

A third aspect of Forlines's brand of transformationalism is seen in his remarks on life's everyday pursuits. For example, he notes that Christians may "climb the ladder of success" in regard to work, career, and material gain.[90] In a society increasingly suspicious of the "wealthiest 1%" and capitalism in general, such remarks seem suspect—certainly not like the Savior Who commanded His disciples to "give without pay," and take "no bag for your journey, or two tunics or sandals or a staff" (Matt. 10:8-10). Moreover, even to some Christians the idea of "improving one's station" (a Forlinesean remark) seems inconsistent with biblical passages such as 1 Corinthians 7:17-24, where the apostle Paul urges Christians to remain with God in "whatever condition" in which they were called. However, a closer examination of the context of Forlines's words (especially with respect to such biblical principles) shows that his views of economic engagement are always subject to the "Christian system of values and priorities."[91] For instance, he emphasizes the importance of sacrificial giving to the church and the poor, and intentional caution concerning the pursuit of wealth. Forlines's views challenge the consumer culture that has deeply influenced the Christian church. His understanding of Scripture also makes space for leisure, recreation, and being enriched by the goods of creation with a grateful spirit (see third basic relationship). Such a perspective also challenges the false asceticism that characterizes so much progressive political rhetoric that lacks the ability to name the common causes of most social ills, such as adultery, divorce, laziness, and apathy. Forlines's transformationalism means that Christians live counter-cultural lives in the midst of a dark and decaying world as they take the whole counsel of God seriously.

Forlines's discussion of realistic idealism and perfectionism is a final aspect where we see how ethics is a humble, lived pursuit, and not a triumphalist one. By recognizing our own limitations as sinners living in a fallen world, we are able to embrace a realistic perspective while also pursuing the good, true, lovely, excellent, and beautiful as much as possible. Such an insight grounds

THE PROMISE OF ARMINIAN THEOLOGY

Christian reflection about political and social activity. We cannot accomplish everything this side of eternity, but we do all we can do by God's grace for His glory. As Andreas Köstenberger reminds us, the pursuit of excellence is personal, moral, and vocational in nature.[92] The Forlinesean ethical agenda helps Christians pursue such excellence.

Personal Reflection

In *The Road to Character*, David Brooks confesses to spending too much of life focused on résumé virtues and not eulogy virtues. He then offers case studies of admirable persons (religious and nonreligious) who conquered some great problem by first conquering an inner weakness. "I have lived a life of vague moral aspiration," Brooks poignantly remarks, "vaguely wanting to be good, vaguely wanting to serve some larger purpose, while lacking a concrete moral vocabulary, a clear understanding of how to live a rich inner life, or even a clear knowledge of how character is developed and depth is achieved."[93] While Brooks discusses some honorable figures, these figures can help us only so much. As Christians we assess true character according to Scripture. In Forlines we see a person who takes seriously God, Scripture, and people; in Forlines we see a man of true Christian character. He began teaching ethics in 1968, but has lived it longer than that. For his contributions I am thankful and count myself a debtor. He has pointed us to the Great Architect, Whose blueprints provide infallible guidance for those seeking to build a life that can withstand whatever waves may come (Eph. 4:14).

---

[1] Theologian John Murray calls attention to this nuance in Greek terms in *Principles of Conduct: Aspects of Biblical Ethics* (Grand Rapids: Eerdmans, 1957), 11-13.

[2] F. Leroy Forlines, *Biblical Ethics: Ethics for Happier Living* (Nashville: Randall House, 1973), 8; hereafter *Ethics*.

[3] President Barack Obama has invoked this doctrine in arguing for the advancement of same-sex marriage and other rights for the LGBT community. Conversely, Senator Marco Rubio has explained that the image of God in humanity has implications

for labor: "For Christians, the centrality of work to human meaning and happiness comes from our being made in the image of God" (*American Dreams: Restoring Economic Opportunity for Everyone* [New York: Sentinel, 2004], 74.)

[4] See F. Leroy Forlines, *The Quest for Truth: Answering Life's Inescapable Questions* (Nashville: Randall House, 2001), 148-49; hereafter *Quest*.

[5] See Forlines, *Quest*, 135-66, for Forlines's expanded discussion of this topic.

[6] As exceptions, Ellen T. Charry frames moral life around the theme of happiness in *God and the Art of Happiness* (Grand Rapids: Eerdmans, 2010); however, the most influential conception of happiness arises from Aristotle and his explanation of *eudaimonia*, which refers to the types of right actions that lead to individual well being or flourishing.

[7] Forlines, *Ethics*, 8.

[8] Cf. Mark Rooker, *The Ten Commandments: Ethics for the Twenty-First Century* (Nashville: B&H Academic, 2010); Stanley Hauerwas and William Willimon, *The Truth about God: The Ten Commandments in Christian Life* (Nashville: Abingdon, 1999).

[9] Cf. Robertson McQuilkin and Paul Copan, *An Introduction to Biblical Ethics: Walking in the Way of Wisdom*, 3rd ed. (Downers Grove: IVP Academic, 2014).

[10] Cf. Arthur Holmes, ed., *War and Christian Ethics: Classic Readings on the Morality of War* (Grand Rapids: Baker, 1991); Gene Edward Veith, *Christianity in An Age of Terrorism* (St. Louis: Concordia, 2002); Daniel R. Heimbach, *True Sexual Morality: Recovering Biblical Standards for a Culture in Crisis* (Wheaton: Crossway, 2004); and Richard Bauckham, *The Bible and Ecology: Rediscovering the Community of Creation* (Waco: Baylor University Press, 2010). Some authors make admirable attempts at exploring most of the major ethical challenges for contemporary Christians, such as John Jefferson Davis in *Evangelical Ethics: Issues Facing the Church Today*, 3rd ed. (Phillipsburg: P&R, 2004).

[11] Cf. David W. Jones, *An Introduction to Biblical Ethics* (Nashville: B&H Academic, 2013). This is perhaps the best recent example of this type of holistic approach.

[12] Cf. Norman Geisler, *Options in Contemporary Christian Ethics* (Grand Rapids: Baker, 1984). These various options are also explored in Arthur Holmes's *Ethics: Approaching Moral Decisions*, 2nd ed. (Downers Grove: IVP Academic, 2007).

[13] O'Donovan's most significant books have been *Resurrection and Moral Order: An Outline for Evangelical Ethics*, 2nd ed. (Grand Rapids: Eerdmans, 1994) and *The Desire of the Nations: Rediscovering the Roots of Political Theology* (New York: Cambridge University Press, 1996).

[14] Most of Hauerwas's work has been in the form of essays and sermons, though some of his earlier books were more systematic volumes. E.g., *A Community of Character: Toward a Constructive Christian Social Ethic* (Notre Dame: University of Notre Dame Press, 1981) and *The Peaceable Kingdom: A Primer in Christian Ethics* (Notre Dame: University of Notre Dame Press, 1983).

[15] John S Feinberg and Paul D. Feinberg, *Ethics for a Brave New World*, 2nd ed. (Wheaton: Crossway, 2010).

[16] Grand Rapids: Baker Academic, 1989; the second edition (2010) has the subtitle of "Contemporary Issues and Options."

[17] Scott Rae, *Moral Choices: An Introduction to Ethics*, 3rd ed. (Grand Rapids: Zondervan, 2009).

[18] E.g., Wayne Grudem and Bruce Ware, *Biblical Foundations for Manhood and Womanhood* (Wheaton:Crossway, 2002); Wayne Grudem, *Politics According to the Bible: A Comprehensive Resource for Understanding Modern Political Issues in Light of Scripture* (Grand Rapids: Zondervan, 2010); Wayne Grudem and Barry Asmus, *The Poverty of Nations: A Sustainable Solution* (Wheaton: Crossway, 2013); Wayne Grudem, *Business for the Glory of God: The Bible's Teaching on the Moral Goodness of Business* (Wheaton: Crossway, 2003).

[19] One example is the Free Will Baptist National Executive Committee's decision to establish a special committee in 2013 to study the moral and legal implications of same-sex marriage on Free Will Baptist churches in the near future.

[20] Leroy Forlines, *Morals and Orthodoxy* (Nashville: Commission on Theological Liberalism, 1974).

[21] F. Leroy Forlines, *Contending for the Faith: Practical Answers for Perplexing Problems* (Nashville: Randall House, 1984).

[22] On the other hand, Karl Barth, the famed Swiss theologian of the early-mid twentieth century, may be the only other twentieth century Protestant theologian to publish a dogmatics/systematics work, a Romans commentary, and a serious ethical treatise.

[23] Forlines speaks favorably of Henry in many places. E.g., *Issues Among Evangelicals* (Nashville: The Commission on Theological Liberalism, 1968), 76.

[24] Henry's *The Uneasy Conscience of Fundamentalism* is the work primarily discussed by Forlines (Grand Rapids: Eerdmans, 1947). Other important early, ethical works by Henry include *Christian Personal Ethics* (Grand Rapids: Baker, 1957) and *Aspects of Christian Social Ethics* (Grand Rapids: Baker, 1964).

[25] Forlines, *Ethics*, 19.

[26] Ibid., 25.

[27] Such sentiments make difficult the task of placing Forlines strictly in either a conventional "deontological ethic" camp (act-oriented) or "consequentialist" camp (outcome-oriented).

[28] The concept of self-deception is very strong in Forlines, just as in other more presuppositional apologists. See Forlines, *Ethics*, 24-28.

[29] Forlines, *Ethics*, 20.

[30] Ibid., 27. Forlines calls this the "principle of immediacy."

[31] Ibid., 28.

[32] Ibid., 29

[33] Forlines, *Quest*, 1.

34 The Dalai Lama's *Beyond Religion: Ethics for a Whole World* constitutes a significant attempt to develop such an ethic (New York: Mariner, 2011).

35 Forlines, *Ethics*, 20.

36 Keith Loftin, ed., *God & Morality: Four Views* (Downers Grove: IVP Academic, 2012), 8.

37 For Christians (and Forlines specifically), the question is whether we can be righteous without God. The answer is no.

38 Like Forlines, O'Donovan is careful to observe that while one might connect their discussion on ethics and the gospel to one key movement in Christ's redemptive work (the resurrection, Christ's death, the incarnation), all of them are integral to ethical motivation (13).

39 Forlines, *Ethics*, 29-30.

40 Ibid, 30.

41 Ibid.; see also Forlines, *Quest*, 312-13.

42 Henri Blocher, "Sanctification by Faith?" in *Sanctification: Explorations in Theology and Practice*, ed. Kelly M. Kapic (Downers Grove: IVP Academic, 2014), 74.

43 Forlines, *Ethics*, 35.

44 Ibid., 129-44.

45 G. K. Chesterton, *Orthodoxy* (Mineola: Dover, 2004), 7.

46 Forlines, *Ethics*, 29.

47 Ibid., 27.

48 Stanley Hauerwas in Michael J. Quirk, "Stanley Hauerwas: An Interview," *Cross Currents*, Spring 2002, Vol. 52, No. 1; http://www.crosscurrents.org/Hauerwas-spring2002.htm; accessed May 25, 2015; Internet.

49 Ibid.

50 David Brooks, *The Road to Character* (New York: Random, 2015), 54.

51 Forlines, *Ethics*, 29.

52 Ibid., 9.

53 Ibid., 15.

54 Forlines, *Morals and Orthodoxy*; see also W. Jackson Watts, "In One Accord: Bridging the Divide Between Doctrine and Practice," *Integrity* 6 (Summer 2016): 53-79.

55 Forlines, *Ethics*, 80-81, 99-107.

56 Ibid., 112-13.

57 Ibid., 78-82.

58 Dennis P. Hollinger, *Choosing the Good: Christian Ethics in a Complex World* (Grand Rapids: Baker Academic, 2002), 13.

59 E.g., Arianna Huffington, *Thrive: The Third Metric to Redefining Success and Creating a Life of Well-Being, Wisdom, and Wonder* (New York: Harmony, 2014).

[60] Forlines, *Ethics*, 85.

[61] Ibid., 86.

[62] Ibid., 88.

[63] Ibid., 91.

[64] Ibid., 55.

[65] Ibid., 56.

[66] Ibid., 170-76.

[67] Murray, 13.

[68] Forlines uses the term "ecological" as opposed to "environmental."

[69] Forlines, *Ethics*, 57.

[70] Ibid., 58-59, 179-80.

[71] Many contemporary theological works on ecology also frame this relationship in terms of reconciliation. E.g., Fred Bahnsen and Norman Wirzba, *Making Peace with the Land: God's Call to Reconcile with Creation* (Downers Grove: IVP, 2012).

[72] Forlines, *Ethics*, 161-76.

[73] Forlines, *Quest*, 145.

[74] E.g., Alasdair McIntyre, *After Virtue*, 3rd ed. (Notre Dame: University of Notre Dame Press, 2007). This subject also has a significant presence in Stanley Hauerwas's work.

[75] In *Ethics*, Forlines gives a chapter to discussing when values conflict.

[76] Forlines, *Quest*, 73.

[77] Forlines, *Ethics*, 39.

[78] Ibid., 43.

[79] Ibid.

[80] Ibid.

[81] Andreas Köstenberger, *Excellence: The Character of God and the Pursuit of Scholarly Virtue* (Wheaton: Crossway, 2011), 33-34.

[82] Forlines, *Ethics*, 32.

[83] David F. Wells, *God in the Whirlwind: How the Holy-Love of God Reorients Our World* (Wheaton: Crossway, 2014), 85-86.

[84] Hollinger, 12.

[85] Cf. Tullian Tchividjian, *One Way Love: Inexhaustible Grace for an Exhausted World* (Colorado Springs: David C. Cook, 2012), 211-19; and Timothy Keller, *The Prodigal God: Recovering the Heart of Christian Faith* (New York: Riverhead, 2008). Keller's account of the two lost sons is very similar to Forlines's formulation of the two forms of legalism.

[86] H. Richard Niebuhr, *Christ and Culture* (New York: Harper & Row, 1951), 190. Sometimes this is referred to as "transformational" or "transformationalist."

[87] Contemporary evangelicals should note that this was broached long before the Council for Biblical Manhood and Womanhood was ever formed.

[88] This point is certainly not as developed in Forlines's work as in many contemporary publications, nor does the term "creation care" occur. However, I think his framework would easily accommodate much of the work being done in this area today. Cf. Mark Liederbach and Seth Bible, *True North: Christ, the Gospel, and Creation Care* (Nashville: B&H Academic, 2012). Another example more proximate to Forlines's generation would be Francis Schaeffer and Udo Middelmann, *Pollution and the Death of Man: The Christian View of Ecology* (Carol Stream: Tyndale, 1970).

[89] Such concerns can be found in D. A. Carson, *Christ and Culture Revisited* (Grand Rapids: Eerdmans, 2008).

[90] Forlines, *Ethics*, 182.

[91] Ibid.

[92] This three-fold form of excellence is fully developed in Köstenberger, *Excellence*.

[93] Brooks, 14.

CHAPTER NINE

CONFRONTING SECULARISM

Matthew Steven Bracey

In the past half-century, many voices have contributed to studies in secularism. In 1986, historian James Turner's *Without God, Without Creed* traced the history of modern belief and unbelief from the Reformation period onward. About ten years later, Kramnick and Moore published *The Godless Constitution* (1997), arguing the American founders intended to create a secular state with a strict separation of church and state. In 2004, Susan Jacoby drew similar conclusions as Kramnick and Moore in *Freethinkers: A History of American Secularism*. The so-called New Atheists have also emerged, giving voice to a polemical account of religion and secularism in American history.

Amidst these developments, philosopher Charles Taylor released his tome *A Secular Age* in 2007. So significant is this book that late sociologist Robert Bellah commented that it "recast[s] the entire debate about secularism,"[1] and referred to it as a "breakthrough book—one of the most important books to be written in [his] lifetime."[2] Taylor challenges simple subtraction theories of secularization, which hold that secularity arises in a culture when religion is subtracted, arguing instead that history and present realities are more layered than these theories allow for. Modern culture has not subtracted religion; it has exchanged one belief system for another.[3]

In 2009, Hunter Baker released *The End of Secularism*, positing that secularism is "a dead end."[4] Reminiscent of Richard John Neuhaus's *The Naked Public Square* (1984), Baker argues for an open public square, where participants convince rather than coerce—something modern secularism does not permit. More recently sociologist Peter Berger has rejoined the conversation with *The Many Altars of Modernity* (2014). His landmark *The Sacred Canopy* (1967) had advanced his secularization thesis that modernity leads to secularism, and predicted the secularization of the modern world. Later rejecting that theory, Berger has come to argue for a new paradigm, where modernity leads to pluralism, not necessarily to secularism. With such a diverse sampling of contributions—constitutional, historical, philosophical, and sociological—how does theologian F. Leroy Forlines contribute to this field of study?

Forlines's Contribution: An Overview

For well over a decade, Forlines has given his attention to a yet-to-be-published secularism manuscript, which presently comprises fourteen chapters and more than 150,000 words. In the manuscript secularism is the story of history, philosophy, theology, the church, morality, worldview, culture, society, universities, and law. As he interacts with these topics, he courageously stands in opposition to many of the prevailing moods driving secularism studies today.

In summary, Forlines traces the epistemological assumptions and adjustments throughout American history with specific reference to the development of secularism. He concludes that America was not founded on secularism, and that a balanced accommodationism, rather than a strict separationism, better fulfills the founders' intentions regarding the church-state relationship in the public square. The recent contributions of Taylor and Berger would serve generally to complement Forlines's case. Methodologically, Forlines engages the reader's "total personality,"[5] and critically, his analysis is careful, considerate, and calculated.

America's Founding and the Timeline of Secularism

In *The Godless Constitution*, Kramnick and Moore refer to "the intentionally secular base on which the Constitution was placed."[6] Frank Lambert suggests that the Constitution's "stated purposes were secular, political ends," and that it "established a secular state."[7] Jacoby opens her book by making similar claims.[8] Dawkins writes that America was "founded in secularism" and discusses "the secularism of its [America's] constitution."[9] Forlines challenges these positions by contending that America was not founded on secularism.

He begins by considering the actual movement of secularism. In a very literal sense he argues America could not have been founded on secularism because the movement had not yet begun. It began in the mid-nineteenth century with Englishman George Jacob Holyoake (1817-1906), who coined the term "secularism" in 1846. "The name of Secularism," wrote Holyoake, "was given to certain principles which had for their object human improvement by material means, regarding Science as the Providence of man, and justifying morality by considerations which pertain to this life alone."[10] Secularists, many of whom were atheists, understood secularism to be the absence of religion in society and law, and sought to build a movement for the advancement of human society in which religion had no part. This was different from the American founders' views of religion's role in society.

Yet if America was founded on secularism, Forlines queries, a curious question of chronology arises, since the founding occurred in the late 1780s.[11] The claim, then, that America is founded on secularism is technically, Forlines writes, "an anachronism."[12] Such claims have resulted in widespread confusion and misinformation about the founding. Even if we disregard the anachronism, secularist scholars have made an interpretive move concerning the intentions of the founders. To address this question, Forlines begins with their epistemic background.

The Founders' Epistemological Background: Bacon, Locke, and Newton

Forlines accounts both for the American populace generally, and Jefferson and Madison particularly, who were chief architects of the American church-state arrangement at the founding. By exploring the founders' epistemologies, Forlines avoids simply reviewing what they said, seeking rather to understand what they meant to avoid any hindsight bias: "We gain very little insight into thinkers of the past or present if we read their conclusions, but do not know the sources of data they accept and reject. The only truth a person can discover is that which is allowed by his epistemology."[13] Forlines illustrates his total personality methodology (see chapter one) not simply in reference to his readers, but to his subjects as well; people are more than their words. Specifically, he surveys Jefferson's "trinity of English heroes": Bacon, Locke, and Newton.[14] Their contributions to epistemology and knowledge were central to the founders' understanding of the world.

Francis Bacon (1561-1626) "puts the subject of epistemology on center stage," Forlines writes, for he fundamentally changed the way people acquired and interpreted knowledge.[15] Bacon emphasized an inductive method of logic, and an empirical, scientific approach to understanding. The philosophical, scientific, and the Christian worlds are indebted to Bacon.[16] John Locke (1632-1704) also contributed to the founders' epistemology, especially with reference to political philosophy. Locke advocated for natural law; life, liberty, and property; religious toleration; and the right to revolution. Finally, Forlines considers Isaac Newton (1642-1727), whose *Principia* (1687) represented "a major turning point in human knowledge" in the scientific revolution.[17] He also dispenses with the notion that the scientific revolution disproved Christianity: "To claim the major battle was between the Bible and science is a mistake."[18] To the contrary, Christianity was an "essential ingredient for the introduction of modern science."[19] The Copernican revolution was a "victory for science" and "Christian thought," since "all the players from Copernicus to Newton operated in a Christian worldview."[20]

Forlines argues in summary that Bacon, Locke, and Newton contributed greatly to the founding era by informing its epistemological assumptions about life, knowledge, and the world. With each figure Forlines shows that they were not secularists in any strict sense, not to mention that they predated secularism, as the term is commonly understood by many contemporary scholars, and thus they could not and did not provide the founders with a secularist paradigm for government.[21]

The Founding Era

Forlines then focuses on the founding era. He analyzes the general population as well as Madison and Jefferson, whom he terms "major players" for church-state relations.[22] Not only do their epistemological backgrounds preclude a secular founding, but their words do also.

General Populace

Scottish philosopher David Hume (1711-1776) had contributed toward an "epistemological skepticism"[23] among some in the eighteenth century, and increasingly into the nineteenth century. Some secularists have pointed to this development as possible evidence of a secularist founding, which Forlines describes, again, as anachronistic. Harvard law professor Noah Feldman also makes this point: "Her [Jacoby] approach—anachronistic, in my view—is to identify what I have called secularism as an outgrowth of earlier American religious skepticism, thus projecting secularism backward onto Thomas Paine, Jefferson, and others of the framing generation."[24] Even assuming that some skepticism existed on the fringes, Forlines explains that "atheism was almost non-existent at the time of our Founding Fathers."[25] The founding generation "operated within a Christian frame of reference."[26] "Almost everybody was a Protestant of some kind," writes Feldman.[27] Mark Noll describes America as "overwhelmingly Protestant" at this time.[28] And, excepting Joel Barlow, writes Turner, "America does not seem to have harbored a single individual before the nineteenth century who disbelieved in God."[29]

At the same time, Forlines is not suggesting that the founding generation was orthodox, or that they consistently applied Christian morality in their lives: "There was surely a gap in many people's lives between Christianity's ideals and people's lives."[30] Forlines's point, for which he has good support, is that "the moral ideals of Christianity were deeply embedded in the psyche of the culture,"[31] and an atheistic outlook did not shape the Constitution and First Amendment.[32]

Madison and Jefferson

James Madison (1751-1836), who emerges from this period, contributed significantly to the American church-state articulation. In 1784, Patrick Henry proposed A Bill Establishing a Provision for Teachers of the Christian Religion. In response, Madison issued his Memorial and Remonstrance (1785), advocating for religious freedom and liberty of conscience. Forlines refers to this as "one of the greatest moments in our history,"[33] and the Memorial as "the most important document in support of religious liberty in American history."[34] Madison's explication of religious freedom, Forlines explains, "rest[ed] on a theological foundation," [35] because he made reference to the Governor of the Universe, Universal Sovereign, Creator, and Supreme Lawgiver of the Universe.[36] Forlines holds that this has important implications for appreciating the founders' understanding of the First Amendment.

Thomas Jefferson (1743-1826) is also important for understanding American church-state relations. Jefferson authored the Declaration of Independence (1776) and the Virginia Statute for Religious Freedom (1786). While the Declaration does not make explicit reference to religious freedom, it holds, "We hold these truths to be self-evident, that all men are created equal, that they are endowed by their Creator with certain unalienable Rights, that among these are Life, Liberty and the pursuit of Happiness."[37] It also mentions the laws of nature, nature's God, the supreme Judge of the world, and divine providence.[38] For Jefferson the foundation for these liberties, one being religious freedom, is God. One year after Madison's Memorial, the Virginia General Assembly passed Jefferson's Virginia Statute. A "major influence in the First

Amendment's wording and adoption,"[39] the Virginia Statute begins, "Almighty God hath created the mind free."[40] Like Madison's Memorial, Forlines writes Jefferson's bill "rest[ed] on a theological foundation."[41] While Jefferson was not orthodox (likely a deist) Edwin Gaustad writes he "was the most self-consciously theological of all America's presidents."[42] Thus Forlines holds that neither Madison nor Jefferson were secularists, and certainly not by any strict definition.[43]

The Founding, the First Amendment, and Religious Freedom

Forlines points to the epistemological background and assumptions of the founding generation, Madison's Memorial and Jefferson's Virginia Statute, and the timeline of secularism, as evidence that America was not founded on secularism. If by secularism one means the absence of religion in society and law, which is how the mid-nineteenth century secularists understood it, then it simply does not fit. The founders could not and did not mean what modern secularists would have them to mean, an interpretation that scholars such as Forlines and Feldman refer to as anachronistic. On the other hand, Forlines is not saying America was founded as a Christian nation in any legal sense, even if it has been true as a description of America's people and culture in the past.[44] Instead, Forlines opts for a middle road.

The First Amendment reads: "Congress shall make no law respecting an establishment of religion, or prohibiting the free exercise thereof."[45] While the founders guarded against religious establishment, they never intended to forbid religion from public life. The First Amendment itself guarantees the people's right to exercise their religion, which includes public and civic involvement. This is what Jefferson and Madison themselves had done when they invoked God in formulating the very documents that serve as foundations for the First Amendment. "If the term 'religious liberty' is limited to what goes on in the privacy of a person's mind and conscience," Forlines explains, "it is a contradiction of religious liberty. There can be no law against what goes on in the privacy of his or her mind."[46] Therefore, Forlines shows that America is not founded on secularism.

Nevertheless, secularists argue to the contrary. Dawkins writes, "Whatever their [the Founding Fathers] individual religious views in their own time, the one thing they collectively were is *secularists*."[47] However, Forlines has shown this to be untrue, because "secularism was not available at that time."[48] Other secularists, pointing to America's separation of church and state, express bewilderment that religion has played as significant a role as it has for America and its people throughout its history.[49] In addition, these secularists assert that America's founders believed that secular government with a church-state separation would serve to protect the liberty of people to believe what they want.[50] Forlines explains that the separation of church and state does not establish a secular nation so much as it protects against the institutional establishment of any one religion or sect; guarding against establishment is not the same as establishing a secular government. The founders did not see secular government as the guarantor of liberty of conscience; they saw religious freedom, in contrast to establishment, as that guarantor. In summary, the institutional separation of church and state is not the separation of religion from public life, or morality from the public square; and it is not the establishment of a state founded on secularism.[51]

Finally, Forlines interprets First Amendment religious freedom as the right of all people to exercise their religious beliefs, whether Christian, secularist, atheist, or whomever. Forlines thus stands in the tradition of universal religious liberty articulated by his General Baptist forefather, Thomas Helwys, who said: "For men's religion to God is between God and themselves. The king will not answer for it. Neither may the king be judge between God and man. Let them be heretics, Turks, Jews, or whatsoever, it does not appertain to the earthly power to punish them in the least measure."[52]

Objection: Treaty of Tripoli

Throughout his project Forlines considers various objections to his thesis that America is not founded on secularism. One of these is the Treaty of Tripoli, which concerned American-Muslim relations. Secularists often point to article 11 to support their belief in America's secularist founding: "The

Government of the United States of America is not, in any sense, founded on the Christian religion."[53] For example, Lambert interprets this as "assur[ing] the world that the United States was a secular state."[54] How does Forlines deal with this objection?

First, government not being founded on the Christian religion does not mean that it is founded on secularism; it simply demonstrates disestablishment. "To say the United States did not have a Church-State union does not mean that it was a 'Secularist' nation," Forlines writes.[55] And even from a historical perspective, "John Adams and the Senate were playing a technicality game."[56] That is, the treaty and statement do not concern church-state relations but American-Muslim relations. Even *God Is Not Great* author Hitchens writes, "Those secularists like myself who like to cite this treaty must concede that its conciliatory language was part of America's attempt to come to terms with Barbary demands."[57] Michael Meyerson similarly concludes that this treaty "hardly resolves the question of the religious nature of the American government."[58]

Conclusions about the Founding Era

Secularism as such had not yet begun by the founding era; it is a mid-nineteenth century development. The general populace's epistemology functioned from a broadly Christian framework and structure. Madison's Memorial and Jefferson's Virginia Statute, which served as foundations for the First Amendment, explicitly invoked theological notions. America was therefore not founded on secularism or as a secularist nation. Forlines concludes with this assurance: "You may wonder if I am playing a technicality game with the word 'secularism.' Maybe the concept was around, but called by another name, you might suggest. I have considered this question, but after examining the evidence, have concluded that secularism was not around under a different name."[59]

Epistemological Developments Through American History

Forlines continues his study in secularism by analyzing the epistemological developments in American history and its relationship to secularism from the founding era to the present day. He gives each period its own chapter, tracing developments in culture, society, universities, and law.

Founding Until Civil War

During the period from the founding until the Civil War, Forlines holds that the influences of secularism and atheism were minimal at best. Holyoake pioneered the movement in the 1850s, but that was in England, and its influence took some time to reach American shores. This is not to suggest that people did not doubt, simply that most people were theists. True atheism was a rarity. "When Ralph Waldo Emerson actually met a real live atheist," writes Turner, "he could hardly contain his excitement at the unique chance to dissect the exotic specimen."[60]

Civil War Until World War I

However, transitions began to occur in the mid- to late-nineteenth century. In considering the history of secularism, Forlines distinguishes between "popular secularism" and "epistemological secularism." With popular secularism, several groups began calling for the separation of church and state in the 1870s. Francis Ellingwood Abbot founded a newspaper committed to this purpose, the *Index*; published "The Nine Demands of Liberalism"; and hoped for a constitutional amendment assuring church-state separation. These goals resulted in the formation of organizations like the National Liberal League and American Secular Union. Still popular secularism remained on the fringes, Forlines explains, and the United States still operated within a Christian framework.[61]

On the other hand, universities led the way toward epistemological secularism, which would have greater influence for American secularism. Academicians began restricting data to reason, observation, and experience, which Forlines refers to as "absolute rationalism" and "absolute empiricism."[62] He points to Immanuel Kant, who had divided reality between the noumenal and phenomenal worlds, as providing a way for university professors to maintain their religious and academic opinions, even if contradictory—what Julie Reuben refers to as the "separation of facts and values."[63] In addition, administrators began reforming university curricula from a classical, unified knowledge approach to a modern, specialized knowledge approach, which would inflict a "blow to the concept of a unified worldview," and lead to a "fragmentation of knowledge."[64]

Nevertheless, Forlines explains, these changes "did not immediately set in motion a move to abdicate the morals that had characterized the antebellum institutions of higher learning."[65] Julie Reuben writes that these reformers "continued to view piety and moral discipline as one of the aims of higher education."[66] In fact, "almost all state universities still held compulsory chapel services," according to George Marsden, and some "required Sunday church attendance as well" as late as the 1890s.[67] Still, this separation between facts and values could not last, as Francis Schaeffer detailed in *The God Who Is There* (1968). Absolute empiricism, which had "the greatest influence on American culture,"[68] would win the day, and lead ultimately to epistemological secularism and postmodernism.[69]

World War I Until 1960

The developments from the late nineteenth and early twentieth centuries came slowly to roost in the universities, the Court, and the culture itself. Forlines explains the "separation of facts and values became the undoing of the concern and understanding of morality that had shaped American culture from its beginning."[70] In this section readers will notice Forlines's total personality methodology as he mixes personal anecdote with professional scholarship, thus making use of a more classic, historiographical approach.

American sentiment was generally optimistic at the turn of the twentieth century. However, "when World War I failed to be the war that would end all wars," Forlines writes, "the optimism of modernism began to wane."[71] What followed were the Roaring Twenties and Great Depression.[72] Forlines explains that the twenties did not represent a new direction for knowledge and truth, but disobedience to the old direction. Even with their facts-values division, the universities still placed a high premium on morality, at least temporarily. While the general culture was not "perfect," it also considered Christian values important, even most non-Christians.[73] Moving into the 1940s, by "the end of World War II, many who were at the forefront of secular thought began to see that modernism as a worldview was a failure."[74] The war affected Americans greatly: "Everybody knew somebody who lost their lives in the War," Forlines recalls.[75] Of particular interest during this period with reference to America's founding, the Supreme Court released two holdings regarding public education: *Everson v. Board of Education* (1947) and *McCollum v. Board of Education* (1948). Forlines gives an entire chapter to each case, both contributing significantly to a strict separationist interpretation of the First Amendment, which "did not bode well" for an accommodationist approach.[76]

In *Everson*, Justice Hugo Black, author of the majority opinion, famously wrote, "The First Amendment has erected a wall between church and state. That wall must be kept high and impregnable. We could not approve the slightest breach."[77] By so stating, Black echoed a statement from a letter that Thomas Jefferson had written to the representatives of the Danbury Baptist Association in Connecticut in 1802, in which he interpreted the First Amendment's Establishment and Free Exercise Clauses as "building a wall of separation between Church and State."[78] Forlines convincingly argues that a separationist interpretation is incorrect: "It seems obvious to me that he [Jefferson] simply meant that there was not a union between the State and Church as was common in Europe."[79] In fact, Jefferson made statements subsequent to the Danbury letter that seriously challenge a separationist interpretation.

A year after *Everson*, *McCollum* further reinforced the Court's separationist trajectory: "For the First Amendment rests upon the premise that both religion and government can best work to achieve their lofty aims if each is left free from the other within its respective sphere."[80] But as Forlines has shown, the First Amendment guarded against the establishment of religion; it did not require strict separation. Forlines hopes to untangle what modern scholarship seems to have confused. From a practical standpoint, Justice Robert Jackson questioned whether strict separationism is even desirable or possible. In reference to the arts, for example, he wrote, "Music without sacred music, architecture minus the cathedral, or painting without the scriptural themes would be eccentric and incomplete, even from a secular point of view," and, "Certainly a course in English literature that omitted the Bible and other powerful uses of our mother tongue for religious ends would be pretty barren."[81] "The fact is," he continued, "that, for good or for ill, nearly everything in our culture worth transmitting, everything which gives meaning to life, is saturated with religious influences, derived from paganism, Judaism, Christianity—both Catholic and Protestant—and other faiths accepted by a large part of the world's peoples."[82] Although Jackson concurred with the holding, he critiqued it as "uniform" and "rigid," and would have allowed for "flexibility to meet local conditions."[83]

Justice Stanley Reed, who had voted with the *Everson* majority, emerged as the sole dissenting voice in *McCollum*: "Passing years, however, have brought about acceptance of a broader meaning, although never until today, I believe, has this Court widened its interpretation to any such degree as holding that recognition of the interest of our nation in religion . . . was equivalent to an establishment of religion."[84] In reference to Jefferson's Danbury letter, Reed wrote, "The difference between the generality of his [Jefferson] statements on the separation of church and state and the specificity of his conclusions on education are considerable. A rule of law should not be drawn from a figure of speech."[85] Nevertheless, Forlines explains, the *McCollum* majority, like *Everson*, "interpreted Jefferson to be on the side of a hard separation between church and state."[86] These holdings are vital for the modern understanding of church-state relations.

Moving into the 1950s, with the failures of modernism exposed, Forlines analyzes some popular developments that undermined traditional beliefs and morality. One such group was the Beat Generation, a group of authors and artists who tore down received tradition, and in its place erected drugs, eastern mysticism, and free sexual expression. While they anticipated the 1960s hippie movement, such groups did not represent the general populace in the 1950s. Even with the epistemological and legal developments, the culture still operated generally in a Christian framework. Forlines illustrates this through academic research and anecdotal evidence. The general populace were not "batting a thousand,"[87] but even those who lived like the devil generally still believed in God. As a personal example, he recalls only knowing of two people during his childhood who were believed to be atheists.[88] Though such remarks may come as "a surprise to most people to see how strong the influence of morals and ideals remained until the 1960s," Forlines emphasizes that his claims are not the result of a "faulty memory."[89] In fact, historians Rosenzweig and Thelen explain that eyewitness testimony usually makes for the most reliable history. "Historians," they write, "have long believed that participants make the best observers."[90]

Nevertheless, change was afoot. While "there were rumbling noises of change," Forlines explains, "no one had any thoughts about the fact that our culture was on the verge of a revolution."[91] "No one surveying the campus scene in 1959 could have predicted the 1960s," is how Helen Lefkowitz Horowitz states it.[92] What happened? In the words of cultural commentator Ken Myers, "What happened was The Sixties."[93]

1960s to the Present

While various movements prior to the 1960s had attempted to undermine the moral ideals of the Ten Commandments, both on popular and epistemological levels, they had not constituted a "mass movement."[94] Yet with the epistemological changes that had previously transpired, and the failure of modernity, a major "paradigm shift" occurred in the 1960s.[95] Forlines refers to this as "the beginning of an 'Epistemological Continental Divide.'"[96] "The lives of all Americans have been changed by it [The Sixties]," writes Myers, "whether or not they are aware that anything happened."[97] Bob Dylan simply says, "It was like a flying saucer landed."[98] This shift is none other than postmodernism finally finding large-scale expression. To help us think through what happened, Forlines proposes a distinction between "revolutionary postmodernism" and "philosophical postmodernism." Both, he explains, "fly the banner of Secularism."[99] By making such distinctions—whether between popular and epistemological secularism, revolutionary and philosophical postmodernism, or something else—Forlines shows his strengths, being careful not to conflate differing developments, or differing aspects of a movement.

Revolutionary postmodernism refers to the overthrow of modernism in the 1950s and the Student Revolution Movement in the 1960s and 70s,[100] what Myers refers to as the "twenty year decade" (1952-1973).[101] Forlines writes, "It is almost impossible for most people living in America today to grasp the devastation inflicted upon us by the takeover of Revolutionary Postmodernism"; echoing Myers, he continues, "I do not think that most people have a clue about what has happened."[102] And yet Forlines lived through it, serving as the Welch College Dean of Students during this period. While Welch was not as affected as other institutions, it was not unaffected. Forlines shares, "This book never would have been written had it not been for the experiences I had as a student dean."[103]

Whereas universities had taught qualities like aesthetics, excellence, etiquette, good taste, manners, propriety, and refinement, they became places that were not simply "unconcerned" with these things, but altogether "disdainful" toward them.[104] "There was more concern about excellence and civility in the darkest days of the Great Depression than existed in the prosperous times of the 1960s," Forlines writes; "sad to say that this is still the case."[105] What resulted in the Student Revolution Movement, which "hit full force" around 1965,[106] was "rioting, demonstrations, and physical destruction on university campuses."[107] And though universities had functioned *in loco parentis*, they increasingly abandoned this role and became centers for the sexual revolution. "The sexual revolution," Horowitz explains, "destroyed the older dating codes that had persisted since the 1920s."[108] Forlines describes "the abandonment of the standards of sexual morality" as "one of the saddest chapters in American history."[109] However, the revolution could not be sustained. "The 1970s followed the thesis of the 1960s as its antithesis. Students were not only quiet," Horowitz explains, "they were unnaturally quiet. Young high school radicals arrived on campus ready for action, to find little there. No one was interested in protest."[110]

In addition to revolutionary postmodernism, Forlines discusses philosophical postmodernism, which refers to an academic movement that aims "to give academic respectability to Postmodernism."[111]Modernism's optimism had slowly given way to postmodernism's nihilism. Forlines points to Friedrich Nietzsche (1844-1900) as having "blazed the trail for Postmodernism" with his death of culture, art, music, philosophy, morals, ideals, and truth.[112] While developments were occurring throughout the twentieth century leading up to this point, Forlines points to Jean-François Lyotard in particular. Lyotard introduced the term "postmodernism" to philosophy in *The Postmodern Condition* (1979), in which he posited the end of "grand narratives."[113] "The postmodern Worldview," Forlines explains, "is that there is no Worldview. You might say that their Worldview is an 'Anti-Worldview-Worldview.' Rather than a Worldview, they speak of a multiplicity of 'Narratives'"[114] (see chapter two). Forlines points to Francis Schaeffer as "a man ahead of his times,"[115] who anticipated these developments in *Escape From Reason* (1968). Forlines describes that period between 1960 and 1990 as "a period of transition" in which there was an "ongoing battle" between modernism and postmodernism; in many areas, postmodernism has won, at least to this point in history.[116] By 1987, Allan Bloom introduced *The Closing of the American Mind* by saying, "There is one thing a professor can be absolutely certain of: almost every student entering the university believes, or says he believes, that truth is relative."[117]

Prospects

Christians today live with the consequence of these developments. Forlines writes that this is "the most confusing time in United States history," and that these are "truly strange times."[118] The marriage of American secularism and postmodernism would produce a society in which religion and the concept of "true truth" are altogether stamped out.[119] "It is the whole society that is now engaged in this massive experiment to do what no other major civilization has done," David F. Wells explains, "to rebuild itself deliberately and self-consciously without religious foundations. And the bottom line of this endeavor is that truth in any absolute sense is gone. Truth, like life, is fractured."[120] How do we respond in such a society?

Church and Culture

Forlines expresses deep concern for the church's integrity and influence (see chapter ten), and about the impact these historical developments have had and are having on the church. In addition, "Christians today seem to be in a state of confusion about how and whether we should confront what is happening both in and outside the churches in this regard."[121] Within the church he says, we must maintain biblical integrity and avoid cheap-easy believism. Beyond the church, we must "get involved and confront the evils from postmodernity's influence on our communities, universities, nation, and world."[122] Forlines writes that modernism was "haunted" by the "presence of 'something' that could not be explained in terms of materialism or naturalism,"[123] an image Taylor invokes in A Secular Age. The same is true with postmodernism. "[The] knowledge of God and knowledge of basic morality," Forlines writes, "are written into our very being."[124] He has also articulated this general idea as the inescapable questions of life.[125] The point is that the church must understand the times in which it lives, and go forth into the secular, postmodern age, remembering that those captured in its grip are persons with the knowledge of God written on their hearts, who God created and for whom Christ died.

Throughout his work, Forlines shows how the epistemological changes and development of secularism have affected our culture, morals, and ideals. This is not without consequence. "I hope that we can learn how these morals and ideals became imbedded into the American psyche," he writes.[126] "When we can make sense of how this has happened, then maybe we can contribute to a reawakening of these morals and ideals in the psyche of our present culture. This will require a transformation of our culture."[127] Forlines proposes we do this by engaging persons' total personalities as thinking, feeling, acting beings: the church must offer more than "correct information,"[128] but must also "make a connection and evoke a personal response in a postmodern culture."[129]

Balanced Accommodationism

"My guiding interest in this study has always been to gain an understanding of the founding fathers' real intent concerning the relationship between the State and the Church."[130] I believe Forlines has achieved this goal. He has shown that America was not strictly founded on secularism, and that a strict separationist interpretation of the First Amendment is more recent. In contrast, Forlines proposes a balanced accommodationism, such that persons of all beliefs—Christian, secularist, agnostic, atheist, or whomever—can receive a fair hearing for their ideas in the public square and university. Unequivocally, he respects the right of others to the free exercise of religion and the freedom of speech. "But don't push me off the platform," he says.[131] He hopes his work will "be introduced to the Supreme Court,"[132] "lead to some changes in the way the First Amendment has been interpreted,"[133] and "reshape the way that state owned educational institutions deal with God and morality."[134] Whether Forlines's hopes come true may depend on which justices sit on the Court and their jurisprudential hermeneutic. Whatever the case, his work in this area is original and compelling.

Conclusion

With Forlines a study in American secularism is a journey through the epistemological assumptions and developments from the 1500s onward. It touches on science, philosophy, jurisprudence, government, culture, morals, the university, and more. Forlines's project will fit well in studies on secularism, especially for Christians working in these areas, as he offers insight, synthesis, and wisdom. In addition, it will prompt the church to faithfulness in belief and behavior, challenge her to understand the times in which she lives, equip her with important tools for facing this world, and direct her toward the transformation of culture and the change of society. For all of this and more, we can be thankful to F. Leroy Forlines.

[1] Robert Neely Bellah, "A Secular Age: Secularism of a new kind;" *The Immanent Frame: Secularism, religion, and the public square*, October 19, 2007; http://blogs.ssrc.org/tif/2007/10/19/secularism-of-a-new-kind/; accessed November 14, 2015; Internet. See also James K. A. Smith, *How (Not) to Be Secular: Reading Charles Taylor* (Grand Rapids: Eerdmans, 2014).

[2] Bellah.

[3] Cf. Martin E. Marty, *The Protestant Voice in American Pluralism* (Athens: The University of Georgia Press, 2004).

[4] Hunter Baker, *The End of Secularism* (Wheaton: Crossway, 2009), 14.

[5] F. Leroy Forlines, *The Quest for Truth: Answering Life's Inescapable Questions* (Nashville: Randall House, 2001), xiv-xvi; hereafter *Quest*.

[6] Isaac Kramnick and Laurence Moore, *The Godless Constitution: The Case Against Religious Correctness* (New York: W. W. Norton & Company, 1997), 14.

[7] Frank Lambert, *The Founding Fathers and the Place of Religion in America* (Princeton: Princeton University Press, 2003), 2.

[8] Susan Jacoby, *Freethinkers: A History of American Secularism* (New York: Metropolitan Books, Henry Holt and Company, 2004), 1-2.

[9] Richard Dawkins, *The God Delusion* (Boston: Houghton Mifflin, 2006), 40.

[10] George Jacob Holyoake, *The Origin and Nature of Secularism; Showing That Where Freethought Commonly Ends Secularism Begins* (London: Watts & Co., 1896), 50.

[11] Some secularists are aware of this problem; cf. Jacoby, 2.

[12] F. Leroy Forlines, "Theism and Western Culture," 1. All citations to Forlines, excepting *Quest*, refer to chapters in his yet-to-be-published secularism project.

[13] Forlines, *Quest*, 9.

[14] Edwin S. Gaustad, *Sworn on the Altar of God: A Religious Biography of Thomas Jefferson* (Grand Rapids: Eerdmans, 1996), 20.

[15] Forlines, "Thomas Jefferson and the Timeline of Secularism," 20.

[16] Ibid., 22.

[17] Ibid., 23.

[18] Forlines, "Theism and Western Culture," 9.

[19] Ibid., 11.

[20] Ibid., 9.

[21] Forlines, "Thomas Jefferson and the Timeline of Secularism," 23-24; "Theism and Western Culture," 14; cf. Forlines, *Quest*, 9-11.

[22] Forlines, "Understanding Thomas Jefferson's View on Religious Freedom," 2.

[23] Forlines, "From Francis Bacon to the Opening of the University of Virginia," 9.

[24] Noah Feldman, *Divided by God: America's Church-State Problem—And What We Should Do About It* (New York: Farrar, Straus and Giroux, 2005), 272, n. 11.

[25] Forlines, "Understanding Thomas Jefferson's View on Religious Freedom," 7.

[26] Ibid.

[27] Feldman, 51.

[28] Mark A. Noll, *A History of Christianity in the United States and Canada* (Grand Rapids: Eerdmans, 1992), 145.

[29] James Turner, *Without God, Without Creed* (Baltimore: The Johns Hopkins University Press, 1986), 44.

[30] Forlines, "Understanding Thomas Jefferson's View on Religious Freedom," 8.

[31] Ibid.

[32] Forlines, "Theism and Western Culture," 21; cf. Turner, xi-xii.

[33] Forlines, "In Search of Thomas Jefferson's View of the Relationship Between the Church and the State: *Everson v. Board of Education*," 22; hereafter "*Everson*."

[34] Forlines, "Understanding Thomas Jefferson's View on Religious Freedom," 3.

[35] Ibid., 2.

[36] James Madison, *Religious Freedom: Memorial and Remonstrance* (Boston: Lincoln & Edmands, 1819), 1, 5-6, 12.

[37] Declaration of Independence; http://www.archives.gov/exhibits/charters/declaration_transcript.html; accessed November 21, 2015; Internet.

[38] Ibid.

[39] Forlines, "Understanding Thomas Jefferson's View on Religious Freedom," 3.

[40] Thomas Jefferson, Virginia Statute for Religious Freedom, in Lenni Brenner, ed., *Jefferson & Madison on Separation of Church and State: Writings on Religion and Secularism* (Fort Lee: Barricade, 2004), 48.

[41] Forlines, "Understanding Thomas Jefferson's View on Religious Freedom," 12.

[42] Edwin S. Gaustad, *Sworn on the Altar of God: A Religious Biography of Thomas Jefferson* (Grand Rapids: Eerdmans, 1996), xiii.

[43] See Forlines, "Understanding Thomas Jefferson's View on Religious Freedom," 12.

[44] Forlines, "Summing It Up: A Case for an Accommodationist Relationship Between the State and the Church," 21; hereafter "Summing It Up."

[45] United States Constitution Amendment I.

[46] Forlines, "*Everson*," 20.

[47] Dawkins, 39.

[48] Forlines, "Understanding Thomas Jefferson's View on Religious Freedom," 4.

[49] See for example Jacoby, 3-4.

[50] Ibid.

[51] Even some Christian historians have failed to make these careful distinctions that Forlines makes; cf. Noll, 144ff. In addition, I appreciate J. Matthew Pinson who has helped me think through how to articulate these points.

[52] Thomas Helwys, *A Short Declaration of the Mystery of Iniquity* (1612), in Joe Early, Jr., ed., *The Life and Writings of Thomas Helwys* (Macon: Mercer University Press, 2009), 209. The General Baptists in seventeenth century England were the forefathers of Free Will Baptists in America.

[53] See Forlines, "Thomas Jefferson and the Timeline of Secularism," 3.

[54] Lambert, 11; see also Dawkins, 39-40.

[55] Forlines, "Thomas Jefferson and the Timeline of Secularism," 3-4.

[56] Ibid., 3.

[57] Christopher Hitchens, "Jefferson Versus the Muslim Pirates," *City Journal*, Spring 2007; http://www.city-journal.org/html/17_2_urbanities-thomas_jefferson.html; accessed November 22, 2015; Internet.

[58] Michael I. Meyerson, *Endowed by Our Creator: The Birth of Religious Freedom in America* (New Haven: Yale University Press, 2012), 202. A point of interest: Dawkins holds that the language of article 11 "caused no dissent at the time, among either politicians or public" (*The God Delusion*, 40). That is false. Secretary of War James McHenry did. See Meyerson, 201; and George Gibbs, *Memoirs of the Federal Administrations of George Washington and John Adams, Edited from the Papers of Oliver Wolcott, Secretary of the Treasury*, vol. 2 (New York: William Van Norden, 1846), 421.

[59] Forlines, "Thomas Jefferson and the Timeline of Secularism," 15. Although the term "secular" existed prior to 1846, as well as several derivations, including "secular clergy," "secularist," "secularity," and "secularization," none of these uses had the same meaning as secularism; they did not connote godlessness or an irreligious society.

[60] Turner, 102.

[61] Forlines, "From the End of the Civil War Until the End of World War I," 4.

[62] Ibid., 25ff.

[63] Julie A. Reuben, *The Making of the Modern University: Intellectual Transformation and the Marginalization of Morality* (Chicago: The University of Chicago Press, 1996), 4.

[64] Forlines, "From the End of the Civil War Until the End of World War I," 31.

[65] Forlines, "Looking to the Future: The Influence of Epistemology on Worldview and Lifeview Development," 3; hereafter "Looking to the Future."

[66] Reuben, 12.

[67] George M. Marsden, *The Soul of the American University: From Protestant Establishment to Established Nonbelief* (New York: Oxford University Press, 1994), 3.

[68] Forlines, "Summing It Up" 20.

[69] Forlines, "From the End of the Civil War Until the End of World War I," 44.

[70] Forlines, "From the End of World War I Until 1960," 2.

[71] Forlines, Quest, 15.

[72] Forlines, "From the End of World War I Until 1960," 3, 13.

[73] Ibid., 4.

[74] Forlines, Quest, 15.

[75] Forlines, "Looking to the Future," 5.

[76] Forlines, "Everson," 3.

[77] Everson v. Board of Ed. of Ewing, 330 U.S. 18 (1947).

[78] Thomas Jefferson to the Danbury Baptist Association, January 1, 1802, in Brenner, 163; see also Ralph Ketcham, ed., Selected Writings of James Madison (Indianapolis: Hackett, 2006), 305-06.

[79] Forlines, "Summing It Up," 11.

[80] McCollum v. Board of Education, 333 U.S. 212 (1948).

[81] McCollum, 333 U.S. at 236 (Jackson, R., concurring).

[82] Id.

[83] Id. at 237.

[84] Id. at 244 (Reed, S., dissenting).

[85] Id. at 247.

[86] Forlines, "Theism and Western Culture," 25.

[87] Forlines, "From the End of World War I Until 1960," 4; cf. Charles Taylor, A Secular Age (Cambridge: The Belknap Press of Harvard University Press, 2007), 745.

[88] Forlines, "Looking to the Future," 5.

[89] Forlines, "From the End of World War I Until 1960," 35.

[90] Roy Rosenzweig and David Thelen, The Presence of the Past: Popular Uses of History in American Life (New York: Columbia University Press, 1998), 38.

[91] Forlines, "Looking to the Future," 6.

[92] Helen Lefkowitz Horowitz, Campus Life: Undergraduate Cultures from the End of the Eighteenth Century to the Present (Chicago: The University of Chicago Press, 1987), 220.

[93] Kenneth A. Myers, All God's Children and Blue Suede Shoes: Christians and Popular Culture (Wheaton: Crossway, 1989), 104.

[94] Forlines, "From the 1960s Until the Twenty-first Century," 1.

[95] Forlines, "From the End of World War I Until 1960," 12; see also Forlines, Quest, 419-65.

[96] Forlines, "From Francis Bacon to the Opening of the University of Virginia," 1.

[97] Myers, 104.

[98] Cited in James Miller, *"Democracy Is in the Streets": From Port Huron to the Siege of Chicago* (Cambridge: Harvard University Press, 1987), 315.

[99] Forlines, "From the 1960s Until the Twenty-first Century," 33.

[100] Ibid., 26, 32.

[101] Myers, 103-06.

[102] Forlines, "From the 1960s Until the Twenty-first Century," 31.

[103] Ibid., 3.

[104] Ibid., 27; cf. Forlines, *Quest*, 232-33.

[105] Ibid., 28.

[106] Ibid., 2.

[107] Ibid., 11.

[108] Horowitz, 228.

[109] Forlines, "From the 1960s Until the Twenty-first Century," 38.

[110] Horowitz, 245.

[111] Forlines, "From the 1960s Until the Twenty-first Century," 32.

[112] Forlines, "Looking to the Future," 22.

[113] See Jean-François Lyotard, *The Postmodern Condition: A Report on Knowledge*, trans. Geoff Bennington and Brian Massumi (Minneapolis: University of Minnesota Press, 1979), 37-41.

[114] Forlines, "Looking to the Future," 17.

[115] Forlines, "From the 1960s Until the Twenty-first Century," 25.

[116] Ibid., 31; Forlines, *Quest*, 64.

[117] Allan Bloom, *The Closing of the American Mind: How Higher Education Has Failed Democracy and Impoverished the Souls of Today's Students* (New York: Simon & Schuster, 1987), 25.

[118] Forlines, "Looking to the Future," 14, 26.

[119] Francis A. Schaeffer, *Escape from Reason*, in *Francis A. Schaeffer Trilogy* (Wheaton: Crossway, 1990), 218.

[120] David F. Wells, *No Place for Truth Or Whatever Happened to Evangelical Theology?* (Grand Rapids: Eerdmans, 1993), 80.

[121] Forlines, "From the End of World War I Until 1960," 5.

[122] Forlines, "Looking to the Future," 10.

[123] Forlines, "From the 1960s Until the Twenty-first Century," 32.

[124] Forlines, *Quest*, 33.

[125] Ibid., 1.

[126] Forlines, "From the End of World War I Until 1960s," 5.

[127] Ibid.

[128] Forlines, "Looking to the Future," 9.

[129] Ibid.

[130] Forlines, "Summing It Up," 3.

[131] Forlines, "Looking to the Future," 27.

[132] Forlines, "From Francis Bacon to the Opening of the University of Virginia," 19.

[133] Forlines, "Understanding Thomas Jefferson's View on Religious Freedom," 60.

[134] Forlines, "From the 1960s Until the Twenty-first Century," 36.

CHAPTER TEN

COMMUNICATING THE GOSPEL: THE CHURCH'S MISSION AND MINISTRY

Christopher Talbot

In 2006 at a Desiring God conference Tim Keller gave a lecture entitled "The Supremacy of Christ and the Gospel in a Postmodern World."[1] In it he made a considerable claim: America has largely been inoculated to the gospel. For many Americans, he argued, we have had just enough of the gospel not to believe in it, and instead have become immune to it. Much of the United States is no longer Christ-centered, but as Flannery O'Connor stated, "Christ-haunted."[2] Keller proceeded to explain that the general population had the basic "worldview furniture" of the Christian mind only a few generations ago. Whereas they may not have believed in the gospel, they at least had the basic framework to understand it. However, in our postmodern context this is no longer true. People lack the basic, intellectual furniture of "God, truth, or sin, or of peculiar Christian ethical practices."[3]

Keller was not the first to discuss how to communicate the gospel in such a changing environment. D. Martyn Lloyd-Jones, C. S. Lewis, Francis Schaeffer, Leslie Newbigin, and David F. Wells are among the many who have addressed the difficulties of modern ministry. They were not alone though. Free Will

Baptist theologian F. Leroy Forlines was and is among these ranks. Forlines, while in a smaller realm of influence, wrote perceptively on the intersection of gospel ministry and postmodern secularization (see chapter nine). One could even argue that this intersection is the nucleus for much of Forlines's thought. He writes, "We have the same Bible and the same gospel we have always had. But it takes a different preparation to rescue those who are being held captive by Postmodernism than was the case when modernism was the predominant secular influence."[4] Like others, Forlines keenly sensed the increasing clash of worldviews.

Today, many argue that the American church is either on the decline, or is simply waiting for the ecclesiastical surgeon to pronounce her dead.[5] Books, blogs, conferences, and ministry leaders posit ways in which the American church can adjust and better minister to this generation. The answers range from extreme pragmatism to complete cultural withdrawal. In this chapter, I will strive to articulate a Forlinesean understanding of how the church should minister in an increasingly pluralistic, secular society. Forlines's conclusions are helpful in an increasingly post-Christian era, because they are thoroughly rooted in biblical and historical foundations. Additionally, his perspective points the way forward on how we might fulfill the church's mission in the twenty-first century.

Forming a Gospel Perspective

Ecclesiology (the doctrine of the church) and gospel proclamation are two sides of the same theological coin. To consider one is to ponder the other. Mark Dever writes, "[Ecclesiology] is the most visible part of Christian theology, and it is vitally connected with every other part. A distorted church usually coincides with a distorted gospel."[6] Forlines would agree with Dever that the church and gospel are fundamentally linked; however, Forlines begins with gospel proclamation. In a Forlinesean framework, getting the gospel right properly orients the church.[7] Forlines is certainly not silent on how the church should minister and proclaim the good news in today's times. He presents five components that are vitally important to the church's ministry in the world: (1) gospel worldview, (2) Christian epistemology, (3) holistic/unabridged Christianity, (4) biblical anthropology, and (5) costly discipleship.[8] Forlines suggests that this framework will equip us minister to those "held captive by Postmodernism."[9]

Gospel Worldview

To proclaim transcendent good news in a morally ambiguous age requires the best thinking from every Christian (Rom. 12:2; 1 Cor. 2:16; 2 Cor. 10:5). This not only includes a robust biblical understanding of God and revelation, but also a thoughtful understanding of our cultural moment. As John Stott's famous book articulates, Christians minister "between two worlds."[10] Our thinking on ecclesiology and the gospel must bridge the gap between the spheres of Scripture and culture. As Graham Johnston writes, "God's truth transcends culture; for God's truth to penetrate today's culture we have only to find ways to bridge the biblical and the postmodern worlds—to speak meaningfully to people where they are."[11] For Forlines, this comes by understanding the paradigm shift that has occurred in our culture from modernism to postmodernism, and the difficulty it has added to communicating the Christian message.[12] In this, our ministry effectiveness depends critically on our understanding of our present-day cultural milieu.

We might pause to wonder why the church should be so concerned with the philosophy *du jour*: postmodernism. If we faithfully follow and understand historical biblical truth, why should we worry about the prevalent worldview of our time (cf. Matt. 16:3)? The answer is simple: Never before has America's leading worldview and the Church's historic worldview been at such odds.[13] Philosophies and worldviews change and develop, and yet major scale paradigm shifts, like what we see in postmodernism, are rare.[14] Foundationally, Christianity and postmodernism understand truth in diametrically opposed ways.[15] Therefore, if we fail to understand postmodernism and its wide reaching effects, not least of which concerns truth and epistemology, we will fail to minister adequately to the surrounding society. If we truly are between two worlds, we are charged with bridging a monumental chasm. Forlines notes the staunch contrast, "Christianity is truth based. Postmodernism denies the existence of ultimate truth. Christianity is rational. It believes in the law of non-contradiction. Postmodernism is irrational. It is not bothered by the law of non-contradiction. Christianity believes in absolute moral truth. Postmodernism believes in moral relativism."[16] Nevertheless, the difficulty is larger than a clash of understanding. Postmodernism, more than a list of propositions, has come to pervade much of society and thus exerts widespread influence.[17]

Still, the problem of postmodernism should lead us deeper into the gospel (Rom. 11:33; Phil. 1:9; Eph. 3:18). When we realize how these worldviews conflict, we are spurred to understand how the gospel of Jesus Christ affects our understanding for all of life. Knowing how false worldviews challenge the Christian notion of truth, we should seek to understand the Truth, or as one author articulates "true truth."[18] This is what Forlines argues for: "Christian thought embraces the whole of reality. It is a worldview. There is no truth that stands outside the Christian worldview."[19] To understand the gospel and its implications for all of life is to understand this world in its true reality.

Echoing Abraham Kuyper and Francis Schaeffer, Forlines argues for a complete biblical worldview for the church and ministry. That means church members peer through the "biblical-gospel lens" to understand culture's different spheres: politics, work, literature, art, and so forth. To have anything less would fall short of articulating the breadth of Christian faith (Col. 3:17). Forlines would affirm that this method of gospel ministry is inherently apologetic. To defend and proclaim a holistic gospel rightly, we must understand how it speaks authoritatively to every sphere of life.[20] To understand the gospel's implications for life is preparation to defend the gospel (1 Pet. 3:15). As Forlines remarks, "Christianity is comprehensive. It touches all the bases. It speaks to the whole of life and thought."[21]

When arguing for a biblical worldview, we can fail to place the gospel at the center. Wells states, "Gospel truth . . . is about the triune God acting in this world redemptively, in the course of time, in the fabric of history, and bringing all of this to its climax in Christ."[22] It is more than obedience, association, and even our Christian life. God's action within reality reorients all of life. In this worldview, the gospel is the epicenter of a world completely turned upside-down. Therefore, church leaders must articulate and demonstrate for their people how the gospel affects all of life. They must show, in Christ's gospel, a new and better understanding of marriage (Eph. 5:22-33), work (2 Thess. 3:6-12), ministry (2 Cor. 5:20), children (Mark 10:13-16), and much more. Carl F. H. Henry explained, "Historically, Christianity embraced a life view as well as a world view; it was socially as well as philosophically pertinent."[23]

Christian Epistemology

A gospel worldview must begin with an understanding of epistemology. As we proclaim the good news to our congregations, we must formulate how we know it to be true (cf. John 18:38). Certainly, we concur with Augustine's thoughts that all truth man discovers ultimately belongs to God.[24] Therefore, we have to communicate the authority by which we speak. In a Forlinesean framework, the Bible, a living book, pours forth an indispensible well of life-giving truth (Heb. 4:12).[25] As we urge congregants to know God fully (cf. Matt. 7:7), we must also instruct them in how God's divine revelation has the answers to their inescapable questions of life. Only through divine revelation can we fully know any truth.

Because divine revelation is rooted in a biblical worldview, it stands at odds with postmodern epistemology. Forlines posits that when these worldviews collide epistemologically, the ultimate question concerns authority, rather than purpose: "It is a question of 'Who's to say?' rather than 'Why?'"[26] "Who?" rather than "why?" presupposes a lack of authority. When we ask "why?" we assume a reasonable answer. When we ask "who?" we assume the authority is flawed.[27] Even so, we should be sympathetic to these questions. Honest questions deserve honest answers. This resonates with what Martyn Lloyd-Jones described in his classic *Preaching and Preachers*: the decline of biblical preaching is primarily connected with "the loss of belief in the authority of Scriptures, and a diminution in the belief of the Truth."[28] We must fight this loss of belief and orient people to the morality found within divine authority.[29] Forlines notes,

"To believe that something is right and wrong depends on a standard of Truth that declares some things to be right and some things to be wrong."[30] Thus we come full circle to the question of which authority is reliable as we minister. Historical Christian faith asserts that our reliable authority is the special revelation we have received from God. As Forlines explains,

> The Christian view of a personal God who creates and speaks furnishes an adequate basis for knowledge of God and His will. The Bible, as God's Word, is adequate as a source of knowledge about God, morals, the identity of man, human need, redemption, etc. Such a view takes away our lostness. It identifies man's needs and tells how to deal with them.[31]

This understanding of purpose and revelation stands up against today's prevailing thoughts. The gospel offers us answers to the questions we cannot escape. Conversely, in postmodernism, we have neither purpose, nor meaning, nor shared human experience, nor answers—save what we conjure up ourselves.

If the church will fulfill its mission, it must demonstrate where it stands biblically and how it arrived there (Matt. 24:14, 28: 18-20; Mark 16:15; 1 Pet. 2:9-10). Thus, we must educate ourselves on how to confront those who have been deeply influenced by relative truth. In Forlines's words, we must "do this in such a way that it gives hope. We must help those who have been deluded into thinking that there is no meaning and purpose for life with the only message that gives people meaning and purpose for life. That is what we have been commissioned by Jesus Christ to do."[32]

Unabridged Christianity

Unabridged Christianity is a faith free from doctrinal minimalism. While a holistic Christianity intrinsically overlaps with a gospel worldview, it is the foundation on which a worldview is built (cf. Eph. 4:21). Christians must seek to have the most full-orbed understanding of the Christian faith as possible. A holistic, gospel worldview and an unabridged Christianity must walk hand-in-hand, working in tandem. Yet we live in a time where Christianity is often reduced to a sound byte. Forlines notes, "The gospel has been restricted by many to that minimum truth that is essential to be grasped for conversion. There can be no doubt that this is the gospel. The question, however, is: Is this all [of] the gospel?"[33]

Fred Sanders in *The Deep Things of God* argues that modern-day evangelicalism is broadly weak in its theology. This claim is hardly surprising. However, what is intriguing is Sanders's analysis. He states that American evangelical theology has been reduced to four basic doctrines, or better yet, four words: Bible, cross, conversion, and heaven. Essentially if we believe these four statements, then we have evangelicalism's basic elements: (1) the Bible is God's Word, (2) Jesus died on the cross, (3) you have to be saved, and (4) you will go to heaven when you die.[34] While these are certainly fundamental doctrines, the truth about God and us is not limited to these doctrines.[35] Likewise, Forlines states, "This abridged or truncated approach to Christianity has been one of the greatest contributing factors to a weakening of Christianity."[36] In many ways, the church have defaulted to a lowest-common-denominator theology in its teaching and preaching.

Forlines maintains that doctrinal minimalism will ultimately hurt and hinder the church (cf. Heb. 5:11-14). Commenting on the Fundamentalist-Modernist controversy,[37] Forlines insightfully explains,

> This combination of an emphasis on the fundamentals of the faith and the new zeal for making it clear that we are saved by faith alone created an interest in the *minimalism*: the minimum that is required for salvation. . . . The emphasis on the fundamentals of the faith tended to draw attention away from other areas of thought. The emphasis on the minimum that is required for evangelism caused many to label doctrines that were not a part of this minimum as being non-essential. . . . A seemingly deliberate abridgement of Christianity began to develop.[38]

Forlines's account of the dangers of minimalism expresses the same concerns as many had before. For example, "The Christian movement at its inception was not just a way of life in the modern sense," J. Gresham Machen wrote, "but a way of life founded upon a message. It was based, not upon mere feeling, not upon a mere program of work, but upon an account of facts. In other words it was based upon doctrine."[39] The Christian faith, historically and biblically, is founded upon doctrine (Tit. 1:9, 2:1; 1 Tim. 6:3; 2 Tim. 4:3). From the New Testament period and throughout church history, Christianity has been rooted in and directed by scriptural teaching (1 Cor. 1:17-29; 1 Tim. 3:16, 4:13; 2 Tim. 2:15, 4:2-4). Thus abridging Christian teaching is like laying an ax to its roots. Forlines argues that the failure to preach and teach the whole counsel of God and all of its implications for every sphere of life leads to a superficial understanding of what it means to be a Christian.[40] Although faith like this is founded on doctrine, and begins in the head, it does not leave the heart and hands untouched. To have an unabridged Christianity is to show how the truth of God—that is, theology—is for all of life and for the whole person.

Forlines postulates that a full-orbed Christianity bears the fruit of a fully experienced humanity. He likens unabridged Christianity to playing the piano. When we seek to know God's whole counsel, we will avoid a bull-in-the-China-shop approach to playing our instrument.[41] We can move past the elementary songs of our youth into more marvelous sonatas. Knowing all the scriptural and theological notes allows us to make the best use of the doctrinal piano. Instead of hammering on a few notes we know well, we can play the sweet music of God's grace as we ascend and descend the spiritual scales. While we always come back to those first notes (e.g., Bible, cross, conversion, and heaven), we can now play more complicated melodies; we can explore the implications that these basic doctrines have for others.

In light of the danger of doctrinal minimalism, we should remember that every minister is fundamentally a theologian. Albert Mohler states, "The pastoral calling is inherently theological. Given the fact that the pastor is to be the teacher of the Word of God and the teacher of the gospel, it cannot be otherwise. The idea of the pastorate as a non-theological office is inconceivable in light of the New Testament."[42] Charles Ryrie stated the same in his *Basic Theology* twenty years earlier. Everyone is a theologian, he argues, the issue being whether one is a sloppy or informed theologian.[43] The question, then, becomes, "How do we bring our theology to bear on the gospel and church?" Theology should be allowed to inform our ecclesiology and evangelism. Biblical terms must not be redefined from how they have been understood through church history because these changes have theological implications. Forlines remarks, "The problem that plagues us is: How do we avoid leaving the impression that salvation can be a superficial experience if faith is the only condition for salvation? . . . We do not safeguard ourselves from superficial Christianity by the way we define faith."[44] Biblically-informed faith is not (and should not be) complicated, but that should not lead to a watered-down Christianity. As Marva Dawn has said, we can "reach out without dumbing down."[45] In the simplest way, the pastor-theologian should communicate God's whole counsel, and yet strive to articulate it in a way both the mature believer and spiritual infant can understand (1 Pet. 2:1-3). However, a costly discipleship is needed. Before we turn our attention to discipleship in this postmodern era, we will first dive deeper into the specific theological area of anthropology.

Biblical Anthropology

A Forlinesean framework of ministry emphasizes biblical anthropology, which is both helpful and insightful. One could summarize Forlines's thought in the following mantra: whole theology for the whole church for the whole person. Forlines writes, "This responsibility of helping people must be shared by the whole church. . . . Working together we can send out the message to a hurting world that through Christ and Christianity there are answers to their problems."[46] This is built on and consists of a robust theology of the gospel that coheres with our anthropology. Biblical anthropology entails a consistent understanding of human identity.[47] Forlines argues that we understand humanity thoroughly as designed human beings (Ps. 139:13-16; Jer. 1:5; Job 33:4; Eph.

2:10), but also fallen, sinful human beings (John 8:23; Rom. 3:23, 5:12-14).[48] In addition, biblical anthropology mandates an applied anthropology. As believers we bring our redemption to bear as we minister to others. As the new humanity, we minister fully to people in their humanness.

First, we must focus on understanding our anthropology and ask what being human truly means. Ultimately this lies in what Forlines calls the "total personality." In this framework, to be fully human is to be someone designed and created to think, feel, and act (Gen. 1:27; 3:6). Forlines would disagree that ministry should work from an anthropology that sees humans as solely thinking things.[49] The gospel engages and transforms each dimension of the person: mind, heart, and will. According to Forlines, God did not create us as mindless mechanisms. He created us to think, feel, and act. Therefore, the ministry should reflect this. As Forlines says, "We are not mere instruments being used by God. We are persons being transformed in our basic, inner nature into the likeness of Jesus Christ."[50]

Though designed and created in the image of God, each person is now fallen due to original sin. This is why Henry states, "Only an anthropology and a soteriology that insists upon man's sinful lostness and the ability of God to restore the responsive sinner is the adequate key."[51] Forlines writes elsewhere,

> The mind, heart, and will are involved in saving faith. With the mind, the truth about sin, Jesus Christ, and salvation is comprehended objectively. The content of the truth is grasped and understood. With the heart, what is grasped objectively by the mind is grasped subjectively. The truth about sin becomes real. Conviction takes place. The truth about Jesus Christ and salvation becomes real. The reality of the truth conditions the heart for action to follow. The emotions are definitely involved in the experience of faith and the total Christian experience. We feel what we believe. We are not emotional blanks. Emotions are a part of the human personality by creation. Emotions need to be based on truth and

disciplined by truth, but emotions must not be downgraded. With the will there is the commitment of the personality to Jesus Christ. We receive Jesus Christ. The will can act only where there is a prepared mind and heart. The will, out of the prepared mind and heart, sets in action the response of faith. What is objectively perceived by the mind is subjectively felt by the heart, and subjectively appropriated by the will.[52]

For Forlines, no part of the human person is left untouched when we both communicate and receive the gospel message. This is the pastor's role in all he does: to appeal to a person's heart, mind, and will in such a way that his people will want to worship and obey God (Matt. 22:35-40).[53]

Forlines argues that much of this ministry is found in what he refers to as the inescapable questions of life. These include, but are not limited to: Is there a God? If so, how can I know Him? How can I know what is right and wrong? Is there life after death? If so, how can I get ready for it?[54] Forlines notes that people may receive the wrong answers, but they never ask the wrong questions. As Christians, and specifically as pastors, we must articulate biblically based answers to these fundamental questions. Forlines emphasizes that human beings are designed beings: "[Truth] is designed to minister to his needs. Every human being is designed for truth. We are not a blank tablet upon which we can choose what we want to be written and be happy with any choice we might make. Our needs have been designed in us by God. They are innate."[55]

Understanding human identity is not enough, though. We must also look at how this anthropology is applied. Forlines states we must minister to people in their pain. This can take various forms, applying to the categories just mentioned. We minister to people as they hurt cognitively, emotionally, and physically—all while focusing on their biggest need: sin. Forlines writes, "When people find an answer for their hurts, many of their intellectual problems with unbelief will either vanish or diminish."[56] Thus deed ministry (helping hurts) should ultimately point to and find its fulfillment in word ministry (gospel proclamation). Emphasizing this very thing, Forlines states we should have compassion for people's pain and problems, while never losing sight of their eternal context (Matt. 9:36). This means that our ministries should also be characterized by discipleship.

Costly Discipleship

The final component of a Forlinesean framework for Christian ministry is an unavoidable outcome of each preceding component.[57] As we communicate the gospel, all of our thinking, feeling, and acting should manifest itself in a costly discipleship reminiscent of Dietrich Bonhoeffer. As Bonhoeffer asserts, "Christianity without discipleship is always Christianity without Christ."[58] If our evangelism efforts and local church ministry do not bring the believer into a life of discipleship, we have failed to fully lead them to Christ—truly, we have only given them cheap-easy believism. Bonhoeffer notes, "Cheap grace is the deadly enemy of our church. We are fighting to-day [sic] for costly grace."[59] In many ways this is precisely what Forlines argues as he points us to the price of discipleship in the Gospel of Luke (e.g., 14:26-33). We simply cannot ignore these words if we want to make a difference for God in our times.[60] To not communicate the cost of discipleship is to fail to articulate an unabridged Christianity.[61]

In this discussion of discipleship we see some of Forlines's most explicit commentary concerning ministry methodology. He connects cheap grace closely to doctrinal minimalism. He argues against the consumeristic, selective religious culture we have developed in the United States. In a rare exacting tone, Forlines questions, "How dare we challenge popular and dynamic senior pastors who communicate a minimalist gospel? This is a gospel which calls us to receive Jesus as our personal Savior so that God can begin to fill our lives with the things we *really* need—purpose, success, happiness, health, and eternal life as a bonus for the hereafter."[62] Strikingly, this "preaching" seems too similar to what sociologist Christian Smith calls "Moralistic Therapeutic Deism."[63] This "deism" is not biblical Christianity, but consists of five main tenets:

(1) A God exists who created and orders the world and watches over human life on earth.

(2) God wants people to be good, nice, and fair to each other, as taught in
the Bible and by most world religions.

(3) The central goal of life is to be happy and to feel good about one-self.

(4) God does not need to be particularly involved in one's life except
when he is needed to resolve a problem.

(5) Good people go to heaven when they die.[64]

Some of these affirmations parallel Christianity, but they do not represent
biblical Christianity. Moreover, this articulation of faith is intensely man-cen-
tered—almost explicitly stating that God exists solely for the purpose of man's
happiness and comfort. This sounds consistent with Bonhoeffer's definition
of cheap grace: "the preaching of forgiveness without requiring repentance,
baptism without church discipline."[65] Yet we do not preach moralistic therapeutic deism, but a Christian life that is costly.

Costly discipleship always proves itself in a transformed life. Forlines
writes, "The free salvation that forgives our sins and changes our destiny also
changes our lives. Those whose lives are not changed have not received the
forgiveness of sins."[66] Faith and works are inseparable in a Christian life (Jas.
2:18). Unfortunately this is where much of our preaching and teaching falters.
Forlines notes, "[Cheap-easy believism] arises when faulty reasoning is applied
to the idea of salvation by faith apart from works."[67] The new believer's life
has been utterly transformed, and the new ground is cultivable soil.[68] To be a
Christian and believe in the gospel is to be transformed by the word and person of Christ. We are boldly to proclaim this message. "In communicating the
Christian message," Forlines writes, "we are in the business of rescuing people
from the damning effects of sin in the next life and the detrimental effects of
sin in this life."[69] We are cosmic messengers of reconciliation (2 Cor. 5).

The balance always needed in discussing discipleship is to ensure we do
not add anything to the gospel's requirements. "We do not need to make a
distinction between being saved and being a disciple," Forlines explains.[70] "It

is assumed in the gospels that a saved person is a disciple. The only question is with regard to the quality of his discipleship."[71] Authentic discipleship is characterized by willful obedience and personal holiness.[72] Forlines himself quotes Bonhoeffer, sharing much of his sensibilities on this topic.[73] Bonhoeffer writes in his classic, "The only man who has the right to say that he is justified by grace alone is the man who has left all to follow Christ."[74] Forlines summarizes this discipleship well: "As the Bible plainly teaches, it is certainly not true that those who have experienced the new birth and have become new creatures have habits that are no different from those of the world about them."[75]

Moving Forward

Forlines has given us an extraordinary gift by articulating how we should communicate the precious gospel in contemporary culture. These five components in gospel ministry can aid us in rescuing people from the eternal effects of sin. Yet we should also consider how we could move further down the path that Forlines has brought us and build on the sturdy foundation he has laid for us. Two applications are especially relevant in contemporary ministry. First, since the church ministers and communicates with words, we must consider ministry in an increasingly image-driven, digital age. Second, we must examine how we might continue to articulate and exemplify a theology of preaching for the church.

Media and the Messengers

Because Forlines has laid a superb foundation for a ministry aimed toward God's glory through gospel proclamation, we are able to build upon it, rather than over it. One area in need of further development concerning proclamation and communication is media ecology. Although Forlines does not explore this explicitly, it is an important area for reflection. Because we live in a new media frontier, we minister to people deeply shaped by technological media of various kinds. This forces us to exercise discernment about how we minister in a media-driven age.

Our technological society is molded and ordered by the scenes we see on our electronic screens. We live in a time dominated by what Richard Weaver called the "great stereopticon": the television. That is not to say that all we see on a television, computer, tablet, or smartphone is inherently bad (or good). It simply means that our culture is being changed by how it processes information.[76] Regarding digital media, we must engage in what Kevin Vanhoozer calls "cultural hermeneutics."[77] We must equip ourselves with the exegetical tools necessary to understand the spirit of the age and go in reverse of what John Stott has argued for—taking the biblical message to contemporary times. We should rather see how our contemporary times are positively or negatively affecting our understanding and embodiment of biblical truth. If we love our neighbors, as Christ has commanded, we must then do our best to understand both them and the cultural trends within which they live. Too often, as Vanhoozer writes, culture is too familiar, "so close to us—our social 'skin,' as it were—that we have a hard time stepping back and examining [it] at a distance."[78]

For all of electronic technology's many benefits, its inherent sensibilities tend to make it easier to jettison the past, and press us more toward what is new, innovative, and on the cutting edge. As Weaver wrote, "Technology emancipates not only from memory but also from faith."[79] As we utilize various technologies within the church's ministry (electronic or not), we must consider how they affect our content. Concerns over technology should be more than just taste and style, or even history or tradition; they must be rooted in a careful theological conviction and judgment, less they remain stylistic preferences.[80] Moreover, if our ministry ethos is connected to the God Who has revealed Himself to us—one Who spoke the cosmos into existence and has communicated Himself to us—then we should be thoughtful about current and future mediums of communication. Simply, Christianity is founded and sustained through communication. We are messengers of reconciliation (2 Cor. 5). Therefore, we must be thoughtful on how we communicate in our technological age.

The Power of Preaching

God has also given us the tool of preaching for the benefit of His people. We must possess a robust theology of preaching in order to fortify the church. Often the focus on communication in ministry is quarantined to simple technique. While important, it is but one aspect of an ever-important topic. After all, Lloyd-Jones defined preaching as "theology coming through a man who is on fire."[81] Communication in ministry must fuse the best of our thinking with the best of our practice—orchestrating our head, heart, and hands together.

In light of Forlines's discussion of postmodernism, how much more important is this topic in a time in which pragmatism is king? We often hear skeptics and congregants alike bemoan the current state of pulpit preaching. This leads some like T. David Gordon to ask, "So if the church is not effectual in convincing, converting, and comforting sinners, is it because preaching will not accomplish this, or because the preaching is poorly done?"[82] At its essence, it is not so much a matter of efficiency, but of theological practice. Therefore, in our preaching and teaching, the question is not one of whether our services are contemporary or traditional, but one of authority. By Whose authority does the minister preach? Ultimately he must be God's servant, empowered by God's Spirit, proclaiming God's truth, from God's Word, to God's people, for God's kingdom. Biblical preaching leaves no room for man-centeredness. We must preach the redemptive revelation as revealed in Jesus Christ.[83] When our God, through His revealed Word and Spirit has affected us in thought, emotions, and will, our preaching will be renewed. Thus, as we think more deeply on this topic, we must shine a light on current and future ministerial trends to see how they may be understood in the kingdom work.

Still, as we think about ministry's challenges and burdens, we can easily become discouraged. Yet we can find hope within the pages of Scripture. In Ezekiel 37 God commanded Ezekiel to speak to a valley of dry bones. He faithfully followed the LORD's command, and as he did so he saw the transformation God's Word had on those bones. Flesh began to come upon them, and life entered into them. In many ways this is a parable for our own preaching.

As we preach to the spiritually dead and lifeless, we have the privilege of watching God's Word enter into them and bring life, and life more abundantly. We must realize, as Jonathan Leeman states, "God's Word, working through God's Spirit, is God's primary instrument for growing God's Church. In fact, God's Word is the most powerful force in the universe."[84] Only through the proclaiming, sharing, and living of God's Word can we accomplish anything for the kingdom of Christ. Only through the proclamation of God's Word, applied by God's Spirit can the church grow and flourish. As the Father, Spirit, and Son were at work within the creation of the universe, as the Word is declared, they are at work within the creation and transformation of each believer.

As we minister in this culture and think further toward a theology of preaching and ecclesiology, we can fall back upon this Forlinesean framework. We have been given the self-revealed truth of God through His Scriptures on which we can develop a worldview that orbits the gospel and a complete Christianity. Furthermore, as we embody these elements in our practice, we will see them speak deeply to the individual person, as humans made in the image of God. This all culminates in a Christian life that takes Christ's commands and truths seriously and lives fervently under Christ's Lordship.

Conclusion

I recently asked Leroy Forlines, "Have you ever thought about writing a book or chapter on ecclesiology?" He answered with a grin, "I've thought about *not* writing a book or chapter on ecclesiology."[85] While Forlines has written extensively on a wide array of theological topics, he has encouraged us here to develop and define a Reformed Arminian ecclesiology for the next generation. While focusing on this daunting task, we should be thankful for the thoughtful gift he has given us in intentionally paving the way onward.

Forlines writes in one essay, "I feel that in some way I owe an apology to the young people of this generation for not having done a better job in my contribution to preparing the way. We cannot lay all the blame on this generation. Those of us who went before have failed them."[86] I was startled at this comment when I consider all of the wonderful preparation he has given us as we charge forward in transforming our ministries into outposts for Christ's kingdom. While Forlines may second-guess his contributions, he gives us a foundation that serves as a nucleus of any good ecclesiology: the message.

What then is the way forward for Free Will Baptists specifically, and evangelicalism broadly? There are difficult days ahead for churches in America who hold fast to God's Word. Kevin DeYoung argues,

> You've heard it said that Christianity in America is a mile wide and an inch deep. Well, it's more like a half a mile wide now. I'm convinced that if Christianity is to be a mile wide again in America, it will first have to find a way to be a mile deep. Shallow Christianity will not last in the coming generation, and it will not grow. Cultural Christianity is fading. The church in the twenty-first century must go big on truth or go home.[87]

We no longer live in a nation that deeply shares our Christian ethos. But we do not have to panic or withdraw. In many ways the way forward is backwards. As we think about the future, we must go back to the gospel. We have a blessed, transcendent hope that is not altered by our culture's problems. As Forlines says, "The wonderful thing is that though all of us have sinned and [are] worthy of eternal death, God has intervened in to human history and is offering to all who have sinned a new hope of a glorious eternal future with God."[88] He writes elsewhere,

> Our challenge is great. We must take our responsibility seriously. Every human being is made in the image of God. . . . For that one who is away from God, there is an emptiness that only God can fill. . . . There is something within that longs for a right relationship with God. It is our responsibility under God to learn how, with the help of God, to reach these

people and when we do reach them to given them the whole counsel of God.[89]

Wells may have put it best: "The key to the future is not...capitulation. . . . It is courage."[90] Faithfulness to biblical Christianity in doctrine and practice—for the church's mission, ministry, worship, and witness—is the answer for the church today and tomorrow.

---

[1] Timothy J. Keller, "The Gospel and the Supremacy of Christ in a Postmodern World," in John Piper and Justin Taylor, eds., *The Supremacy of Christ in a Postmodern World* (Wheaton: Crossway, 2007).

[2] Flannery O'Connor, *Mystery and Manners: Occasional Prose* (New York: Farrar, Straus and Giroux, 1969), 44. O'Connor wrote, "I think it is safe to say that while the [American] South is hardly Christ-centered, it is most certainly Christ-haunted."

[3] Keller, 105. The list of prophetic, cultural commentators about this cultural shift is innumerable. Whereas a litany of pastor/scholars have articulated the importance of contextualing the gospel message for this new philosophical era, a host of media ecologists (among others) have similarly foretold the difficulty of simple communication in the coming years.

[4] F. Leroy Forlines, *The Quest for Truth: Answering Life's Inescapable Questions* (Nashville: Randall House, 2001), 432; hereafter, *Quest*.

[5] "America's Changing Religious Landscape: Christians Decline Sharply as Share of Population; Unaffiliated and Other Faiths Continue to Grow," *Pew Research Center: Religion and Public Life*, May 12, 2015; http://www.pewforum.org/2015/05/12/americas-changing-religious-landscape/; accessed May 21, 2015; Internet. Generally, the denominations that have seen a relatively drastic decrease in attendance are primarily mainline Protestant, whereas evangelical churches have largely maintained their numbers.

[6] Mark Dever, "The Doctrine of the Church," ed. Daniel Akin, *A Theology for the Church*, rev. ed., (Nashville: B&H Academic, 2014), 603.

[7] One could argue that Paul took this approach with the Galatians. Breaking from his regular epistolary introduction, Galatians 1:6-10 focuses on the gospel's content first, rather than the ecclesiological manifestations in the church at Galatia.

[8] These are my terms, used to articulate consistent themes in Forlines's work.

[9] Forlines, *Quest*, 432.

[10] As John Stott rightly notes, preaching in its very essence is more than just exposition, but is inherently communicating a "God-given message to living people who

need to hear it" (John Stott, *Between Two Worlds: The Art of Preaching in the Twentieth Century* [Grand Rapids: Eerdmans, 1982], 137).

[11] Graham Johnston, *Preaching to a Postmodern World: A Guide to Reaching Twenty-First Century Listeners*, (Grand Rapids: Baker, 2001), 10.

[12] Forlines, *Quest*, 426.

[13] F. Leroy Forlines, "Are We Preaching the Gospel?" (paper presented at The Commission for Theological Integrity's Free Will Baptist Theological Symposium, Hillsdale Free Will Baptist College, Moore, Oklahoma, October 2009), 112.

[14] Leroy Forlines, "Dealing with the Influence of Postmodernism" (paper presented at Theological Seminar at the National Association of Free Will Baptists, Tulsa, Oklahoma, 1998), 6.

[15] See Diogenes Allen, *Christian Belief in a Postmodern World: The Full Wealth of Conviction* (Louisville: Westminster/John Knox Press, 1989); Leslie Newbigin, *The Gospel in a Pluralist Society* (Grand Rapids: Eerdmans, 1989); and D. A. Carson, *The Gagging of God: Christianity Confronts Pluralism* (Grand Rapids: Zondervan, 1996).

[16] Forlines, "Dealing with the Influence of Postmodernism," 4.

[17] Forlines, "Are We Preaching the Gospel?", 112.

[18] Francis A. Schaeffer, *Escape from Reason*, in *Francis A. Schaeffer Trilogy* (Wheaton: Crossway, 1990), 218.

[19] Forlines, *Quest*, 447.

[20] While a gospel worldview speaks authoritatively to every sphere of life, it does not speak exhaustively. We can learn about a variety of things (e.g., farming, music, and work) via God's common grace.

[21] F. Leroy Forlines, "A Plea for Unabridged Christianity," *Integrity: A Journal of Christian Thought* 2 (Summer 2003), 102.

[22] David F. Wells, *The Courage to Be Protestant: Truth-lovers, Marketers, and Emergents in the Postmodern World* (Grand Rapids: Eerdmans, 2008), 52.

[23] Carl F. H. Henry, *The Uneasy Conscience of Modern Fundamentalism* (Grand Rapids: Eerdmans, 1947), 18.

[24] "A person who is a good and true Christian should realize that truth belongs to his Lord, wherever it is found" (Augustine, *On Christian Doctrine*, trans. R. P. H. Green [Oxford: Oxford University Press, 1997], 72).

[25] Forlines, "Are We Preaching the Gospel?" 126.

[26] Ibid., 108.

[27] Ibid.

[28] Martyn Lloyd-Jones, *Preaching and Preachers* (Grand Rapids: Zondervan, 2011), 20.

[29] Forlines writes, "There is authority that goes with preaching because it is a message from God. It is dealing with the gospel and the indisputable truths of Christianity. To believe Christianity true is to believe that which is preaching, in the New Testa-

ment age of the word, to be true." Leroy Forlines, "The Pastor and His People," TH 302 Systematic Theology 2, 7.

[30] Forlines, "Are We Preaching the Gospel?" 109.

[31] Leroy Forlines, "Christian Thought in Life" (unpublished manuscript, 1987), 6.

[32] Forlines, "Dealing with the Influence of Postmodernism," 6-7.

[33] F. Leroy Forlines, Cheap-Easy Believism (Nashville: Commission for Theological Liberalism, National Association of Free Will Baptists, 1975), 10.

[34] For more on the dilution of American Evangelicalism, see Carl Trueman, The Real Scandal of the Evangelical Mind (Chicago: Moody, 2011).

[35] Fred Sanders, The Deep Things of God: How the Trinity Changes Everything (Wheaton: Crossway, 2010), 15.

[36] Forlines, "A Plea for Unabridged Christianity," 91; italics removed from original.

[37] By "fundamentalist," I mean those who subscribe to the fundamentals (e.g., inspiration of Scripture, the Virgin Birth, Christ's deity and atonement, bodily resurrection and return, etc.), and not to what has become the modern-day nomenclature of the term.

[38] Forlines, "Are We Preaching the Gospel?" 124-25.

[39] J. Gresham Machen, Christianity and Liberalism (Grand Rapids: Eerdmans, 1946), 21.

[40] Forlines, Cheap-Easy Believism, 11.

[41] Forlines, "A Plea for Unabridged Christianity," 102.

[42] R. Albert Mohler, Jr., He Is Not Silent: Preaching in a Postmodern World (Chicago: Moody, 2008), 106.

[43] Charles C. Ryrie, Basic Theology: A Popular Systematic Guide to Understanding Biblical Truth (Wheaton: Victor, 1988), 9.

[44] F. Leroy Forlines, Classical Arminianism: A Theology of Salvation, ed. J. Matthew Pinson (Nashville: Randall House, 2011), 255.

[45] Marva J. Dawn, Reaching Out Without Dumbing Down: A Theology of Worship for This Urgent Time (Grand Rapids: Eerdmans, 1995).

[46] Leroy Forlines, "Understanding Yourself and Others: A Biblical, Theological, and Practical Approach to Personality" (unpublished manuscript, 1994), 3.

[47] James K. A. Smith, Desiring the Kingdom: Worship, Worldview, and Cultural Formation (Grand Rapids: Baker Academic, 2009), 32.

[48] Forlines, Quest, 431.

[49] See Smith, Desiring the Kingdom, 26-32, Smith argues that people are not so much "thinking things" as much as they are "worshipping things." This is a helpful perspective, but fails, I believe, in moving toward a total personality of the human person.

[50] Leroy Forlines, "Conformity to the Personality of Christ: The Extent," *Free Will Baptist Convention Sermons: 1935-2010* (Antioch: Executive Office of the National Association of Free Will Baptists, 2011), 137.

[51] Henry, 15.

[52] Forlines, *Classical Arminianism*, 257.

[53] Forlines, "The Pastor and His People," 6.

[54] Forlines, *Quest*, 1.

[55] Ibid.

[56] Ibid.

[57] See Robert E. Picirilli, *Discipleship: The Expression of Saving Faith* (Nashville: Randall House, 2013).

[58] Dietrich Bonhoeffer, *The Cost of Discipleship* (New York: Simon & Schuster; reprint: Touchstone, 1995), 59.

[59] Ibid., 43.

[60] Forlines, *Quest*, 426.

[61] Ibid.

[62] Forlines, "Are We Preaching the Gospel?" 133; italics added.

[63] Christian Smith, "On 'Moralistic Therapeutic Deism' as U. S. Teenagers' Actual, Tacit, De Facto Religious Faith," Princeton Theological Seminary; https://www.ptsem.edu/uploadedFiles/School_of_Christian_Vocation_and_Mission/Institute_for_Youth_Ministry/Princeton_Lectures/Smith-Moralistic.pdf; accessed June 10, 2015; Internet.

[64] Ibid.

[65] Bonhoeffer, 44.

[66] Forlines, *Cheap-Easy Believism*, 4; italics removed from original.

[67] Ibid., 1.

[68] F. Leroy Forlines, *Biblical Ethics: Ethics for Happier Living* (Nashville: Randall House, 1973), 35.

[69] Forlines, *Quest*, 433.

[70] Ibid., 426. While the culture-at-large seems to move toward buzzwords such as "authenticity," emphasizing the sincerity of the Christian life over his or her actual obedience, Forlines argues we should double-down, as it were, on preaching biblical commands and holiness. Both Jerry Bridges, *The Pursuit of Holiness* (Colorado Springs: NavPress, 1978), and Kevin DeYoung, *The Hole in our Holiness: Filling the Gap between Gospel Passion and the Pursuit of Godliness* (Wheaton: Crossway, 2012), affirm this line of thought.

[71] Forlines, *Quest*, 426.

[72] Forlines, *Biblical Ethics*, 33.

[73] Forlines, "Are We Preaching the Gospel?" 133.

[74] Bonhoeffer, 51.

[75] Forlines, "A Plea for Unabridged Christianity," 96.

[76] See Nicholas Carr, *The Shallows: What the Internet is Doing to Our Brains* (New York: W. W. Norton, 2010); Neil Postman, *Amusing Ourselves to Death* (New York: Penguin, 1985); Richard Weaver, *Ideas Have Consequences* (Chicago: The University of Chicago Press, 1948); T. David Gordon, *Why Johnny Can't Preach: The Media Have Shaped the Messengers* (Phillipsburg: P&R, 2009); Kenneth A. Myers, *All God's Children and Blue Suede Shoes* (Wheaton: Crossway, 1989); and Marva J. Dawn, *Is It a Lost Cause? Having the Heart of God for the Church's Children* (Grand Rapids: Eerdmans, 1997), especially chapters 10-11.

[77] Kevin J. Vanhoozer, Charles A. Anderson, Michael J. Sleasman, eds., *Everyday Theology: How to Read Cultural Texts and Interpret Trends* (Grand Rapids: Baker Academic, 2007).

[78] Ibid., 17.

[79] Weaver, 101.

[80] Warren Cole Smith, *A Lover's Quarrel with the Evangelical Church* (Colorado Springs: Authentic, 2008), 168-69.

[81] Lloyd-Jones, 97

[82] Gordon, 32.

[83] Forlines, *Classical Arminianism*, 255.

[84] Jonathan Leeman, *Reverberation: How God's Word Brings Light, Freedom, and Action to His People* (Chicago: Moody, 2011), 19.

[85] Conversation with F. Leroy Forlines on May 5, 2015 at Welch College.

[86] Forlines, "A Plea for Unabridged Christianity," 98.

[87] Kevin DeYoung, ed., *Don't Call It a Comeback: The Old Faith for a New Day* (Wheaton: Crossway, 2011), 29.

[88] Forlines, "Are We Preaching the Gospel?" 139.

[89] Forlines, *Quest*, 465.

[90] Wells, 21.

CHAPTER ELEVEN

UNDERSTANDING AND HELPING PEOPLE

Edward E. Moody, Jr.

A Helper Is Born

Throughout his life, F. Leroy Forlines has been on a quest to understand and help people. His journey led him to become a student at Welch College, where he heard guest speakers and others give testimony which seemed to indicate they were much happier than he was. Usually they described being saved and following God and then seeing others saved. Others described victorious living, saying things like, "Trust, don't try." This did not work for Forlines. He wondered why his experience was different.[1] Later as a pastor, and still later as Welch College's Dean of Students for seventeen years, Forlines would minister to many kinds of people. He observed that many sought God's help and may have even responded to numerous altar calls. Despite their efforts, though, they did not seem to find the help they so desperately sought from God. Although they may have poured their hearts out to Him, their problems remained or returned after a brief period.[2]

Most people know others like this. Unfortunately, church members have sometimes distanced themselves from people with complicated problems after trying to help them with routine efforts and simple answers. Too often people with complex problems have been ignored or abandoned. Conversely, many Christians feel inadequate and ineffective as helpers when simple answers do not seem to work for those they tried to help. Forlines saw too many people as sheep without a shepherd. He concluded that Christians have a responsibility to help people find the answers to face life's harsh realities. This is what it means for Christians to love their neighbors as themselves.[3] Forlines does not believe in giving simple answers to people's complex problems. But he also refuses to give up on helping such people. He has often noted that he never spoke to a person about his or her problems without believing there was an answer for them: "I know that answers may not be easy but I believe they exist, and by God's help they can be found and experienced."[4] Forlines acknowledges that some have more difficulty finding answers than others, but nonetheless there are answers. He has thus developed an approach to help people who are walking away from Christianity, no longer considering it as the source for answers.[5]

Forlines served as Dean of Students in the turbulent sixties and seventies. Though this was a difficult time to find answers, he did. As the culture around him increasingly became antagonistic to the Christian worldview, Forlines articulated biblical answers about human nature, self-image, and sexuality. He understood the problems that people face, especially the many youth who follow the "route of sin" (drugs, alcohol, crime, sexual immorality), as well as the church's need to help them.[6] What arose might be called "Forlines's Doctrine of Humanity," which is a biblical, theological, and practical approach to answering the inescapable questions of life. His wisdom is needed now more than ever.

The Correct Diagnosis

Forlines has spent countless hours counseling others. That said, he has received little formal training in it. In fact, his training consisted of only two, two-credit hour courses he took in 1958 and 1959. These courses were primarily reading courses, and he has indicated the only thing he really learned from them was that people with problems spend considerable time thinking about themselves.[7] These courses were not the beginning of his thoughts on self-image though; that had already been shaped by Scripture and by his time with people.

Forlines has frequently described and discussed what he terms the inescapable questions of life: "Is there a God? If so, what is He like? How can I know Him? Who am I? Where am I? How can I tell right from wrong? Is there life after death? What should I and what can I do about guilt?"[8] According to Forlines one cannot have peace without answering these questions. For example, Forlines's early writings show he was concerned about the impact that teaching evolution would have on the culture. He noted that "naturalism finds itself completely inadequate" in answering life's inescapable questions, and "bankrupt where the need is greatest."[9] As early as Biblical Systematics in the seventies, Forlines devoted an entire chapter to man's creation.[10] In order to help people, Forlines argues that we must properly identify and understand them; this is something evolution cannot do. Proper identification of anything is critical. A motor requires proper identification to select the right kind of fuel. The same can be said for plants—what can be fatal to one plant may not be harmful to another. Consider how dangerous the improper identification of animals can be (e.g., mistaking a coral snake for a milk snake). Likewise, he concludes there is danger in an inaccurate description of human nature and purpose. To help people truly we must study what God designed them to be.[11]

This task is challenging since the secularist views man as part of the animal world in which there is no transcendent morality and no moral absolutes. The existentialist concludes that life has no meaning apart from that which each individual determines. To them, one person's opinion is as good as another's. On the other hand, Christianity views man as created by and for God. Since God creates man, he is accountable to Him and must look to Him for answers. Christianity teaches that truth is eternal and universal, and that every human is designed for it. "In the basic sense," Forlines writes, "every human being has the same needs programmed into his being."[12] If real truth exists, one opinion cannot be as good as another. Only one of these worldviews has the truth that can set people free; rather than prescribing a remedy, non-Christian worldviews contribute to the problem because they result in false diagnoses of man's problems.[13]

The Image of God

Instead of secularism, existentialism, and other false options, understanding and helping people requires a worldview that answers people's questions and addresses their needs. Forlines begins by focusing on what is meant by man being created in God's image. We must examine what man was meant to be before trying to repair him. If one were attempting to restore a wrecked car, they would do much better by focusing on what the automobile looked like before it was wrecked. Therefore, Forlines asks what it means for the human personality to be created in God's image.[14] It means, he concludes, that people's questions are in fact inescapable, because God has designed us with them. It also means that, because we have God's constitutional likeness within us, we have a mind, heart, and will with which we think, feel, and act.[15] This means we have a rational and moral likeness, and we are personal beings.

Man being made in God's image means he is a rational, moral creature. Colossians 3:10 and Ephesians 4:24 offer clues about these features. Colossians 3:10 refers to the new self, which is renewed in knowledge after the image of the Creator. Forlines explains, "We do not make people rational by educating them. We can educate people because by the design of creation they are rational."[16] Because God created people to think, reason, and learn, people need answers to life's inescapable questions, and they should be able to apprehend those answers. A proper worldview offers this.

Ephesians 4:24 teaches a moral likeness when it refers to the new self that is "created after the likeness of God in true righteousness and holiness." Forlines notes, "We do not make people moral by teaching them morals. We can teach them morals because by the design of creation they are moral."[17] Although some believe they can disregard God's moral standards, such actions only lead to more problems since God did not create us this way. Therefore, a human being cannot depart from God's moral law without suffering consequences.[18]

Finally, man was created in God's likeness with respect both to his personhood and personality.[19] The "person" sums up what a human being should be. Each individual is rational and moral (Matt. 22:37; Rom. 14:5; Heb. 8:10). People think with their minds. They feel with their hearts, the seat of emotions. They can make choices as embodied by the will, which is the constitutional likeness of God in man. Since God and man are both personal, and God has made man in His image, they can enter into relationships.[20] And special revelation is God's ordained means of conveying the knowledge of Himself (a personal being) to us (also personal beings).

The Four Basic Relationships

Since God has created every person in His image as a personal being, every person has the same basic needs. The only difference between people is that some people's needs are being met while others are not. If a person would find happiness and satisfaction in life, they must discover what these needs are and, by God's grace, bring their experiences into conformity with the means God uses to meet our needs.[21] Human need is displayed through four basic relationships: a relationship with God, others, self, and the created order. Therefore, all problems are relationship problems in some manner. If we would understand and help people, we must have a basic grasp of these relationships.[22]

God the Creator has designed people for a relationship with Him, without which they cannot have a whole personality.[23] Additionally, since every person is created in God's image, every person has great value. Interaction with others, however, is also necessary to having a healthy personality. These interpersonal relationships must be guided by values such as holiness, love, wisdom, and ideals (see chapter eight).[24] Regarding our relationship with self, every person has intrinsic value as being created in God's image. Believers are especially able to appreciate this value because they are part of God's family. The Christian who takes his or her responsibility as a member of God's family seriously has a stronger basis for self-respect (2 Tim. 4:7) and concern for others.[25] Finally, God has designed us for relationship with the created order. Humans are given dominion over the earth, which entails a type of wise stewardship. God meant for us to enjoy the physical, material realm. The created order also provides a context in which we experience beauty, excellence, and order. Man is designed for these relationships; to live the good life involves living in harmony with Him, others, self, and the created order.

The Impact of Sin

Despite our creation in God's image, sin has marred each of these four relationships. The constitutional likeness has not been demolished, but these relationships have all been distorted in various ways, which explains people's problems.[26] Because the Fall has negatively affected man's personality, we long for these relationships to be made right, which only God can accomplish. Forlines observes that though our culture has made many scientific and technological advances, similar advances have not been made in the areas of human behavior and personality.[27] Indeed, only God's truth can fill this void.

Our Relationship With God

Everything in life depends on one's relationship with God. It is impossible to have a true worldview without a proper relationship with God. Only God can meet our needs. The more a person tries to deal with personality and life's problems without God, the more inadequate and flawed their view will be. In Forlines's later career, he has observed the rise of postmodernity as the prevailing worldview. He challenged these forces as early as the 1950s, sounding the alarm about the precursors of postmodernism and the slide away from orthodoxy.[28] These developments have led to even more confusion (see chapter nine). In contrast to a postmodern worldview, Forlines notes, if God is real and the Bible true, everything adds up: "It is unthinkable that we could be created by God and live in a universe created by God, and not be adversely affected if we are not in a right relationship with God."[29] How then can we know man needs a relationship with God, Forlines asks. He answers that we do not make people religious by teaching them about God; instead, we teach them about God because they are inherently religious. Left alone, most people believe in God. They have to be taught not to.[30]

Because God's law (the moral law of the Ten Commandments) is written on our hearts, Forlines notes, the categories of right and wrong still remain within the sinner even if they stop believing in God. In effect they use a plus value for right and a negative value for wrong, because no person can completely suppress instilled morality. God's image in man is never totally silent in a person's life since man is morally constituted. When man revolted against God, he revolted against himself, leaving himself to exist in conflict and inner contradiction. This problem can only be remedied with a proper relationship with God, leading to proper moral and ethical standards and experiences. Until this relationship is righted, a person will experience trouble in all of life's relationships.[31]

Our Relationship With One Another (Interpersonal Relationships)

Healthy, interpersonal relationships are also essential, and yet sin has also marred these. The longer Forlines has lived, the more he has come to believe that good interpersonal relationships are important. Anyone who has observed people's problems knows what damage can come from a person being socially maladjusted. Loners, for example, which often describes those who seem to commit terrible crimes, are never happy.[32] Through the course of his ministry, Forlines has observed how sexual problems also mar interpersonal relationships: "It would be impossible to overestimate the seriousness of the problems that are being caused in our culture by sexual immorality."[33] When he was dealing with people who were having problems, Forlines was amazed at how often the subject of sex arose; and yet, he concludes, one cannot make right and wise decisions without a positive perspective on sex.

Proper sexual intimacy is described in Hebrews 13:4: "Let marriage be held in honor among all, and let the marriage bed be undefiled, for God will judge the sexually immoral and adulterous." The word "honorable" could also be translated "precious." This indicates the unique nature of sexual intimacy. In marriage sex is appropriate and sacred. Unless a person understands the value of sex when experienced in the proper context, he cannot understand the seriousness of sexual sin. Similarly 1 Corinthians 6:18-19 indicates that sexual sin is unique, and sexual intimacy sacred. Christians must understand the pathway of destruction that takes place when moral ideals are violated.[34] Why are sexual sins so devastating? Forlines answers, "When a person by strength or seduction forces himself into the inner shrine of a sexual experience with another person, it would be, at least in some way, analogous to an act of desecration of the Temple in the Old Testament."[35] This points to why thwarting biblical standards on sexual intimacy has been so destructive and pervasive.

Some of those whom Forlines has counseled came to him with an issue unrelated to sex. Eventually he would often learn the father had abused the young lady for three years or something similar. "At some point along the way," Forlines writes, "it dawned on me that problem people are troubled people."[36] The sexually abused are frequently troubled by guilt and feelings of worthlessness. Unless the issue is properly addressed, the person may feel dirty, and even end up living an immoral life. When one male abuses another male, this can be especially devastating to the latter's identity, and many times he suffers alone.[37] The church will have to prepare to help people with these issues.

Our Relationship With Ourselves (Intrapersonal Relationships)

Forlines's interactions with those he tried to help convinced him of the need for a proper sense of self-worth. Thus, he began examining and developing his ideas concerning self-worth and self-image from Scripture. Because sin mars our relationship with ourselves, it leads us to struggle with both pride and feelings of inferiority. He observed that deeply troubled people spent too much time in self-examination, asking questions like "What's wrong with me?" and "Why can't I be happy as other people?" These questions continually occupy their minds.[38]

Though many Christians seem to promote self-deprecation under the guise of humility, the real aim is for people to have self-confidence. Some Christians have not understood this due to misinterpreting passages such as Isaiah 6:5 ("And I said: 'Woe is me! For I am lost; for I am a man of unclean lips, and I dwell in the midst of a people of unclean lips; for my eyes have seen the King, the LORD of hosts!'"). Yet Forlines notes this does not represent the state of mind in which we should always remain: "It is quite obvious that, in spite of our imperfections in this life, we can be acceptable with God. If an absolutely holy God has a standard that we can measure up to in this life, certainly we should be able to accept ourselves."[39]

In Philippians 2:3, Paul instructs readers to esteem others as better than themselves. Forlines explains that Paul is asking us "to be quicker to say good things about others than to say good things about ourselves."[40] In fact, Paul appears to have had a healthy self-image. Consider 1 Corinthians 4:16: "I urge you, then, be imitators of me." For Paul to tell people to imitate him suggests he had a healthy self-image. People may appropriately think positively about themselves when what they are thinking is true. In Ephesians 3:8, Paul explains that he was the least of all Christians, and yet God in His grace had allowed him to preach the gospel. Paul realized his shortcomings as well as his ability to minister. Do you want a surgeon who is about to perform surgery on you with a downtrodden look, who says, "I don't know why they chose me! I don't think I can do this," Forlines asks. No, we want someone with self-confidence doing our surgeries; the same is true with those who minister to us.[41]

Proper confidence frees a person's mind to devote attention to other things. Rightly understood, self-confidence does not lead to pride and is preferable to a lack of self-confidence. We certainly do not believe that the worst Christians should be our pastors and evangelists, much less for such a person to be an apostle and the author of more books in the Bible than anyone else. Jesus' statement "You are of more value than many sparrows" (Matt. 10:31) clearly suggests that people are important.[42] Again, Forlines notes, "Christianity does not call upon us to set aside self-interest."[43] Why else would Jesus call on us to love your neighbor as ourselves (Matt. 22:39; Lev. 19:18) if He did not assume care for self to be normal?[44]

Our Relationship With the Created Order

Sin impacts everything including our relationship with creation. It leads to the exploitation of the created order, and its effect can be seen in our attitude toward it. Forlines notes that if we ignore this need to experience beauty, excellence, and order, we do so to our own harm. God calls us to exercise dominion over the earth, though not to exploit it. We should not think of materiality as inherently evil, nor to worship it. Rather, the Christian should concern himself with beauty and strive for excellence in the natural and material realm. Forlines believes the fragmentation of music is one of the signs of the impact of a secular worldview. In contrast, by surrounding ourselves (and families) with excellence, beauty, and order, we promote a positive relationship with the created order, and positive growth in other relationships that are exercised in the world.[45]

Making Personality Changes

As believers find themselves struggling with an entangling sin, they may wonder how they can change. For many this has been a source of confusion. Forlines gives the example of someone with a temper problem. If they ask God to take their problem away, they may begin to wonder why God does not take it away immediately as they continue to have problems with angry outbursts. They may wonder if they have enough faith. However, physical relationships are different from personal relationships. Physical relationships are governed by cause and effect. If you hit a nail with a hammer, it will be driven into the wood. Personal relationships do not respond in the same way, since they are characterized by influence and response. Objects do not have a will, while human beings do.[46]

Consider how Jesus healed a blind man instantaneously. Eyes are part of the physical body. However, the apostle Peter arguably did not become a mature believer until later in the book of Acts after Jesus had already ascended into heaven. Personality change and development, which entails the way people think, feel, and act, take time. This is why instructions like "trust, don't try" discourage some; "trust and try" is perhaps better advice. After all, Paul "learned" to be content (Phil. 4:11). This indicates that the virtue of contentment was not instantaneous for him either. He told Timothy to "discipline" himself (1 Tim. 4:7) for the purpose of godliness. The writer of Hebrews tells us to train to eat solid food so the intake of truth can help us exercise discernment better (Heb. 5:14). Indeed, Scripture teaches us to trust and try.[47] God Himself works in us to accomplish His will (Phil. 2:13). Though the Fall has marred God's image in us, we still have a mind and will to do God's work. We have an influence and response relationship with God. Just as a mechanic rebuilding an engine takes time, so there is a natural passage of time as God works to bring us into compliance with His will and spiritual maturity.[48]

As a component of personality, Forlines addresses the mind. He defines the conscious mind as what we are aware of at a given time. He notes that everything else is stored in the subconscious mind, which is mainly retrieved by asking a question. He often entertained his students by talking about the "boys downstairs" as an analogy for the unconscious mind. The boys downstairs remind you of something you have read from a book. He also explains that the subconscious mind (or the boys downstairs) works on problems when we are not consciously thinking about them. That is the positive side of our personality. Our subconscious minds work to render our engagement in positive practices easier than they might otherwise be. At the same time, if we have developed negative habits over the years, breaking them often takes more time—again, because of the subconscious mind.

But we know that Christ has made a way for us to be a different person (2 Cor. 5:17).[49] Change requires motivation. Forlines describes life as an escalator going down, only you want to go up. As life's escalator is going down, we do not have to do anything if we do not mind being put off at the basement floor. This might be the minimum wage earner, the one addicted to drugs or alcohol or on the public dole. If you do not want to live in life's basement, you must exert some effort. Forlines acknowledges that some people's escalator runs faster than others, but we cannot control this. We must do whatever is necessary to achieve the goals God has set before us.[50] When the value becomes great enough, one can break a bad habit.

What does this mean for those entangled in addiction or another sin? Can we have hope? Our hope comes from understanding we have divine aid, as well as a responsibility to make changes in our life. We also have aid from others that can be received, and those who have struggled with similar difficulties can help us.[51] Forlines encourages us to think of change by going through steps:

1. "There is nothing in my basic nature that requires me to be this way": One may struggle with sexual sin or feelings of inferiority, but it does not have to be that way.

2. "I am this way because of my previous programming": I am this way because my habits have programmed me to be this way—nothing more. Because I have conceded to my sinful nature, I have developed tendencies or habits that have led me further down this path.

3. "I do not have to be this way. I can reprogram myself": God is in the change business. We can be different.

4. "I am not going to continue to be this way. I will reprogram myself": Make a commitment by God's grace that you will change and be changed.

5. "I am no longer that way. I have reprogramed myself."[52] You are changed. As Scripture states, "And such were some of you" (1 Cor. 6:11). Now you walk with newness of life.

"Regardless of how unfortunate the past might have been," Forlines writes, "the past does not have to predict the future."[53] It is hard, if not impossible for us to do this alone. How then does Forlines's approach enable us to understand and better help others?

The Role of Christians and the Church

God calls Christians to help through preaching, teaching, and reaching. If our efforts are ineffective, some dimension is missing somewhere. Certainly the impact of secular thought and practice in our culture has made reaching people with the gospel more difficult. However, Forlines believes the greatest hope that most of us have of a breakthrough with today's world is with God's help to minister to the broken people's hurts. When people find an answer for their hurts, many of their intellectual problems with unbelief will either vanish or diminish. This is the whole church's responsibility. We may meet some needs through a formal counseling program, friendships, and even support groups. By working together we can send the message to a hurting world that Christ and Christianity offer answers to their problems.[54] God has called us all to help, but how? We can begin by focusing on the four basic relationships and what we can do to help. This leads to and is reinforced by good interpersonal relationships.

Developing Healthy Interpersonal Relationships

Interpersonal relationships are especially relevant in family life. The strength of the parent-child relationship helps prepare a child for the future: "When there is not a good relationship with parents, the foundation is laid for the development of personality problems."[55] Forlines notes that life's two most difficult periods are being a teenager and being a parent of a teenager. He suggests that the church should do more to help families and teenagers during this important time of life. They especially need our aid in navigating the day's sexual issues, which we will consider more below.

Developing a Proper Worldview

The church can also help people think and live with a Christian worldview that impacts the culture. This is necessary to help people develop a relationship with God that will be durable and influential in the world. The secular worldview has introduced the strong influence of moral relativism into our society. This has led many to think that abortion is as good as parenting, that homosexuality has the same moral value as heterosexuality, and that sex outside of marriage has the same moral value as sex inside of marriage. People have exchanged moral convictions for preferences.

This kind of thinking fails to provide the happiness and satisfaction people seek. The result is that the only thing wrong is to think a behavior or action is wrong! The influence of moral relativism has made it much harder for people to recognize their need for a Redeemer. This will require a great deal of work on our part. Though preaching with more zeal with the same approach was perhaps adequate a generation ago, Forlines warns that this will not reach people today. Because our culture is brainwashed with moral relativism, we must remember where people are when we begin to minister to them. And as it becomes evident that we care about them and can help them, they will come to us for help, and we should go to them.[56]

Dealing With Discouragement and Developing Gratitude

People have a choice about how to deal with suffering. When one experiences depression, stress, rejection, loneliness, boredom, or any other problem, they can choose to turn to God or sin.[57] This underlies the importance of intervening with the hurting. It is also a major responsibility for the church to support people during difficult times. Forlines describes that many bad decisions are made in low moments (Heb. 12:12-16). On the other hand, he notes that some of the best decisions are made in low moments (Ps. 18:6), like the prodigal son's decision to go home (Luke 15:17-19). The pain of others gives us both an opportunity and responsibility to help. If we fail to seize the opportunity to help people, they can easily go in the wrong direction.[58] Related to this, Forlines observes that deeply troubled people are not strong on thanksgiving or gratitude for the most part. He has often said, "You will never see a happy person who is unthankful, nor will you see an unhappy person who is thankful."[59] Therefore, we should help people develop gratitude toward others.

Overintrospection

Forlines writes, "It is extremely important that we do all of our thinking about self-image and self-interest in the context of loving God and loving others."[60] We can help people by getting them to get their mind off themselves. Forlines discerns that those with inferiority complexes often have deep feelings of insecurity and spend excessive time thinking about themselves. The reason many people think often about themselves is that they are experiencing great difficulty. For example, if your car works well, you probably do not think about it much. However, when you experience car problems, you think about your car. Similarly, people who are well do not spend much time thinking about sickness.[61]

Simply telling people not to think about themselves does not solve the problem though. Sometimes the answer is to help them with a problem they are having. How do we know when someone is struggling? People who talk about themselves are often struggling in a particular area of their life. Even when one area works well, feelings of inferiority can quickly arise when one feels that one of their strengths is criticized. Suppose a baseball player with a poor self-image is good at pitching. If his pitching is criticized, he may become extremely defensive. Instead, this person needs to develop self-confidence. How do we know when introspection has become hurtful or helpful? A good rule for introspection is that it is good when you are learning something new about yourself, and you can control it. Introspection is bad when you are not learning anything new, and you cannot control it.[62]

Dealing With Sin

A Forlinesean approach also helps people resist temptation and deal with sin. Much confusion has resulted over Christ's command to "crucify self." Many have looked to this passage, and others like it, as a command to adopt a low view of one's self. However, a more accurate assessment interprets this as relating to the call to crucify the flesh—our sinful, fallen nature. To crucify self is to deny self of inappropriate desires. The flesh would like to operate on the principle of immediacy (see chapter eight), but Christian ethics requires thinking and living in view of the long-term and eternal rather than the immediate. Desires that are legitimate in their time and place are sinful when they are fulfilled at the wrong time and place (e.g., Heb. 13:4). Self-denial always means saying no to sin's pull. This is good and necessary for sanctification, and success in life. In a way, to deny self is a way of loving self.[63]

Fostering and Maintaining Unity

Forlines talks about the danger of looking at only one side of things. For example, if one listened only to Christians who gave their testimonies, he notes, they would have a distorted view of Christianity. In fact, this led to some of the problems he helped people address in their lives. A second example he observes regards why Christians have difficulty getting along with one another. There are absolute truths, such as the Ten Commandments, as well as areas of life where we have general principles that God has given to guide us. Sometimes problems occur when one believer makes one side of the truth into an absolute, and another makes another side of the truth into an absolute.

These examples illustrate the principle of what Forlines calls tension and counterbalance. We see it throughout Scripture. For instance, God tells us He will supply all of our needs (Matt. 6:33; Phil. 4:19). As a general rule then God will meet our needs and protect us in times of danger. However, that is only one side of the truth.[64] The general rule will not fit every circumstance. God will generally meet our needs, but we must also work hard, pursue excellence, and live wisely in accordance with Scripture as stewards over the gifts God has given us. We would do well to recognize this principle in order to promote unity among believers in interpreting, teaching, and living out the Word.

Forlines and Our Contemporary Challenge

Forlines believes the church should do more to help people properly deal with sex, though he notes that discussions about sex in church settings should be treated with great respect. No longer do children spend their early years in relative innocence. Sadly, the culture is robbing children of their opportunity to be children. Sexual sin has led to many inferiority complexes. For many with whom Forlines has counseled, problems began by finding pornography, often that belonged to a father or some other adult male. "This acquaintance with pornography at an early age had programmed itself in his memory and several years later it was seeking to bring about his downfall," Forlines recalls.[65] He observes that those who were more prone to be loners were more likely to struggle with pornography than the socially active.

Forlines's discovery that righteousness is not only right but also good marked a good day in his life. By the same token, sin is not only wrong, but also bad. In a manner of speaking, living a Christian life is simply easier. In regard to sexual sin, certain suggestions for maintaining sexual purity may prove difficult, since the culture and church has become desensitized to sexual issues. One solution then might be that we help people develop a passion for purity (Matt. 5:6); righteousness is not only right, but also good. Forlines observes that if you are hungering and thirsting after righteousness, it is almost useless to spend much time thinking about what is permissible. How do we help people do this? We help them safeguard themselves. People should plan to be pure. "I trust myself because I distrust myself," Forlines would say. By this, he meant that his distrust of himself helped him make proper precautions to avoid sexual sin.[66]

We can assist families by helping them build storm shelters. Storm shelters are built while the weather is good before life's storms beat down upon a person. Forlines would say, "It is the sober man who decides to get drunk." The point is that we must make decisions about dealing with sexual sin early in life before we find ourselves battling with discouragement. Part of a good storm shelter is to get into the habit of making right decisions. Forlines notes that he did not get up in the morning on a Sunday and decide whether he would attend church; he made that decision years ago and that decision dictates much about his behavior on a weekend. Therefore, getting up and going to church is easier for him. Similarly, we wish to instill in our young people the importance of sexual purity by noting the high value of entering marriage as a virgin. This decision impacts how one dresses because of the message one's appearance conveys. It also dictates the kind of storm shelter a person builds to deal with the risks associated with the inevitable down periods of life. We make plans for how we will conduct ourselves even then (Rom. 12:17). In a way avoiding sexual sin involves strengthening all of life's relationships.[67]

When people have been marred by sexual sin, we can help them move on by finding peace and self-forgiveness. When Jesus was invited to the Pharisee Simon's home, He met a woman who was tired of her sin (Luke 7:36-50), and said, "Your faith has saved you; go in peace." "Go in peace" implies that Jesus instructed her to forgive herself. Sometimes we have the most trouble with forgiving ourselves. Thus we should help others forgive themselves, and write "past tense" on their sins. Paul indicates this very thing (1 Cor. 6:9-11). We are no longer that kind of person. God had turned us into a new creature (2 Cor. 5:17). As a church we must help people deal with the pull of past sins and realize that past sins do not have to define their present or their future. If people cross the line in courtship, Satan will often tell them they have no right to speak on the issues of purity and modesty. That is a lie, and we must help them see that they have a role in helping people in the future deal with sexual issues. We can go a long way in helping people overcome sexual sin if we as a church create an environment where they feel a strong sense of acceptance.[68]

Forlines grasped the problems of his time. In the midst of our current sexual confusion and general cultural confusion about personal identity, his tireless work in Scripture and with people has led to some powerful teaching that helps us all better understand and help people. As we examine the current landscape of our culture, we can see that his warnings are well founded. His contributions on these subjects deserve a fresh hearing, given their benefit to help us answer the questions and meet the needs of a culture that so desperately needs what he has offered.

---

[1] F. Leroy Forlines, "Understanding Yourself and Others: A Biblical, Theological, and Practical Approach to Personality" (unpublished manuscript, 1994), 6.

[2] Ibid., 1.

[3] Ibid.

[4] Ibid, 7.

[5] Ibid, 33.

[6] Ibid, 3.

[7] Ibid, 35.

[8] F. Leroy Forlines, *Biblical Systematics: A Study of the Christian System of Life and Thought* (Nashville: Randall House, 1975), 1.

[9] F. Leroy Forlines, *Evolution* (Nashville: Randall House, 1973), 6.

[10] Forlines, *Biblical Systematics*, 87.

[11] F. Leroy Forlines, *Classical Arminianism: A Theology of Salvation* (Nashville: Randall House, 2011), 1-2.

[12] Leroy Forlines, "Understanding and Helping People" (unpublished manuscript, 2007), 8.

[13] Ibid, 18.

[14] Forlines, *Classical Arminianism*, 3.

[15] Ibid., "Understanding and Helping People," 9.

[16] Forlines, *Classical Arminianism*, 3.

[17] Ibid., 4.

[18] Ibid.

[19] Ibid, 6-7.

[20] Forlines, "Understanding and Helping People," 14.

[21] Ibid, 17.

[22] Ibid, 18. For purposes of conceptual clarity and practical significance, I have inverted the original order of Forlines's third and fourth basic relationships as they originally appear in *Biblical Ethics* (1973).

[23] F. Leroy Forlines, *A Theological Approach to Personality* (Nashville: Free Will Baptist Bible College, n.d.), 4.

[24] Ibid., 7.

[25] Ibid.

[26] Leroy Forlines, *The Quest for Truth: Answering Life's Inescapable Questions* (Nashville: Randall House, 2001), 154.

[27] Forlines, "Understanding and Helping People," 12.

[28] Leroy Forlines and Robert Picirilli, *Orthodoxy, Modern Trends, and Free Will Baptists* (Nashville: Free Will Baptist Bible College, 1957).

[29] Forlines, "Understanding and Helping People," 19.

[30] Ibid., 19.

[31] Ibid., 11.

[32] Ibid., 26.

[33] F. Leroy Forlines, "The Prostitution of Sex and the Pathway of Devastation that Follows" (unpublished manuscript, 2007), 1.

[34] Ibid., 3.

[35] Ibid., 4.

36 Ibid., 6.

37 Ibid., 8.

38 Ibid., 28.

39 Ibid., 51.

40 Ibid., 53.

41 Ibid., 56.

42 Ibid., 57.

43 Ibid., 72.

44 Ibid., 70-71.

45 Ibid., 193.

46 Ibid., 77.

47 Ibid., 80.

48 Ibid., 82.

49 Ibid., 84.

50 Ibid., 31-32.

51 See also Edward E. Moody, *First Aid for Emotional Hurts: Helping People Through Difficult Times* (Nashville: Randall House, 2008).

52 Forlines, "Understanding and Helping People," 94-95.

53 Ibid., 51.

54 Ibid., 4.

55 Ibid., 39.

56 Ibid., 51.

57 See also Edward E. Moody, *First Aid for Your Emotional Hurts: Sexual Issues* (Nashville: Randall House, 2015).

58 Forlines, "Understanding and Helping People," 5.

59 Ibid., 51.

60 Ibid., 39.

61 Ibid., 40.

62 Ibid., 41.

63 Ibid., 66.

64 Ibid., 38.

65 Forlines, "The Prostitution of Sex," 9.

66 Ibid., 20-21.

67 Ibid., 32-33.

68 Ibid., 37-38.

PART IV

PERSONAL
TRIBUTES

F. LEROY AND FAY FORLINES: A TRIBUTE TO OUR PARENTS

James and Jon Forlines

We, James and Jon, the sons of F. Leroy and Fay Forlines, have been fortunate to hear songs of tribute from many who have expressed deep appreciation for our parents' work as we have traveled around the United States and world. Certainly we add our voices of praise to this chorus that has rung in our ears—this amazing refrain that has challenged us to honor our Lord in this way. We do not wish to use poetic license to paint an unrealistic fairy tale picture of Mom and Dad. Instead, our hope is to reflect the deep, abiding beliefs and faith practices that have carried them through life's journey.

Leroy and Fay are united in the belief that God has spoken to the human race through His Word. They believe He reveals Himself to this world through excellence, order, and beauty. Hope and guidance for this life come from valuing these gifts from God, which give meaning and purpose. Mom and Dad have offered us, beyond their human frailties, unmoving reference points, which have always served to guide us through life's uncertainties to God's will for our lives. Many times they have helped us find our way when selfish desires would lead us otherwise.

The best place to find these reference points are in Dad's book, *Biblical Ethics*, where he points to four basic values that give rise to principles for all Christians to live by: holiness, love, wisdom, and ideals. So strongly was he convinced that his students should memorize these values and their meanings that he would often exhort his ethics class, "If someone were to call you at 2 a.m. and wake you out of a deep sleep to ask you these four basic values, you should be able to say them without thinking." He regarded these truths so sincerely that they resided in the very core of his being, where he wanted them to be vested in his students. And so it happened that, with sophomoric humor, one of his students actually did call him once at 2 a.m. to ask him what the four basic values were. Dad is a very deep sleeper. To his credit, he responded with the correct answers, and then asked, "Who is this?" The student quickly hung up.

As beings created in God's image, these values are seen by Mom and Dad as life principles to be lived out. They are not just theory. We believe our parents have sought to live them out as best as possible, and for this we hope to honor them with this tribute.

Holiness

Our parents helped us understand that we were born into this world, falling short of a holy God's expectations; however, God offers the gift of salvation through faith in Christ as Lord and Savior. They also taught us that, with changed hearts, we should aspire to honor Christ by living obedient lives before Him. Examples of this were recited through family stories. One example includes our grandparents. Dad's beliefs were strongly shaped by watching his parents live lives of faith before him. Perhaps one of the most indelible memories came when his father was dying. Though poor in this world, our grandfather's dying requests included strict instructions to make sure to pay the doctor what was owed for his care. Dad often spoke of the good name his father had in the Winterville community. His father was a Christ-follower. To those who knew him, he was a man of integrity. His word meant something: John Forlines could be counted on to do what he said he would do.

Sinful lifestyles and practices also bothered our parents because they had witnessed how such lifestyles had destroyed the lives of many family members and friends. What we, as kids, would think was being old fashioned and judgmental was, instead, warning us of the perils that so easily beset us all. Yes, it made for awkward moments growing up in the Forlines's home. Prominent in our minds are the rare times Dad would stop to watch television. Usually, it seemed he was checking up on what we were watching. On more than one occasion when he would notice something that was said or done inappropriately, he would say, "That vexes my righteous soul." Sin should bother those who want to please God, who want to live lives that do not invite question otherwise.

Love

No doubt Mom was at the center of expressed love and sacrifice in our home. As the mother of two rowdy and often ungrateful boys, her belief in us was unwavering even when others were wondering when (not if) we would end up on the FBI's Most Wanted List. Mom sacrificed much, because of the demands of Dad's work, to make sure our needs were met and horizons broadened by vast experiences. There was, however, no mistaking Dad's unconditional commitment to his family. James recounts one event that solidly convinced him of that fact:

> I was walking down a perilous path, and there were many things I was doing that were hurting Mom and Dad. One day we were in the car, just Dad and me. I heard later that he had gone to hear a Christian child psychologist speak at Vanderbilt who suggested this approach. He said, "James, your mother and I have done our best to teach you the right way to live, and to follow and serve God. But you are becoming your own man. And you will have to decide what you consider to be right and wrong. And you will have to bear the consequences for those decisions. But I want you to know that if you walk away from everything we have taught you, if you turn your back on everything we believe, and even if you turn your back

on God; you will always be my son, and I will always love you."
That psychologist was James Dobson, who founded Focus on
the Family.

In those days, many in the Christian world held psychology in great suspicion. But Dad recognized godly advice and lovingly urged a wayward son away from danger. We saw him rise early to pray, and we saw him end the day in prayer. We knew he would pray for us, because he told us he would. This was confirmed on at least one occasion when James heard his own name being raised up in love to our heavenly Father from Dad's closet during his evening prayers.

Our parents took this love and showed us, through example, how to meet others' needs also. We cannot begin to tell the stories of the hitchhikers they picked up, meals they gave to the hungry, forgotten servants of God they visited and honored for their service, helping hands they gave, grieving hearts they cared for, and second chances they gave. We saw them care for others, helping them see their place of importance in God's eyes. A helping hand was often followed by words of good news.

Wisdom

Dad also challenged others to desire true wisdom and discernment found only in the Bible with the Holy Spirit's illumination. This is a hard work. It is a work of solitude as well as a reward gained from a multitude of sound opinions and counselors. Dad values the well-thought-out opinions of others. He has settled his own views of Scripture by reading God's Word and varying scholarly opinions, and by debating with others—all worked through meticulously before arriving at his own position. (Did we mention that Dad has been plagued all of his life with the challenge of being a slow reader?) This exhausting pursuit of wisdom continues to this day. Nothing fans his flame, even now, more than a request for his views on a matter, or a lively discussion with differing views on a subject. It seems there is always a book in his hand, or at least one nearby.

Dare we tell you that he has been seen, on more than one occasion recently, sitting in a gown on the side of his own emergency room bed with a book in hand? It only seemed logical to him that, even though he was going through a great health challenge, there was little time to waste waiting on the modern health care system to work its wonders. "Dad, can we just stop a moment here to say that people want to feel their sympathies are needed when they go to the trouble of making hospital visits? They also sort of expect to have discussions about health matters and not trending theological issues!"

On more than one occasion, Dad showed his wisdom when we asked difficult questions. After one of our pets died, one of us asked, "Will Tiger be in heaven?" He thoughtfully replied, "If it will make heaven a better place, he will be there. God loves us." When the questions got trickier Dad was still known to weigh in with thoughtful responses. When one of us began showing interest in one of the neighborhood girls whose family members were Orthodox Jews, we asked, "Dad, is it okay for a Free Will Baptist to marry a Jew?" His simple response avoided what was set-up to be a full out argument: "Why don't you go ask her father that question?"

Ideals

Mom and Dad were perpetual learners, from the printed page to experiencing the world around them with their five senses. Wanting rather to play with our friends, they often made us pile in the car on weekends and help them explore some local fascination they had read about in the newspaper. History was a never-ending lesson to be learned; we are what we are because of great discoveries, accomplishments, and mistakes of the past. They all needed to be relearned and reexamined.

Much to our dismay, Mom was engaged with her surroundings and loved exposing us to new tastes and cultural events. She also had a green thumb and tried very hard to teach us to have the same fascination with helping things grow. Dad enjoyed fixing broken things. He found great pleasure in bringing order from disrepair. This could also be seen in the many hours of godly guidance he offered to students in his office, mending broken lives. We cannot begin to tell you how many people have told us how he helped them put their lives back on track while they were his students. Only in adulthood, and nearly too late, have we come to appreciate the rich knowledge and experience we gained through our parents "weird" attractions and kind hearts.

Our parents view this world as being put into existence in an orderly and purposeful way. Though man's fall began a spiral of destruction, a God-transformed life is best lived out by seeking to emulate orderliness and self-control. Excellence in all things should be sought out and greatly valued. Beautiful landscapes, masterful art works, and well-thought-out writings are revered. They worked hard to expose the two of us to many of these things near our home and as we travelled. They taught us to see and value God's hand in these things, because they direct our attention to ideals—principles that reflected God's essence.

Mom and Dad taught us to be mindful of this in all that we say, think, and do. Anything less is not God-honoring. In this way we were told, among other things, to clean our rooms, dress well, watch how we carried ourselves, be mindful of others' needs, give our reasonable best to tasks we were given, be respectful of God's house, and follow God's leading in His Word and through His Spirit's leading. They expressed great concern to us to consider most, not what others thought of us in these efforts, but to ask ourselves what others would think about the God we loved when they saw what we said, did, or valued. All we do should be an expression of praise to the LORD. We have learned to ask, "Do our lives and handiwork reflect the order and beauty of His creation?"

Conclusion

Through our own reflections and the innumerable conversations we have had with those whose lives have been touched by our parents, we are reminded often how grateful we should be to Mom and Dad for the strong commitment to a belief system that places the highest priority on obedience to God's design for our lives. Through the maze of this postmodern culture, those reference points of holiness, love, wisdom, and ideals have made clear the LORD's design for our lives. By fixing our paths on these benchmarks, and also using them to find our way back when we stray, we know beyond any shadow of a doubt that we have been redeemed from sin and our duty is to reflect the image of the Almighty.

F. LEROY FORLINES AS A COLLEAGUE AND FRIEND

Robert E. Picirilli

I am grateful for the privilege of writing a tribute for this festschrift to F. Leroy Forlines. He has been a personal friend and colleague since we were fellow students at Welch College a long time ago. I first met Leroy in the fall of 1949. He was a second-year student then, from Winterville, North Carolina; and I was a freshman from Pamplico, South Carolina. Neither of us actually lived in the small town from which our mail was distributed—we were both country boys. I soon learned that his nickname was "Pop," probably because he was a few years older than some of us, and more likely because he was very serious-minded and tended to provide fatherly oversight for the younger ones of us, including me. I wouldn't say that he has been a "father figure" to me exactly—more like an older brother.

I remember two things most about him during those student years. First, during one year we were roommates. We were two among six in one of the large rooms on the second floor of what came to be known as "old Ennis." The others were Herbert Waid, Lonnie Sparks, Bob White, and Ray Turnage. Leroy was certainly a steadying influence on that group, a model of maturity in the midst of our immaturity. He was famous for sitting in a straight-back chair and rocking on the two back legs, his open hands all the while in his lap with his fingers and thumbs alternately meeting and pushing away—like a spider doing push-ups on a mirror. To appreciate this fully, one should know that the other five of us often disappointed him, especially during the nightly prayer times, when something funny would happen, and we would be lost in uncontrollable laughter. Leroy could then be seen frowning pointedly and rocking in his chair. Sometimes he was successful in restoring order.

The second memory that stands out is that he and I were in a course called "Arminian Theology," taught by the college president, Dr. L. C. Johnson. It was largely a reading and discussion course, one that has not been offered before or since. Brother Johnson, I think, wanted the course to grapple with the distinctive theological positions of our Free Will Baptist heritage, something that was not done much in the denomination in those days. He picked passages in Jacobus Arminius's writings for us to read, and then raised questions in class for discussion. It was a stimulating and heady time.

Something I remember well from this course is that Leroy the student and Brother Johnson the teacher got locked in an ongoing debate about original sin. The question was whether all three (guilt, condemnation, and depravity) were passed along to the entire human race in consequence of Adam's sin. In agreement with Arminius, Brother Johnson said that they were; Leroy didn't object that depravity passed from Adam to humanity, but he couldn't quite accept that everyone is judged guilty and condemned for our original parents' sin. The discussion went on for many class periods, while the rest of us mostly listened (and not always patiently!). Leroy finally saw the light and became a staunch defender of what I have come to call "Reformation Arminianism"; he calls it "Classical Arminianism." The point is that he wasn't willing to accept anything just because someone else said so—not even the esteemed Arminius or the college president! He had to think it through for himself.

Speaking for myself I was very frustrated. As it turned out, both Leroy and Brother Johnson agreed that the universal guilt and condemnation, which mankind had inherited from Adam, were cancelled by virtue of Christ's atonement for the whole human race. I wasn't certain of that, and so much time had been taken up on Leroy's problem that there was no time left to talk about mine!

Regardless, I do not think it is a stretch to say that Leroy began working out his system of theology in that course in Arminian theology. I am confident that it was an especially formative one for both of us; and that it made a difference for Free Will Baptists—even though most never knew anything about it.

Leroy graduated from Welch College in 1952, and I graduated in 1953. He went first to a church in Warwick City, Virginia (in the Tidewater area) as pastor. Soon the college brought him back with the intention of providing for him to teach extension courses in various places across the denomination (apparently Brother Johnson had been impressed with the student's critical thinking!). Interest in those courses was not strong, however, while interest in the campus program was growing. Consequently, Leroy became, instead, a full-time member of the faculty and began working on a master's degree during the summers in Winona Lake, Indiana. At about the same time, in the fall of 1955, and fresh from graduate school, I also went back to teach too. Except for a couple of years when he was away at Northern Baptist Theological Seminary in Chicago, completing his Bachelor of Divinity (what is now known as an M.Div.), he and I were colleagues for our entire careers as members of the college faculty.

I cannot hope to tell, in full measure, what it has been like to have Leroy Forlines for a close friend and colleague for more than a half century. I begin by speaking more broadly: He has been a mentor, not simply for me, but for a whole denomination. Even those who may disagree with him about one matter or another will have to acknowledge, I think, that his viewpoint provides the touchstone from which the discussion emerges. Before Forlines, Free Will Baptists had no written systematic theology. The old volume by Butler and Dunn, representing the Randall movement and long since out of print, was all that could be claimed in this regard (and it wasn't a very good theology book at that!). From Leroy's teaching theology all those years at Welch College grew first his *Biblical Systematics*, subsequently replaced by *The Quest for Truth*. This work is a very good theology, indeed, and it represents the mature and unique thinking of the man. It would be impossible to estimate the impact that Leroy's teaching of theology has had on students for so long. His thinking has indeed shaped that of a denomination.

I gladly acknowledge that he has been a mentor to me personally. As I write this I am thinking of a particular occasion that illustrates this. For some reason (which I forget now), I was grappling with a question of biblical interpretation. I think it had to do with eschatology, perhaps with the Olivet Discourse in Matthew 24. I found myself inclined to think the passage did not mean exactly what we were used to hearing, and was reluctant to strike out on a different path all by myself. So I called to see if he was in his office. He was and had some time, so I went over; we spent several hours exploring the passage. He saw where I was headed, and was already thinking along similar lines. Needless to say, I was encouraged.

One of the qualities that characterizes Leroy's thinking is the development of useful categories that help define things. A particularly helpful category concerns the difference between *form* and *substance*. That's useful, for example, when one is making a distinction between the things that can change and those that should not. In many ways it is acceptable, or helpful to recognize that the form of a thing can change without changing the substance. I cannot begin to tell how often I have used this very distinction in teaching (in a recent work, for example, I observed that faith is the substance and obedience is the form that faith takes when confronted with a command of God).

Another one of Leroy's adages that has helped me avoid hermeneutical pitfalls is his insistence that when we want to know the biblical view of any matter, we should go to a part of the Bible where that very matter is being discussed, and not settle for passages that make only a passing reference to the matter. Once this is stated, it seems obvious; but Leroy was the first person I ever heard say it. (I think this is significant, for example, when discussing the possibility of apostasy; Hebrews is the very source to which we should repair when formulating doctrine on that subject.)

I should hasten to admit that Leroy and I have not always seen eye to eye on every point of theology or biblical interpretation. In our younger years (younger for me than for him!), when our blood ran hotter than it does in our old age, we were often known to lock horns in verbal battle. These "discussions" could take place almost anywhere: in either of our offices, at the dining table, in the faculty lounge. We didn't avoid others' ears. We could go at it long and loud, each of us getting a little red in the face and raising our voices. Others enjoyed observing—or not! But we both knew that we argued as friends in pursuit of the truth; and thus no ill will was ever involved. We neither gave nor expected any quarter, and my respect for him only grew.

One of our disagreements persists to this day, regarding Romans 7:14-25. According to Leroy, the passage reflects the experience of an unconverted person who has been exposed to the law of God. I see it, instead, as the experience of any saved person instructed by God's revealed will. Each of us has published our views. My respect for his thinking means that I was far more careful in defending my view than I might otherwise have been, and that even now I express my view without the dogmatism I might otherwise have. I regard this as one of the unsettled issues of biblical interpretation, and that is primarily because Leroy Forlines disagrees with me.

At times we have collaborated on various projects. In the mid-1950s we were speaking in chapel along similar lines and decided to write a little booklet, which the college published in 1957 as *Orthodoxy, Modern Trends, and Free Will Baptists*. It was the first thing to be published among us that warned about the dangers of liberal theological thinking, and called attention to those things that we need to do to be sure that Free Will Baptists remain sound in the faith.

Leroy has always been a thinking man's thinker. More than any person I know, he likes to take on a thorny theological issue and think it through, regardless of how long it takes for him to arrive at an understanding that satisfies him. In this he thinks for himself and is not overly influenced by the views of those whom he reads. Even when he was a student, rocking silently on the back legs of his chair with his eyes closed, he was thinking about issues and their solutions. One of the best illustrations of this involves our understanding of apostasy.

During his final years as a student, he tackled Hebrews 6:4-6. As he worked through the passage, he discovered that the apostate described there cannot be recovered. He might have been the first modern Free Will Baptist to set this forth in writing. At the request of Damon Dodd, then director of Free Will Baptist Home Missions, he wrote a little booklet on the subject. They published it in the mid-1950s, entitling it *The Significance of the Doctrine of Perseverance*. Later the FWB Press in Ayden republished it in 1959, and again Randall House in 1986, as *The Doctrine of Perseverance*. (It was also republished once between these two dates by Evangelist Van Dale Hudson.) I am confident that nothing published in our ranks has been so influential in shaping our doctrine of perseverance, and he had it worked out while he was a Bible college student!

That Leroy thinks for himself is indicated in the fact that his way of writing theology isn't exactly like that of the traditional theologians. He has his own way of approaching a subject, and this is seen especially in his concern for personal application of truth to life. He doesn't believe that theology, or Bible study for that matter, is intended to be merely intellectual. Instead, such studies are meant to have deep and permanent effects on what he is likely to call "the whole person." Truth is to be *lived*, and it is meant to change one's thoughts, feelings, and will.

As general editor of the *Randall House Bible Commentary* on the New Testament, the lot fell to me to edit his Romans commentary at the beginning of 1986. When he turned in the manuscript I read it and was immediately impressed that it is exactly what a "theological" commentary ought to be. Of course, Romans lends itself well to that, but not every interpreter manages to achieve what Leroy did: he discerned and expounded the theological themes of this great epistle and set them forth in a way that Christians can *apply*—that is the important word—to their lives.

This concern for application carries over into Leroy's concern for personal wholeness. Many years ago (while he was Dean of Students, I think), he became aware that people, including students, are often hurting emotionally and need help. Therefore, he made himself available. Though he had no formal training in counseling, he developed an effective approach (again, mostly his own) and counseled hundreds of students. Many testified to the very real help he was able to provide in the sessions he had with them, and students loved him for it. He was a firm disciplinarian, but he acted in love and genuine concern for students' welfare. His *Biblical Ethics* manifests this same concern and goes far toward defining the *basis* for ethical behavior, and so anchoring it not in a sterile law but in the personal values that make for wholeness.

Someone has said we are all unique, but some are more unique than others. Leroy Forlines is one of these. He is special. Our denomination, Welch College, and indeed the Christian Church have been graced to have his life and thought influence us. All glory to God for having made him what and who he is and placing him among us.

F. LEROY FORLINES
AS MENTOR

J. Matthew Pinson

I will never forget my first conversation with F. Leroy Forlines. I was an immature freshman at Welch College trying to sort things out, and one of my fellow students admonished me, "Matt, I know just what you need to do to find yourself—go talk to Leroy Forlines. He can help you."

I was very intimidated by this prospect. My only interaction with Leroy Forlines had been when he had come by Goen Hall, the men's dormitory, and rounded up a handful of boys to go help him with yard work. It was that day that I heard my first "Leroy Forlinesism." Miss Fay (the affectionate name I eventually began to call Dr. Fay Forlines, his wife) met us boys out in the yard to give us our assignments. She pointed to a plot of weeds and said, "Boys, Leroy hasn't gotten around to pulling these weeds. I'll need you to do it." To which Mr. Forlines replied, "Too deep for me!"

When that student suggested that I go see Mr. Forlines, I was very hesitant to do so. After all, Leroy Forlines was a gray-headed intellectual old enough to be my grandfather, who used big words like "epistemology" and "traducianism." "Could I ever get up the nerve to approach him?" I thought to myself. And if I could, how could a theologian like Leroy Forlines be of any practical help to a wet-behind-the-ears freshman who had decided he wanted to get on the fast track to law school?

Well, I decided to go and talk to Mr. Forlines anyway. I can remember sheepishly going up to his office on the second floor of the academic building and hesitatingly knocking on his door. He said, "Come in," and I walked in to find him in his characteristic pose, rocking back and forth in his desk chair, his elbows on the armrests, lightly tapping the fingers of both hands together. In his Eastern North Carolina accent and iconic soft voice, he invited me to sit down. Then he asked a question he has asked me hundreds of times since that day: "Whatcha got on your mind?"

There was much more to that question than I first thought. What I thought was just a figure of speech—an ice breaker to get conversation going—was really a question that got to the heart of what Leroy Forlines is all about: getting people to think deeply about who they are, about who God is, about what God's universe is like. In short, what I realized later was that Leroy Forlines was inviting me to think deeply about the answers to what he calls the inescapable questions of life, and to feel deeply about those answers and live my life committed to those answers.

That day was the beginning of a long friendship—a friendship that outlasted my immaturity and shaped me in ways I cannot begin to explain. That day Leroy Forlines, maybe without even knowing it, became a mentor to me. That day I began a journey with Mr. Forlines that would last the next thirty years, and now he is one of the best friends I have in this world.

It would take a book to discuss Leroy Forlines as mentor. But I have only a few pages. So I will mention just a few lessons I have learned from Leroy Forlines that I apply in my own mentoring of others. I have already mentioned the first one: *Leroy Forlines taught me the importance of thinking hard about the inescapable questions of life.*

This was not just abstract, philosophical-theological thinking. That is because the inescapable questions of life are deeply existential, deeply personal, deeply spiritual, deeply communal. He taught me that. The inescapable questions of life have to do with the deepest philosophical questions, which cannot be ignored, as we are wont to do in our anti-intellectual age. They have to be faced squarely. We have to ask honest questions, and in our Christian lives, people will ask us honest questions. And in response to those questions—sometimes tough questions—we have to give honest answers.

Those questions, and those answers, are intellectual in nature. Yet they are not only intellectual. They are spiritual. They are existential. They are relational. And this brings me to the next thing Mr. Forlines taught me about mentoring: *When you are mentoring people, you need to get them to think holistically—as human beings made in the divine image who think, feel, and make free choices.* This is what he calls the "total personality" approach. No doubt this is why he took so well to the counseling aspect of the job Dr. L. C. Johnson gave him as Dean of Men and Dean of Students at Welch College, in addition to his teaching. This side of him would later make it into a yet-to-be-published book on the human psyche and human relationships entitled *Understanding Yourself and Others.*

Another thing he taught me about mentoring people is closely related: *You need to get people thinking in terms of relationships—their relationship with God, and how that reshapes their relationships with themselves, others, and the world around them (the created order, the culture).* This relationally-oriented way of thinking is not a touchy-feely sort of emphasis on relationships. It is an emphasis on understanding and helping people who are divine image-bearers.[1] It is an emphasis on Christian sanctification. It is an emphasis on transforming the culture around us holistically.

These emphases led to the way that Leroy Forlines mentored me. He cared about what I was thinking, and he worked to develop me as a thinker, to draw out my potential as a scholar, to encourage me to further my education, and so forth. However, he also cared about me as a person. He cared about my family, and he wanted me to get to know his family, particularly his wife, Miss Fay, who has also had a great impact on my wife Melinda and me.

Leroy Forlines cared about how I was feeling and what I was going through. He wanted to understand and help me. I have learned from him that mentoring and leadership development can never be—must never be—only about professional or intellectual development. They must also be about personal and spiritual development.

There is another thing I want to mention about Leroy Forlines's mentoring, and that is his scattered comments to me about my *"personal PR."* Some of the young people who have been around me will chuckle at this, because they have heard me use this same language, always referring to Mr. Forlines. I can hear him say this as if it were yesterday, "Matt, you've got to attend to your personal PR."

Frankly, this is refreshing coming from a theologian. I have spent most of my adult life in two worlds—the world of scholarship, the intellect, and academics on one hand, and the world of practical leadership on the other. Too many scholars do not care enough about personal relationships, let alone "personal PR." These scholars make fun of things like that—thinking they sound like something from a motivational seminar. At the same time, I have been to way too many leadership seminars—and read way too many leadership books—that were shallow, not thoughtful, too pragmatic, not "total personality" enough, not "four basic relationships" enough.

What was and is wonderful about Leroy Forlines is that his total personality approach and his four-basic-relationships approach are very practical, without leaving behind depth and intelligence. This has caused him to talk about different frames on how to make practical life decisions.

"You don't just ask, 'Is it right or wrong?'" he would say. "And you don't just live life and make decisions legalistically, avoiding only those things that are prohibited by a chapter and verse in the Bible." Instead, he taught me and so many others, you follow biblical principles. You ask questions like: Does this show my love to God and to others? Is this the wisest course of action for me to take? Does this exemplify excellence and high ideals that others could imitate—ideals on which a culture and civilization could be built?

This holistic thinking naturally would lead people to "attend to their personal PR"—to care, not just about *what* they say, but about *how* they say it, not just about the content of their actions, but about how they might be misperceived or misunderstood by others.

One of the things I remember Mr. Forlines reminding me about in terms of "attending to my personal PR" was when I was in graduate school at Yale, way up in Connecticut, a world away from Welch College and the National Association of Free Will Baptists. Mr. Forlines always encouraged me to be a churchman and a Christian scholar in the context of the Free Will Baptist Church. And he would often remind me that, being far away at Yale, I needed to maintain contact with him and with others at the college and in the denomination. I needed to show an interest in the Free Will Baptist Church and its institutions if I ever hoped to exercise meaningful leadership within them. I did not need just to "do my own thing" and then suddenly show up and expect to be given leadership responsibilities in churches or in the denomination without having labored "in the small places" in those churches and among those people. This was rare wisdom for me as a young man. I took it to heart, and I pass it on to those in the next generation.

I could go on and on about Leroy Forlines as mentor. But I will tell one last story and then close. This story illustrates one other important mentoring lesson I learned from Leroy Forlines: *Make a way for younger people by telling others about them and what they have to offer.*

I have often said that my modest work as an Arminian Baptist historical theologian is simply what it looks like when a trained historian who has sat at the feet of Leroy Forlines begins to study the theology of the sixteenth and seventeenth centuries. I started doing that when I was at Yale and Florida State University in my mid-twenties, and naturally I shared the fruit of my labor with Mr. Forlines.

Well, he was not content just to listen and have nice conversations with me, nor even just to encourage me. He said, "I want others to hear about this." So he set up a meeting with Robert Picirilli, Ralph Hampton, Jack Williams, and himself in Dr. Picirilli's office, for the purpose of my sharing my research with them. Talk about intimidating! I will always remember that meeting. Yet more than that, I will remember what it stood for: Leroy Forlines, whom I held in such high esteem, wanted to tell others about me and what I had to offer to our faith community. This was a tremendous encouragement to me, and I have always hoped that I could do this for others who come after me.

I thank God for Leroy Forlines. He has been a gift of God to the church, specifically to Free Will Baptists, in that he has singularly shaped our theology and ethics. But God also gave Leroy Forlines as a gift to me, as a mentor who has shown the love of Christ to me and has taught me more about Christ and His gospel and His kingdom than I can express. My prayer is that I can play a small role in passing that same love and that same kind of mentoring on to the generations that will follow.

---

[1] He taught a popular night course entitled "Understanding and Helping People."

FORLINES AND THE FUTURE

W. Jackson Watts

One of the many rewarding aspects of bringing this festschrift to the Christian community has been to retread ground once trod in F. Leroy Forlines's works, and discover some new paths that readers can find through reading him. Good authors have the ability to present old ideas afresh and anew. Few are able to present old ideas in ways that will retain their impact and influence beyond one generation. While Forlines is not above the limitations that constrain us all, we believe—as this volume demonstrates—his work is uniquely valuable because of its capacity to mold and motivate multiple generations of scholars to serve Christ's church and world.

Inevitably not every question one may ask about Forlines's theological legacy can be answered in a single volume. There are yet more paths to explore. However, the major themes, arguments, emphases, and overall contributions of Forlinesean theology and ministry have been narrated and discussed across these chapters and tributes. What remains is for students, laymen, leaders, and scholars to consider what has been presented and embrace the weighty heritage bequeathed to them. For some, wrestling with the significance of this material will cause them to return to Forlines's works to read or reread. They will rush headlong into the material written and presented by Forlines over a six-decade ministry, letting their roots go down deep into the same soil that has nourished so many through the years. Others will trace the themes and topics here as treated in the works of other theologians, philosophers, and cultural critics, finding interesting similarities and significant differences. Still others may find value in simply entering the conversation we hope this book generates among Free Will Baptists, other self-described Arminians, and the broader evangelical community.

Entering the dialogue about ideas that matter is an exciting opportunity. It may even be an obligation. In Hebrews 11, the author offers a powerful summation of the stories of those who served God by faith from Abel to those nameless, forgotten prophets and servants who died in faithful service to God. The reader is then brought into the narrative more pointedly in 12:1-3. In light of the great cloud of witnesses which surround us, we are urged to lay aside every weight and sin which entangles us, and run the race set before us, having our eyes fixed on the founder and perfecter of our salvation. Many inspiring sermons (Hebrews included) have contained such exhortations. The images are powerful, even if one has never been an athlete. The word "run" is a metaphor for life itself, which causes us to question what activities this race entails. I think that being conversant in Christian thought, namely theology, is a valuable and critical part of our collective Christian marathon.

God's Word sustains us. It reveals truth, gives life, and bestows wisdom for Christian pilgrims on their earthly journey. Theology itself is a compound word that essentially means "the study of God." Traditionally theology has included the study of God as well as the world He has made. If this is a faithful understanding of theology, and I believe it is, then Andrew Ball is correct in chapter one when he says, "Theology is not just the warp and woof of scholars, but the milk and meat of *every* Christ follower. It meets the needs of our total personality. We need theology because we need God." If we want to run our race faithfully, then we must begin to see theological study as part and parcel of Christian discipleship. Such study confronts us with truths that inform and transform, practices that make and mold, and affections that elevate and encourage. This is why the legacy of Leroy Forlines matters today: It is the legacy of a servant seeking to speak faithful words concerning God, His Word, and His world. They are words we should continue to study with interest and integrity in the coming generation.

In preparation for this festschrift, Matthew Bracey and I reviewed many other similar volumes to gain a fuller understanding of this unique genre of theological literature. Among those consulted was a history of Princeton Seminary. It explored the lives of its most notable leaders from 1812 to 1929—some with whom Forlines dialogues in his work. In the foreword Paul Helseth makes an intriguing observation that provoked me before we began work on this project. Speaking with warm admiration about the contributions of the Old Princeton theologians, Helseth notes,

> They helped me to see the dangers of a kind of dead ortho-
> doxy on the one hand and a kind of unbridled religious en-
> thusiasm on the other, and they persuaded me that because
> theology is an organic enterprise involving the totality of the
> whole soul, it is done most faithfully when there is—by God's
> grace—a symbiotic relationship between the regenerated head
> and heart.[1]

Such words could have easily been said and indeed have been said of Leroy Forlines by those taught and trained by him. His theology offers balance and breadth, and we pray that this book adequately communicates this to our readers. Thank you for reading.

---

[1] Paul Kjoss Helseth, "Foreword," in Gary Steward, *Princeton Seminary (1812-1929): Its Leaders' Lives and Works* (Phillipsburg: P&R, 2014), 14.

ACKNOWLEDGEMENTS

As volume editors we can't quite express the range of emotions that goes into such a unique project throughout its development. However, the one that remains with us the most is gratitude. We're grateful to all those who saw the vision and value behind this project, and helped see it to through completion.

We are grateful to newly-formed Randall House Academic Division for making this their first publication. Ron Hunter, Michelle Orr, and Charles Cook were helpful resources who made this possible and offered invaluable input throughout our work.

We appreciate the hard work and cooperation of our various contributors, making the project the multi-layered work that it has become. Each added something special to this book, which grows from their admiration and appreciation for Leroy Forlines. Additionally, we thank our friends Matt Pinson for help with project development, Darrell Holley and Eric Thomsen for help with editing, and Zach Maloney for help with indexing.

We appreciate the patience and support of our wives who allowed us to be "on loan" for writing, editing, and making emails and telephone calls with one another, volume contributors, and project managers.

We owe a great debt of gratitude to the Forlines family. Mr. Forlines's life and ministry itself was the inspiration for this project. However, his family's cooperation (and confidentiality) has helped make this come to fruition.

Finally, we thank our heavenly Father for His love and truth, and for putting servants in our lives—like Leroy Forlines—who deeply love people, the truth, and the Savior.

Matthew Steven Bracey

W. Jackson Watts

CONTRIBUTORS

Andrew Ball teaches philosophy at the University of Alabama at Birmingham and also serves in the graduate faculty at Welch College. He has degrees in philosophy from the University of Detroit Mercy (B.A.), the University of Windsor (M.A.), the University of Alberta (Ph.D.), and is currently completing seminary studies at Beeson Divinity School. He has previously held teaching positions at the University of Alberta, the King's University College, and Samford University, and has contributed to several scholarly journals. Raised in Free Will Baptist churches in his home state of Michigan, Andy now resides in Birmingham, Alabama with his wife, Ashley.

James Forlines is the Executive Director of Final Command Ministries. Graduating with his bachelors from Welch College, he went on to receive his Master of Arts in Global Leadership with an emphasis in Islamic Studies from Fuller School of Intercultural Studies in Pasadena, California. Previously Forlines served Free Will Baptist churches in Arkansas, Indiana, and North Carolina, and as General Director of Free Will Baptist International Missions. He lives in Nashville with Anita. They have three children, Daniel (wife, Michelle), Rachel (husband, Chris), and Rebekah, as well as four grandchildren, Elise, Lillian, Justus, and Andon.

Jon Forlines is the Vice President for Student Services and psychology professor at Welch College, in Nashville, Tennessee. Forlines is a graduate of Welch College, and also received his master's and doctorate degrees in Counseling

Psychology from Tennessee State University. He lives in Nashville with his wife Susan, Dean of Women at Welch, and their children, Joel, Jared, and Anna.

Kevin L. Hester is Dean of the School of Theology and professor of Theology and Church History at Welch College in Nashville, Tennessee. He teaches courses in church history, theology, philosophy, and New Testament. He is a graduate of Welch College (B.A.), Covenant Theological Seminary (M.Div.) and Saint Louis University (Ph.D.). He is the author of *Free Will Baptists & the Priesthood of All Believers* and *Eschatology and Pain in St. Gregory the Great: The Christological Synthesis of Gregory's Morals on the Book of Job*. He resides in Spring Hill with his wife Leslie and their four sons, Spencer, Seth, Justin, and Jackson.

Matthew McAffee is a graduate of Welch College (B.A.), the Southern Baptist Theological Seminary (M.Div.), and the University of Chicago (M.A., Ph.D.), where he studied Northwest Semitic Philology. Matthew serves as the Biblical and Theological Studies program coordinator and campus pastor at Welch College. He and his wife Anna have four children, Abigail, Lydia, Samuel, and Marianne.

Edward E. Moody, Jr. serves as chair of the Department of Allied Professions, and Professor of Counselor Education at North Carolina Central University. He also serves as pastor of Tippett's Chapel Free Will Baptist Church Clayton, North Carolina. He is the author of *First Aid for Emotional Hurts*, the pamphlet series *First Aid for Your Emotional Hurts*, as well as *Surviving Culture*. Most recently he authored *Ministering in the Midst of a Changing Sexual Landscape*. He is a graduate of Welch College (B.A.), Middle Tennessee State University (M.A.), and North Carolina State University (Ph.D.). Eddie and his wife Lynne have two children, Mackenzie and Mitchell.

Phillip T. Morgan is the youth minister at Heads Free Will Baptist Church in Cedar Hill, Tennessee. He holds a bachelor's degree from Welch College, and is completing a master's degree in history from Middle Tennessee State

University. Phillip has also done theological coursework at Southern Baptist Theological Seminary. He is a regular contributor for the Helwys Society Forum. Phillip lives in Cedar Hill with his wife, Megan, and their children, Isaiah and Julia.

David Outlaw grew up on the Welch College campus as a faculty kid and later as a college student. He received his M.Div. and Ph.D. in theology from Mid-America Baptist Theological Seminary in Memphis, Tennessee. After pastoring for ten years in Arkansas and Tennessee, he lived in Kazakhstan with his wife Angie and their five children. Though they now live in the United States, David still teaches theology for Free Will Baptist International Missions in Kazakhstan, Tajikistan, Russia, Cuba, Panama, and South Korea.

Jesse F. Owens is a Ph.D. candidate at the Southern Baptist Theological Seminary in Historical Theology where he also earned an M.Div. He is an alumnus of Welch College (B.A.), and is actively engaged in pastoral ministry, having served churches in Kentucky and Tennessee. He is a co-founder of and contributor to the Helwys Society Forum. He and his wife Tiffany have one son, Gavin.

Robert E. Picirilli (B.A., Welch College; M.A., Ph.D., Bob Jones University) hails from rural South Carolina and spent his academic career teaching (New Testament, Greek, Philosophy) and in administration (Registrar, Academic Dean) at Welch. He is a widower and father of five married daughters, nine grandchildren, and seven great grandchildren. He is General Editor of the Randall House Commentaries and wrote the commentaries on Mark, 1 & 2 Corinthians, Ephesians, Philippians, 1 & 2 Thessalonians, and 1 & 2 Peter. He has also published *Paul, the Apostle; Grace, Faith, Free Will: Contrasting Views of Salvation; Calvinism and Arminianism; Teacher, Leader, Shepherd: The New Testament Pastor; Discipleship: The Expression of Saving Faith;* and *Little Known Chapters in Free Will Baptist History.* He served stints as Moderator of the National Association of Free Will Baptists and President of the Accrediting Association of Bible Colleges.

J. Matthew Pinson is president of Welch College in Nashville, Tennessee. He holds master's degrees from the University of West Florida and Yale, a doctorate from Vanderbilt, and has authored or edited several books, including *Four Views on Eternal Security*, *Perspectives on Christian Worship*, and *Arminian and Baptist: Explorations in a Theological Tradition*. Matt previously pastored churches in Florida, Connecticut, and Georgia. He lives in the Nashville area with his wife, Melinda, and their children, Anna and Matthew.

Barry Raper serves as Senior Pastor of Bethel Free Will Baptist Church in Chapmansboro, Tennessee, and Program Coordinator for Ministry Studies at Welch College. He holds degrees from Welch College (B.S.) and the Southern Baptist Theological Seminary (M.Div., D.Min.), where his studies focused on spiritual formation. Barry formerly served as a youth pastor and senior pastor in Alabama. He and his wife Amanda have five children.

Christopher Talbot is a faculty member at Welch College in Nashville, Tennessee. He oversees the program of Youth and Family Ministry, along with teaching courses in Bible and theology. Before teaching at Welch, he was a Youth Pastor in Free Will Baptist churches in North Carolina and in Alabama. Chris is a graduate of Welch College (B.S.) and Grace College (M.A.), and also serves as a contributor to the Helwys Society Forum. He regularly writes and speaks on topics concerning theology and ministry. He lives in Gallatin, Tennessee with his wife Rebekah and their child, William.

SUBJECT AND NAME INDEX

Computer, 237

Condemnation, 56, 84, 86, 92, 99, 278

Constantinanism, 176

Conversion, 56, 59, 77, 103, 115, 125, 152, 161, 229-30

Copernicus, 29, 202

Council of Chalcedon, 55, 73, 86

Council of Constantinople, 55

Council of Ephesus, 55

Council of Nicea, 55, 73

Counseling, 3, 248, 259, 283, 287

Courtship, 264

Covenant(s), 69, 94, 126, 141-42, 144-45, 147-51, 153-58, 160, 162-64, 168, 183, 186
Abrahamic, 69, 144-47, 154-55, 160, 164
Grace, of, 105-06, 143
Mosaic, 145, 154, 156-57, 164, 168
Redemption, of, 143,
Reformed theology, 143, 154
Sinaitic, 154, 157
Works, of, 143

Covenantalism, 145, 153-54, 156-57, 170

Created order, 13, 108, 185, 251-52, 256, 287

Creation, 19, 39, 41, 62, 86, 124, 146, 148, 150, 157, 162, 165, 183, 185, 188, 190, 193, 196-97, 232, 239, 249-50, 252, 256, 274

Cultural, 27-29, 35-36, 45-46, 50, 68, 77, 156, 169, 185, 191, 212, 225, 237, 240-41, 243, 245, 264, 273
Critic(s), 292
Engagement, 45, 189-90
Hermeneutic(s), 237
Withdrawal, 45, 224

Culture, 3, 8, 11, 27-28, 35-36, 41-46, 51, 74, 101, 156-57, 168-69, 171, 182, 189, 191, 193, 196, 199-200, 204-05, 208-12, 214-18, 220, 225-26, 234, 236-37, 239-40, 244, 248-49, 252-53, 259-60, 262-64, 275, 287-88

Danbury Baptist Association, 210, 220

Darwin, Charles, 30

Declaration of Independence, 204, 218

Denomination, 1-2, 132, 177, 241, 278-80, 283, 289

Depravity, 33, 56-57, 59-60, 63, 75, 133, 178, 180, 278
Humanity, of, 56, 176

Depression, 10, 28, 209, 213, 260

Desiring God, 232

Determinism, 57, 74, 129

Dever, Mark, 224, 241

DeYoung, Kevin, 240, 244-45

Discipleship, 137, 177, 231, 234-36, 244, 292
Costly, 225, 231, 234-35

Disciplinarian, Discipline, 31-32, 112, 117, 119, 137, 155, 174, 209, 233, 235, 257, 283

Discouragement, 260, 263

Dispensational, Dispensationalism, Dispensationalist(s), 145, 147, 149, 153, 160-61, 163-65, 168, 170

Divine, 14, 38, 58, 61, 63-66, 68, 74-75, 78, 85, 89, 106, 114, 116-17, 123, 125, 143-44, 155, 160, 162, 165, 183, 204, 227, 258, 287
Image-bearer(s), 287
Revelation, 10, 31, 33, 37, 40, 227
Sovereignty, 55, 75, 123, 129

Doctrinal, Doctrine 9-10, 20, 57, 61, 65, 74, 76-78, 81-83, 86-87, 91, 93-98, 100-03, 107, 115, 118-19, 123-24, 128, 131, 134-35, 143, 158, 163, 169, 174, 176, 181-82, 187, 192, 195, 224, 229-30, 241-42, 248, 280, 282
Minimalism, 228-30, 234
Perseverance, of, 122

Dodd, Damon, 282

Dogmatism, 281

Dominican(s), 56

Dormitory, 285

Eastern mysticism, 212

Ecclesiology, 224-25, 231, 239-40

Ecology, 176, 193, 196-97, 236

Education, 9, 209-10, 216, 218, 220-21, 287

Edwards, Jonathan, 98, 135

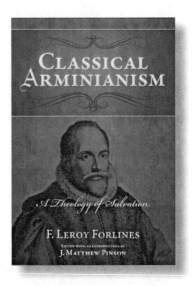

"In this book Leroy Forlines presents a lively, relevant, biblical restatement of classical Arminian theology. In a time when the choice seems to be Calvinism or "free will theism," his classical Arminianism is most welcome. Believing that theology is for life, Forlines writes for every Christian, not just for other theologians. His work appeals to the whole person, sets before us a powerful vision of God's holiness, and calls us to holy living. Every Christian who seeks to be biblically faithful will grow by reading and digesting this nourishing work."

Jonthan R. Wilson
Pioneer McDonald Chair of Theology
Carey Theological College

"Leroy Forlines is an accomplished and seasoned scholar who is the face of Reformed or Classical Arminianism, which is closer to the actual teachings of Jacob Arminius than the more widely known Wesleyan Arminianism. Forlines is, above all, faithful to careful biblical exposition as the foundation of his theology. The perspective offered by Forlines, along with like-minded theologians such as Robert Picirilli and Roger Olson, deserves to be heard on these crucial issues. Although our own perspective differs at points, we have used their books profitably at our seminary."

Steve W. Lemke
Provost
New Orleans Baptist Theological Seminary

randall house

**To order, call 800-877-7030
or visit www.randallhouse.com.**

THE RANDALL HOUSE
BIBLE COMMENTARY SERIES

The *Randall House Bible Commentary* series is a must have for pastors and students alike. With Robert Picirilli as General Editor, and all Free Will Baptist contributors, this series is a great addition to any library.

The series currently contains:

Matthew
Crabtree, Picirilli
13-ISBN: 9780892657377
$39.99 each

Mark
Picirilli
13-ISBN: 9780892655007
$29.99 each

John
Stallings
13-ISBN: 9780892651375
$29.99 each

Romans
Forlines
13-ISBN: 9780892659494
$29.99 each

Galatians-Colossians
Marberry, Ellis, Picirilli
13-ISBN: 9780892651344
$29.99 each

1 Thessalonians-Philemon
Ellis, Outlaw, Picirilli
13-ISBN: 9780892651436
$29.99 each

Hebrews
Outlaw
13-ISBN: 9780892655144
$29.99 each

James, 1 and 2 Peter, Jude
Harrison, Picirilli
13-ISBN: 9780892651450
$29.99 each

1 & 2 Corinthians
Picirilli
13-ISBN: 9780892659500
$29.99 each

1, 2, 3 John & Revelation
Marberry, Picirilli, Pugh, Shaw
13-ISBN: 9780892655373
$34.99 each

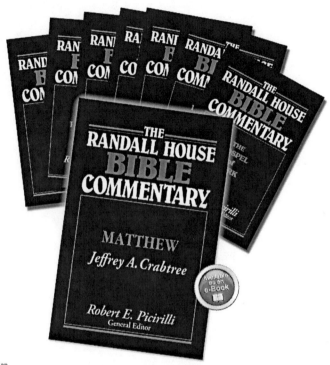

$264.99
FULL SET
(10 Volumes)

TO ORDER: 1-800-877-7030 OR
WWW.RANDALLHOUSE.COM

CPSIA information can be obtained
at www.ICGtesting.com
Printed in the USA
LVOW11s0348080817
544195LV00002B/397/P